Wandering Jews: Global Jewish Migration

The Jewish Role in American Life

An Annual Review of the Casden Institute for the Study of the Jewish Role in American Life

Wandering Jews: Global Jewish Migration

The Jewish Role in American Life

An Annual Review of the Casden Institute for the Study of the Jewish Role in American Life

Volume 18

Steven J. Ross, *Editor*
Steven J. Gold, *Guest Editor*
Lisa Ansell, *Associate Editor*

Published by the Purdue University Press for
the USC Casden Institute for the Study of the
Jewish Role in American Life

Production Editor, Marilyn Lundberg

Cover photo supplied by Steven J. Gold.
Booth for the Israeli Division of the United Jewish Fund, Los Angeles Jewish Festival
in Rancho Park, California, June 2, 1991.

Hardcover ISBN: 978-1-61249-667-2
Paperback ISBN: 978-1-55753-998-4
ePDF ISBN: 978-1-61249-620-7
ePUB ISBN: 978-1-55753-999-1

Published by Purdue University Press
West Lafayette, Indiana
www.press.purdue.edu
pupress@purdue.edu

Printed in the United States of America.

Contents

Foreword

Jews have been in motion for thousands of years, moving across continents, nations, and cities—sometimes voluntarily, often because there was no alternative. How Jews moved, where they moved, what they experienced, and the ways they dealt with their new surroundings is the subject of this innovative volume of The Annual Review. Our guest editor, Steven Gold, has assembled a series of seven cutting-edge essays that examine multiple aspects of Jewish global migration in the twentieth and twenty-first centuries.

Placing their work within the relatively new field of migration studies, our contributing authors reveal that while Jews may share a common religion, their patterns of migration and acculturation were as different as the many nations from which they came. As volume editor Steven Gold notes in his Introduction, the essays are divided into two categories. Several authors explore the hardships Jews faced in migrating to the United States and other countries, while others focus on the problems of adjusting to life in new lands or new cities within the same country. We learn how survivors and refugees in postwar Europe worked with Jewish aid groups to navigate the difficult process of obtaining visas to move the United States. Another essay traces the diverging experiences of Jews migrating to the United States from the former Soviet Union, Israel, and Latin America. Jews who remained in Europe faced their own particular difficulties. One essay focuses on the myriad experiences of Jews who migrated to Paris, Brussels, and Antwerp, while a final essay on migration patterns reveals how the Israeli government attempted to lure highly skilled Jewish émigrés back to their homeland.

Once in the United States, Jewish immigrants encountered a remarkably wide array of experiences. Not only did Jew have to adjust to living alongside Christians, but in the case of Polish Jews, they also had to adjust to living alongside German Jews who often treated them with as much disdain as their American Christian neighbors. Iranian Jews also encountered difficulties in their new land; some were caused by the contempt of Ashkenazi Jews, while other problems emerged from the Iranian community's tendency to isolate themselves from others, Jews and non-Jews alike.

Finally, we learn that internal migration could pose just as many problems as external migration. American Jewish academics who came from large cities with vibrant Jewish life often found it difficult to move their families to college towns such as East Lansing, Michigan, which lacked a Jewish infrastructure.

Taken collectively, the essays in this volume offer new looks at the multiple experiences of Jews as they attempted to immigrate and then adjust to life in a new homeland or new city.

I wish to thank our guest editor, Steven J. Gold, for helping to make this volume a reality. I also wish to thank Marilyn Lundberg Melzian for her wonderful work as our volume's production editor.

Steven J. Ross
Myron and Marian Casden Director
Professor of History

Editorial Introduction: Recent Advancements in Jewish Migration Studies

by Steven J. Gold

A long-standing topic of research, the study of Jewish migration, has recently revealed new levels of growth and innovation. The increased visibility of diverse forms of migration on a global scale—from refugees and labor migrants to transnational entrepreneurs—has contributed to enhanced interest in the subject.

This book brings attention to compelling examples of new scholarship in this field. While available space precludes an exhaustive evaluation of the reasons underlying this development, this introduction reviews three fundamental factors that have contributed to the growth and intellectual expansion in the study of Jewish migration. First is the expansion and broadening of migration studies in general that has occurred in recent decades. Second is the increase in financial and institutional support for Jewish studies. Finally, a third reason for the field's growth is ongoing instances of Jewish migration—both within and across national borders—that compel immigrant-aid organizations and migration scholars to learn about and assist their peripatetic landsmen.

A number of leading scholars have reflected on the transformation of migration studies, noting that the topic is currently examined by a wider range of academic disciplines than ever before.[1] The creation of diverse and innovative approaches to the topic has been widely celebrated.[2] As a case in point, the authors of a recent article devoted to mapping migration studies conclude that the field has finally "come of age."[3]

Observers of migration studies assert that even as the field has expanded and diversified, it has managed to become more rigorous, more international in focus, and more firmly grounded in theory. Moreover, this scholarly endeavor has maintained a significant degree of integration and continuity across disciplines, nations, and world regions. As a consequence, its methods and findings are increasingly applied to a broad range of concerns. Migration research informs policy making by governments, NGOs and immigrant-aid organizations. It also counters the assertions of anti-immigrant movements.[4]

Given the recent upturn in interest and support for studies of migration, a variety of disciplinary associations have established sections, committees, publications, conferences, awards, and other endeavors devoted to the study of migration. This reflects a significant transformation in the field's foci over a relatively short time. As the authors of *What Is Migration History?* point out,[5] until the 1970s, the study of migration was fixed almost exclusively on Western Europe and the US, was androcentric, elitist, overwhelmingly devoted to workforce issues, and indifferent to migrants' interpretations of their own experiences. Subjects such as stratification, slavery, refugees, forced migration, and re-migration were rejected as suitable topics for migration research.

The fact that a significant fraction of contemporary migration scholars are themselves migrants, has helped move migration studies from a narrowly framed undertaking to one now much more ambitious and wider in scope. By and large, scholars who have a personal or familial connection to migration are much better equipped to understand the complex realities encountered by migrants than those with little immediate connection to the process. As a consequence of historical and social factors, Jews have been very well represented among those who have developed the ways through which migration research has been conducted and how knowledge resulting from this examination is put to use.[6]

Historian Tobias Brinkmann[7] has advanced our understanding of how Jewish scholars and activists have fashioned the study of migration. Drawing on his research on the Jewish population of Chicago during the nineteenth century, Brinkmann demonstrated how Jewish communal organizations' efforts to assist recently arrived co-ethnics led to the development of many of the frameworks and methods that are now used in ethnic, migration and community studies.

Arriving in Chicago in the 1840s, Jews from Bavaria recognized the social and economic needs encountered by members of their community as they sought to adjust to life in the US. Drawing upon pre-migration traditions, they formed self-help associations like the United Hebrew Relief Association (UHRA) to provide struggling co-religionists with social support.

Through a detailed examination of UHRA's annual reports, Brinkmann discovered that in order to accomplish its goals more efficiently, the organization shifted its structure from that of a voluntary association to a professional body. "By the 1880s, professional social workers and administrators were replacing volunteers. The communal representatives visited immigrant families in their homes to study poverty and offer advice about hygiene and education."[8] Such a change, Brinkmann asserts, "correlated with a shift from stereotypical perceptions of migrants to more differentiated assessments of social problems."[9] In so doing, Jewish immigrant organizations involved in communal self-help developed the approaches that are used by a wide range of migration scholars today. As Brinkman notes:

> The first detailed studies about immigrants in industrializing cities, so-called social surveys, were compiled by social workers in settlements in London, New York, and Chicago after 1880. When pioneering urban sociologists like Louis Wirth and other students of the Chicago school . . . began to conduct field research in Chicago's immigrant neighborhoods in the 1920s, they acknowledged the work of communal organizations in representing different immigrant groups and social settlements.[10]

In order to record, document and apply practical information about Jewish immigrants and their resettlement, Jewish communal organizations, including the American Jewish Joint Distribution Committee (JDC), commissioned the writing of detailed studies about the experience of migrant Jews. For example, in 1943, the American Jewish Committee commissioned Mark Wischnitzer, himself a German Jewish immigrant with decades of experience assisting migrants in both Europe and the US, to compile a survey of Jewish migration as a reference to inform the resettlement of Jews in the US after WWII. According to Brinkmann, Wischnitzer's book *To Dwell in Safety* remains the most comprehensive study of Jewish migration between 1800 and 1948.[11]

Following Brinkmann's description of the Jewish communal origins of migration studies, we see how an array of Jewish scholars and aid workers contributed in important ways to the growth, conceptual richness, and methodological advancement of the interdisciplinary study of migration.

At the same time, Brinkmann reminds us to recognize the significant contributions of members of other groups who documented the experience of their own and other migrant populations. Among these are Florian Znaniecki, Tamotsu Shibutani, Kian Kwan, W. E. B. DuBois, Alain Locke, Arthur Huff

Fauset and Hanna Arendt. Immigrant scholars' research on a broad range of communities laid the groundwork for contemporary inquiry in migration studies.

Aware of the enhanced interest in and endorsement of studies of migration, a growing number of scholars and students began to produce works in migration, Jewish studies, ethnic studies, and related topics. As E. Cohen,[12] Brinkmann,[13] and others contend, the growth in migration studies has yielded a productive exchange and cross fertilization of concepts, terminology, analytic models and methods between researchers concerned with a variety of groups. Finally, scholars interested in the application of recently developed approaches in migration scholarship have chosen to revisit established concepts and works in the field.[14] Their systematic re-evaluation of classic studies helps contemporary scholars understand the origins of their fields' approaches to research and analysis. In this way, scholars are able to apply contemporary perspectives to the investigation of historical communities and concerns.

A second significant reason for the expansion of Jewish migration studies is the availability of increased levels of financial and institutional support. Philanthropists, institutions of higher learning, academic associations, publishers, students, and audiences interested in works on migration have contributed much to the growth of Jewish migration studies. A sizeable fraction of this programming has been driven by the largess of Jewish donors. However, as Judith Baskin contends in her article "Jewish Studies in North American Colleges and Universities: Yesterday, Today, and Tomorrow," "it is important to point out that there are positions and programs at institutions, both private and public, where external funding has not played a role."[15] Among these are University of Massachusetts at Amherst, the University at Albany, State University of New York and several other state-supported institutions. The allocation of funding directly from college and university budgets demonstrates that such institutions regard the field to be a fundamental component of higher learning.[16]

This increase in resources has generated opportunities for training, employment and publication for scholars involved in Jewish studies generally and Jewish migration research in particular. The Association of Jewish Studies, which began in 1969 with forty-seven members, now has 1,800. The association's website lists more than two hundred Jewish studies programs or departments and 230 endowed positions at North American colleges and universities.[17] Data from the 2000–2001 National Jewish Population Study indicate that 40% of Jewish students take a Jewish studies course during their academic career.[18] Reflecting the field's broad appeal, a significant number of students taking Jewish studies courses and majoring or minoring in Jewish studies are not Jewish.[19]

A third reason for the continued activity of scholars of Jewish migration is that Jewish communities persist in migrating—both within and across national borders. The documentation and analysis of on-going patterns of Jewish migration is important for both practical and scholarly reasons. Indicating Jews' high level of recent involvement with international migration, Pew[20] notes that while only 5% of Christians and 3% of Muslims globally have moved internationally during their lifetime, some 25% of all living Jews no longer reside in their country of birth.

Since the 1950s, Jewish migrants have continued their long record of migration to the US and other countries. From the 1960s to the 1990s, the largest migrant population was Russian-speaking Jews. They settled in Israel, the US, Canada, Australia, and Germany.[21] Since the 1990s, Jewish migrants from France, Israel, Iran, Latin America, the Maghreb, Syria, Yemen, South Africa and Central Asia have settled in Israel, North America, Europe and other locations.[22]

As recent arrivals and bearers of cultural traditions relatively uncommon in their points of settlement, the ability (and for some, the level of interest) of these new migrants in integrating into the host population (Americanized Eastern European Jews) has been limited. Making matters even more complex, recent Jewish migrants' arrival occurred during a time of increasing segmentation and diversity within local Jewish communities. New synagogues, Jewish associations and economic niches maintain disparate ways of life, forms of religious practice, cultural orientations, expressions of nationality, sexuality, politics, and other aspects of being.[23] Faced with such challenges, Jewish, secular and public community agencies, youth programs, synagogues, and immigrant-aid organizations like HIAS (the Hebrew Immigrant Aid Society) whose work has been informed by Jewish migration research, have aided in the resettlement of thousands of Jewish and non-Jewish immigrants in Israel, Europe, Australia, and North and South America.

In addition to documenting the needs, values and concerns of recent migrant populations, scholars devoted to Jewish migrants have created a significant body of research that affirms, contradicts and otherwise elaborates on customary understandings of Jewish migration and adaptation recorded in earlier studies.

In sum, the recent growth and diversity in studies of Jewish migration can be traced to transformations in the way that migration scholarship is conducted, to increases in funding and institutional support for Jewish migration scholarship, and to the on-going migrations of Jewish people throughout the world.

The authors featured in *Wandering Jews* are leaders in the development of inventive scholarship on Jewish migration. The works of these seven scholars are divided into two categories. The first set of chapters addresses the experience of various Jewish groups settling in the United States and other countries. Laura Lamonic compares the experiences of Post-WWII Jewish immigrants from the former Soviet Union, Latin America and Israel living in the United States. Nahid Pirnazar examines the story of Iranian Jewish migration and subsequent acculturation to the United States.

Nir Cohen explores the experience of another contemporary Jewish migrant group—Israeli high-tech migrants—as he evaluates actions pursued by both the Israeli governmental and private sector organizations to encourage their re-migration. Lilach Lev Ari concludes the section by exploring the contexts encountered by three groups of Jewish migrants (Israelis, North Africans, and members of an Orthodox community) who have settled in lucrative but increasingly anti-Semitic Western European locations.

The second set of chapters explore Jewish responses to societal changes imposed by migration. Historian Gil Ribak presents a poignant analysis rooted in the historical perspective of the twenty-first century to reconstruct the evolution of Eastern European Jewish migrants' views of Germans—from admiration to foreboding—during their travel from The Pale of Settlement to the US during the late nineteenth and early twentieth centuries. Libby Garland discusses Jewish Americans' efforts to resettle Jewish refugees after WWII. Finally, Kirsten Fermaglich examines the experiences of Jewish academics and their families building lives and communities in East Lansing, Michigan, from the late 1960s to the present.

The topics of these seven chapters reflect considerable diversity in terms of location, historical period, theoretical and methodological approach, scale of analysis, population characteristics and academic discipline. At the same time, each embodies the energy and excitement that underlies the recent growth and creativity generated in this field. Drawing upon innovative and varied approaches, the volume's authors advance the study of Jewish migration, and migration studies more generally.

Notes

1. Steven J. Gold and Stephanie Nawyn, "Introduction to Second and First Editions," in *The Routledge International Handbook of Migration Studies*, 2nd ed. (London: Routledge, 2019), xxii–xxxi; Christhard Hoffmann, "Jewish History As a History of Immigration: An Overview of Current Historiography in the Scandinavian Countries," *Jewish Studies in the Nordic Countries Today* Scripta Instituti Donneriani Aboensis 27 (2016): 203–22.

2. Erik H. Cohen, "Jewish Identity Research: A State of the Art," *International Journal of Jewish Education Research* 1 (2010): 7–48; Christine Harzig and Dirk Hoerder with Donna Gabaccia, *What Is Migration History?* (Cambridge, UK: Polity Press, 2009); Hein De Hass, Stephen Castles, and Mark J. Miller, *The Age of Migration International Population Movements in the Modern World*, 3rd ed. (New York and London: Guilford Press, 2020).

3. Asya Pisarevskaya, Nathan Levy, Peter Scholten, and Joost Jansen, "Mapping Migration Studies: An Empirical Analysis of the Coming of Age of a Research Field," *Migration Studies* (2019): 1–2.

4. Peter Schrag, *Not Fit for Our Society: Immigration and Nativism in America* (Berkeley: University of California Press, 2010); Peter Skerry, "Opposing Immigration Wasn't Always Racist," *Boston Globe*, April 16, 2017.

5. Harzig and Hoerder with Gabaccia, *What Is Migration History?*

6. Ruben G. Rumbaut, "Immigration Research in the United States: Social Origins and Future Orientations," in *Immigration Research for a New Century: Multidisciplinary Perspectives*, ed. N. Foner, R. G. Rumbaut and S. J. Gold (New York: Russell Sage Foundation, 2000), 23–43.

7. Tobias Brinkmann, "Acquiring Knowledge About Migration: The Jewish Origins of Migration Studies," *Migrant Knowledge*, September 25, 2019, https://migrantknowledge.org/2019/09/25/acquiring-knowledge-about-migration-the-jewish-origins-of-migration-studies/.

8. Ibid.

9. Ibid.

10. Ibid.

11. Ibid., citing Mark Wischnitzer, *To Dwell in Safety* (Philadelphia: Jewish Publication Society of America, 1948).

12. E. H. Cohen, "Jewish Identity Research."

13. Brinkmann, "Acquiring Knowledge About Migration."

14. Calvin Goldscheider, and Frances E. Korbin, "Ethnic Continuity and the Process of Self-Employment," *Ethnicity* 7 (1980): 256–78; Hasia R. Diner, *The Jews of the United States 1654–2000* (Berkeley and Los Angeles: University of California Press, 2004).

15. Judith R. Baskin, "Jewish Studies in North American Colleges and Universities: Yesterday, Today, and Tomorrow," *Shofar* 32, no. 4 (2014): 18.

16. Judith R. Baskin, Personal correspondence, 2020.

17. Penny Schwartz, "Jewish Studies Conference Celebrates 50 Years of Explosive Growth in the Field," *JTA* (December 18, 2018).

18. Baskin, "Jewish Studies in North American Colleges and Universities," 18; National Jewish Population Study, 2000–2001.

19. Baskin, "Jewish Studies in North American Colleges and Universities"; Samuel G. Freedman, "Classes in Judaic Studies, Drawing a Non-Jewish Class," *The New York Times*, Nov. 3, 2004.

20. Pew Research Center's Forum on Religion and Public Life, "Faith on the Move— The Religious Affiliation of International Migrants," 2012, accessed March 1, 2015, http://www.pewforum.org/2012/03/08/religious-migration-exec/.

21. Zvi Gitelman, *The New Jewish Diaspora: Russian-Speaking Immigrants in the United States, Israel and Germany* (New Brunswick, NJ: Rutgers University Press, 2016); Steven J. Gold, "Soviet Jews in the United States," *American Jewish Yearbook* Vol. 94 (1994): 3–57.

22. Steven J. Gold, *From the Workers' State to the Golden State: Jews from the Former Soviet Union in California* (Boston: Allyn and Bacon, 1995); Laura Limonic, *Kugel and Frijoles: Latino Jews in the United States* (Detroit: Wayne State University Press, 2019); Ron Kelley and Jonathan Friedlander, *Irangeles: Iranians in Los Angeles* (Berkeley and Los Angeles: University of California Press, 1993); Steven J. Gold and Mehdi Bozorgmehr, "Middle East and North Africa," in *The New Americans: A Guide to Immigration Since 1965*, ed. Mary Waters and Reed Ueda with Helen B. Marrow (Cambridge, Harvard University Press, 2007), 518–33.

23. Robin Cohen, *Global Diasporas* (Seattle: University of Washington, 1997); Iddo Tavory, *Summoned: Identification and Religious Life in a Jewish Neighborhood* (University of Chicago Press: Chicago, 2016); Hila Amit, *A Queer Way Out: The Politics of Queer Emigration from Israel* (Albany: SUNY Press, 2018).

Bibliography

Amit, Hila. *A Queer Way Out: The Politics of Queer Emigration from Israel.* Albany: SUNY Press, 2018.

Baskin, Judith R. "Jewish Studies in North American Colleges and Universities: Yesterday, Today, and Tomorrow." *Shofar* 32, no. 4 (2014): 9–26.

Brinkmann, Tobias. "Acquiring Knowledge About Migration: The Jewish Origins of Migration Studies." *Migrant Knowledge*, September 25, 2019. https://migrantknowledge.org/2019/09/25/acquiring-knowledge-about-migration-the-jewish-origins-of-migration-studies/.

Cohen, Erik H. "Jewish Identity Research: A State of the Art." *International Journal of Jewish Education Research* 1 (2010): 7–48.

Cohen, Robin. *Global Diasporas.* Seattle: University of Washington, 1997.

De Hass, Hein, Stephen Castles, and Mark J. Miller. *The Age of Migration International Population Movements in the Modern World.* 6th ed. New York and London: Guilford Press, 2020.

Diner, Hasia R. *The Jews of the United States 1654–2000.* Berkeley and Los Angeles: University of California Press, 2004.

Freedman, Samuel G. "Classes in Judaic Studies, Drawing a Non-Jewish Class." *The New York Times*, Nov. 3, 2004.

Gitelman, Zvi. *The New Jewish Diaspora: Russian-Speaking Immigrants in the United States, Israel and Germany.* New Brunswick, NJ: Rutgers University Press, 2016.

Gold, Steven J. *From the Workers' State to the Golden State: Jews from the Former Soviet Union in California.* Boston: Allyn and Bacon, 1995.

———. "Soviet Jews in the United States." *American Jewish Yearbook* Vol. 94 (1994): 3–57.

Gold, Steven J., and Mehdi Bozorgmehr. "Middle East and North Africa." In *The New Americans: A Guide to Immigration Since 1965*, edited by Mary Waters and Reed Ueda with Helen B. Marrow, 518–33. Cambridge, Harvard University Press, 2007.

Gold, Steven J., and Stephanie Nawyn. "Introduction to Second and First Editions." In *The Routledge International Handbook of Migration Studies*, xxii–xxxi. 2nd ed. London: Routledge, 2019.

Goldscheider, Calvin, and Frances E. Korbin, "Ethnic Continuity and the Process of Self-Employment." *Ethnicity* 7 (1980): 256–78.

Harzig, Christine, and Dirk Hoerder with Donna Gabaccia. *What Is Migration History?* Cambridge, UK: Polity Press, 2009.

Hoffmann, Christhard. "Jewish History As a History of Immigration: An Overview of Current Historiography in the Scandinavian Countries." *Jewish Studies in the Nordic Countries Today* Scripta Instituti Donneriani Aboensis 27 (2016): 203–22.

Kelley, Ron, and Jonathan Friedlander. *Irangeles: Iranians in Los Angeles.* Berkeley and Los Angeles: University of California Press, 1993.

Limonic, Laura. *Kugel and Frijoles: Latino Jews in the United States*. Detroit: Wayne State University Press, 2019.

Pew Research Center's Forum on Religion and Public Life. "Faith on the Move—The Religious Affiliation of International Migrants." 2012. Accessed March 1, 2015. http://www.pewforum.org/2012/03/08/religious-migration-exec/.

Pisarevskaya, Asya, Nathan Levy, Peter Scholten and Joost Jansen. "Mapping Migration Studies: An Empirical Analysis of the Coming of Age of a Research Field." *Migration Studies* (2019): 1–27.

Rumbaut, Ruben G. "Immigration Research in the United States: Social Origins and Future Orientations." In *Immigration Research for a New Century: Multidisciplinary Perspectives*, edited by N. Foner, R. G. Rumbaut and S. J. Gold, 23–43. New York: Russell Sage Foundation, 2000.

Schrag, Peter. *Not Fit for Our Society: Immigration and Nativism in America*. Berkeley: University of California Press, 2010.

Schwartz, Penny. "Jewish Studies Conference Celebrates 50 Years of Explosive Growth in the Field." *JTA* (December 18, 2018).

Skerry, Peter. "Opposing Immigration Wasn't Always Racist." *Boston Globe*, April 16, 2017.

Tavory, Iddo. *Summoned: Identification and Religious Life in a Jewish Neighborhood*. University of Chicago Press: Chicago, 2016.

Wischnitzer, Mark. *To Dwell in Safety*. Philadelphia: Jewish Publication Society of America, 1948.

Jewish Identity among Contemporary Jewish Immigrants in the United States

by Laura Limonic

NTRODUCTION

Jewish identity, practice, culture and religiosity are intrinsically tied to the nations where Jews reside. National economic and political structures impact the development of Jewish communities while cultural and social influences are important factors in the construction of Jewish identities. Jews from Latin America, for example, largely function within close-knit, centrally organized communities, ones where non-religious communal life is at the heart of Jewish identity. For Israeli Jews, on the other hand, Jewish religious life is interwoven with the Israeli political and social landscape. Other global Jewish communities have formed under diverse constraints. Some members of global Jewish communities may have little knowledge of Jewish religious rites, as was the case for many of the Jews in the former Soviet Union, whereas other communities might place religiosity and adherence to religious rites at the center of Jewish identity. What happens when members of these communities migrate and settle in the United States? How do American Jewish culture and communal structures affect their lived Jewish experience? In this chapter, I compare three immigrant groups from distinct geographic locations: the former Soviet Union, Israel and Latin America. By comparing demographic and socio-economic characteristics as well as markers of Jewish identity and behavior across these three immigrant groups we can widen our understanding of immigrant communities that comprise the larger US Jewish group. I use data from the Pew Research Center,[1] to construct variables aimed at measuring Jewish identity. Scales of Jewish identity are composed and measured across

Jewish immigrant groups and Jewish native-born adults in the United States—providing insight into the changing nature of Jewish identity and the process of assimilation into the larger US Jewish community.

IMMIGRATION TO THE UNITED STATES

At the turn of the twentieth century, millions of immigrants from multiple countries and of diverse faiths descended upon the shores of the United States. These immigrants brought with them new languages, foods, cultures and religious practices. During the peak of this large migration wave, Protestantism was the dominant US religion. Yet the United States, with its constitutional emphasis on religious pluralism, was primed to accept new religious groups, even if de facto acceptance would arrive decades later.[2] The descendants of this first generation of Catholic and Jewish immigrants from eastern and southern Europe created new ethno-religious communities and eventually forged a path for the integration of Catholicism and Judaism as part of the tripartite Judeo-Christian civil religion in the United States.[3] The children and grandchildren of the large wave of southern and eastern European immigrants not only changed the US religious landscape, they themselves altered their own religious practices. One example of this is the increased participation in Reform Judaism which espouses a Protestant style of convening and practicing religion and is more palatable and adaptable to being Jewish in the United States.[4]

Jewish Immigrants

The majority of the descendant of the first wave of immigrants successfully integrated into US mainstream culture. The children and grandchildren of Italian, Polish, Irish and Jewish immigrants seized opportunities that allowed them to assimilate into the economic, social and political landscape.[5] Jews in particular made deep in-roads into American society, while also influencing US culture.[6] The first group of Jewish immigrants arrived from Germany in the mid-1800s, assimilating into the middle class and gaining a strong economic foothold through commercial activities in the retail and clothing trades.[7] Subsequent waves of Jewish immigrants of varying socio-economic backgrounds and levels of religiosity, largely from eastern Europe arrived in the United States and faced discrimination from native-born Americans and their German coreligionists.[8] Over time, turn of the century Jewish immigrants adapted to the realities of life in the United States and descendants of German as well as eastern European Jews morphed into an "American Judaism," which grew directly out of interaction with US society.

Contemporary Jewish Immigration

The decades following the large wave of immigration to the United States witnessed a paucity of new arrivals due to a combination of factors. The Great Depression and World War II were preceded by the 1924 Johnson-Reed Act which essentially banned new immigrants from "undesirable" regions, particularly southern and eastern Europe. Post-World War II, the United States began accepting refugees from the war, but the majority of contemporary immigrants arrived as a result of the change in immigration laws in 1965. The Hart-Cellar Act of 1965 paved the way for millions of new immigrants from all over the world to enter the United States. Post 1965, Jewish immigrants, many of whom were fleeing politically tenuous situations in their home countries, made the United States their home. The demise of the Soviet bloc was the catalyst for the largest wave of immigrations of Jews from the FSU.[9] Numerous political and economic crisis prompted Jews from Latin America to leave their communities and immigrate to the United States. Latin American regional out-migration streams occurred in waves. Peruvian Jews made their way to Miami during the height of the Shining Path guerrilla movement in the 1980s, whereas the largest wave of Argentine Jews arrived during the economic crisis of 2001. Venezuelan Jews are the newest arrivals, fleeing the political and economic turmoil experienced since Hugo Chavez first took office in 1999.[10] There has been a steady increase of Israeli Jews migrating to the United States since 1970, many of who came for "economic opportunities (including education), family factors, and a need for broader horizons."[11]

JEWISH IDENTITY

Religious identity is multi-layered, nuanced and difficult to measure.[12] Jewish identity is not only layered and multi-faceted; the term "Jewish" represents both a religious and ethno-cultural identity, further complicating the conceptualization of Jewishness and Jewish religious identity.[13] The religious and

ethnic tenets that comprise Jewishness are intertwined in different permuta-
tions for Jews across various generations and geographies. A myriad of factors
affect how one comprises their Jewish identity. Families pass down traditions,
level of religiosity, Zionist ideals as well as rituals and practice. Opportunities
for interaction and identity development also come into play. For example, in
countries with strong Jewish youth movements, Jewish identity formation was
centered around participation in such organizations.[14] In Latin America, the
strength of Jewish institutions, the lack of public services and a strong Zionist
movement are all factors that influenced the development of strong communal
Jewish identity.[15] By comparison, Jews in the former Soviet Union did not have
access to formal religious or ethno-religious organizations, yet their identity as
ethnic Jews was imposed through government classification schemes and overt
discrimination.[16] For Jews in Israel, their Jewish identity is intimately tied to
the nation state, and they often connect participation in Jewish religious rites,
culture and food as "Israeliness" rather than "Jewishness."[17]

A host of literature is dedicated the Jewish experience in the United States,
much of it debating the exceptionality of Jewish integration and Jewish upward
mobility.[18] While the debate ensues, what is certain is that the descendants of
the first large wave of immigrants experienced impressive upward mobility,
social integration and political representation.[19] As the children and grandchildren of Jewish immigrants became wholly integrated into the US mainstream, the ethnic component of Jewish identity began to wane. The demise of
Yiddish language, loss of ethnic enclaves and neighborhoods, integration into
suburban life and assimilation into the white middle-class worked together to
create an American Jewish identity that was symbiotic with American political, cultural and social life.[20] Significant changes to Jewish life occurred in the
post-war period that shaped American Jewish identity. As Jewish life moved
outside of the confines of ethnic neighborhoods, Jewish identity relied on participation in religious organizations (synagogues) and/or religious rites carried
out at home.[21]

Ethnicity or Religion?

A number of scholars[22] have argued that ethnicity and religion among Jews
cannot be separated because the "sacred and secular elements of the culture
are strongly intertwined."[23] Others suggest that religion and ethnicity are not
determinately entangled and that Jews can identify with Jews as a people without identifying with the religious or spiritual component of Judaism.[24] Survey

studies of Jews in the United States decidedly support the notion that Jews and Jewish identity can exist independently of religion. While religious rites, synagogue attendance and belief in God and Jewish law may lie at the center of a religious identity, Jews have demonstrated both changing attitudes over time as well as strong attachment to Jewish peoplehood even in absence of robust religious tendencies. Today in the United States, the majority of Jews identify Jewishness with ancestry over religion, and believe that religious tenets such as working on the Sabbath or not believing in God are compatible with a Jewish identity.[25] American Jews today are at liberty to construct their Jewish identity without external constraints—their participation in Jewish life, among non-Orthodox Jews, is at will and results in looser ties and fluid religious and ethnic Jewish identities.

GLOBAL JEWISH IDENTITY

The social, political and economic structures of countries where Jews reside greatly influence Jewish identity formation. Jewish life in the United States flourished as a result of a myriad of factors specific to the political and economic climate at the time of the great migration peak and subsequent post-war period. In much the same way, Jewish identity across the globe is constructed in relationship to the social structures of the state Jews reside in.

Latin America

Whereas Jews in the United States have pushed for and won entry into the mainstream, in Latin America, Jews are decidedly on the border of mainstream society. Jews from Latin America share a common denominator: they are members of a minority religious group in countries where Catholicism influences both public and private spheres. The strong Catholic presence results in an "othering" of Jews in Latin America. While these boundaries are increasingly blurred, Jews in Latin American countries participate in strong ethnoreligious institutions that have allowed communal Jewish identities to develop in contrast to religious identities. Jewish identity in Latin America leans heavily towards a sense of communal identity, reinforced by strong Jewish institutions such as socio-cultural community and athletic centers, schools, mutual aid societies, political organizations as well as dense networks of co-ethnics.[26]

FSU Jews

Jews from the former Soviet Union do not have a history of strong communities nor strong religious identities. The practice of Jewish culture and Jewish religion in the former Soviet Union was minimal due to state sanction against religious groups and religious observances. The Jewish identity of FSU Jews was linked in part to persecution and antisemitism, and their exclusion from the mainstream enforced their Jewish ethnic identity.[27] The influx of large numbers of Jewish immigrants from the Soviet Union to the United States in the 1990s prompted US Jewish groups (religious, educational, and communal) to reach out to Soviet immigrants and instill a sense of Jewish culture and religiosity among them, with some reluctance and pushback.[28] Today, while the religious and cultural affiliation and identity of FSU vary, Jewish identity for FSU Jews remains, overall, tied to ethnicity. In contrast, a US Jewish identity, while cultural in practice, has strong in roots in religious knowledge and rites.

Israeli Jews

Of the three groups of contemporary Jewish immigrants discussed in this chapter, Israeli Jews have the most complex relationship with Jewish identity. Israeli Jews, unlike Jews from the former Soviet Union or Latin America, are neither political nor economic refugees. They are not fleeing discrimination nor antisemitism. Israeli Jews are both an ethnic and religious majority in their home country. Moreover, leaving Israel is often experienced or perceived as a betrayal of Zionist principles.[29] The social and political fabric of Israeli society is intimately tied to Jewish religious practice. National holidays are religious holidays, the workweek is structured around the observance of the Sabbath; even among secular Israeli Jews, life is lived within Jewish religious boundaries. In the United States, Israeli Jews do not seamlessly merge with the larger American Jewish community; their national Israeli identities diverge in culture and behavior from their US Jewish counterparts. As a result, they create close-knit communities in urban areas such as Los Angeles and New York—areas where there are communities of co-nationals as well as employment and business opportunities—and forge ethnic identities as Israelis within the larger Jewish diaspora.[30]

JEWISH IDENTITY AMONG IMMIGRANT GROUPS

The purpose of this chapter is to explore the different Jewish identity trajectories of contemporary Jewish immigrants in the United States. Jewish identity, both ethnic and religious, is born out of lived individual and communal experiences—for immigrants the construction of Jewish identity comprises elements of pre-migration life and post-migration integration into their host society (the United States in this case). The following section provides an analysis of the identity trajectories among the three groups of contemporary Jewish immigrants that are the subject of this chapter and offers a comparison with their native-born Jewish counterparts in the United States.

DATA AND METHODS

Data for this study are from the Pew Research Center's 2013 Survey of US Jews.[31] The Pew Research Center screened over 70,000 households via random-digit dialing and identified 3,500 households as Jewish. Population weights are applied to the data to yield a nationally representative sample of the US population of Jews. The data estimates there are 6.7 million Jews in the US today, including 5.3 million adults and 1.3 million children, and that Jews are roughly 2.2% of the total US population. For the purposes of this analysis, I limit observations to adults over the age of 18. First-generation immigrants are defined as those born outside of the United States; second generation immigrants are classified as such if they had at least one parent born abroad. All those born in the United States and with US-born parents are defined as native-born Jewish adults. Adults born in Latin America, the Former Soviet Union and Israel are compared to the native-born Jewish population (both second-generation and beyond).

Jewish Identity

Using previous literature on the religious and ethnic identity of Jewish life, I construct two summative scales to measure major components of Jewish identity.[32] Summated factors of religiosity and ethnicity are measured with Cronbach's Alpha measure of internal consistency to test the reliability of these scales.

Research Design

A Jewish religious identity factor was constructed using the following variables:

> Importance of observing Jewish law
> Fasting on Yom Kippur
> Keeping kosher
> Lighting Shabbat candles
> Frequency of synagogue attendance
> Holding or attending a Seder
> Handling money on Shabbat
> Synagogue membership
> Belief in God or universal spirit as essential to being Jewish

The second constructed variable is an ethnic identity scale. Ethnic identity is calculated using factors that pertain to various ways that Jewishness is experienced as part of a communal, group identity and shared history and values. The data from the Pew Research Center asked respondents to rate the importance of certain beliefs and values and on being Jewish. I use the following factors in the construction of ethnic identity:

> Importance of eating traditional Jewish foods
> Importance of being part of a Jewish community
> Importance of being Jewish in your life

In addition, the following variables are included that measure a respondent's ties to Israel:

> Importance of caring for Israel
> Strength of emotional attachment to Israel

I also included two additional variables to measure respondents' social ties and sense of peoplehood.

> Sense of belonging to Jewish people
> Number of close friends that are Jewish

Both summative scales have Cronbach's alpha greater than .78, indicating a reliable measure of consistency among the variables that comprise each scale. These scales serve as dependent variables to understand how Jewish immigrant groups diverge across major Jewish identity markers. I control for a number of variables including sex, marital status, age, education, income, religious denomination, presence of children in household and geographic region (see Appendix A for regression results).

RESULTS

The US Jewish population is overwhelmingly native-born. Eighty-six percent of Jewish adults were born in the United States, slightly higher than the overall US population (83% native-born). While 13% of Jewish adults were born abroad, almost 20% of Jewish adults have at least one parent born outside of the United States. Among those born abroad, immigrants from the FSU were the most highly represented group: FSU Jewish adults make up around 40% of the Jewish adult immigration population. Approximately 13% of Jewish immigrants are from Israel and close to 18% are from Latin America.

Demographics

The median age of both native-born and foreign-born Jewish adults in the United States is between 56 and 57 years old. There are larger differences across national origin groups. The median age for Jews from Latin America is 43. Jewish adults from Israel are slightly older—the median age for this group is closer to 50, while Jewish immigrants from the FSU (median age 65) comprise one of the oldest groups among foreign born Jewish adults.

Immigrant Jews are more likely than their native-born peers to have family incomes within lower brackets. Almost 25% of immigrants reported earnings of $20,000 or less in 2012, compared to only 9.6% of native-born Jewish adults. Native-born Jewish adults were also more likely to report family incomes greater than $150,000. In 2012, 26% of native-born Jewish adults were found in this income bracket. By comparison, only 15.4% of immigrants claimed a comparable family income. In 2012, family income for immigrants from Latin America was overwhelmingly within the $50,000–75,000 bracket (60%) and over 25% reported family earnings of greater than $150,000. In comparison, immigrant Jewish adults from the FSU were more likely to be found in lower income brackets–39% reported family incomes of less than $20,000 and only 8% percent earned more than $150,000. Jewish adults from Israel reported a wide range of annual family incomes. Twenty-five percent of Israeli immigrants reported annual family incomes between $20,000 and $40,000, 30% earned between $40,000 and $75,000 per year, and 16% had annual family incomes of greater than $150,000.

Consistent with scholarly research on educational attainment among Jews, both native-born and foreign-born Jewish adults (25 and older) are highly educated—62% of foreign-born Jews and 66% of native-born Jewish adults have a college degree or higher. Immigrants from Israel had the lowest BA and higher attainment rates (51%), nonetheless a rate considerably higher than the US as a whole (36%).[33] Both immigrant groups from Latin America (67%) and the FSU (62%) reported BA or higher rates in tandem with the general Jewish immigrant population.

Approximately half of the US Jewish adult population (both native- and foreign-born) reported being married in 2012. Jews from Latin America were slightly less likely to report being married—39%—and Israeli born immigrants reported even lower marital rates—32%. Almost 53% of Jewish immigrants from the FSU reported being married. About half of Jewish adults report being married to a partner that is Jewish in some way—either by religion, affinity, no religion, and/or background. Almost 75% of Jews from Latin America are married to someone that is of Jewish background or affinity and more than 60% of Jewish immigrants from the FSU and Israel report a spouse of Jewish identity.

Twenty percent of Jewish immigrants reported one or more children under 18 in their household. Mirroring the trend of the US Jewish population as a whole, 23% of immigrants from Latin America had a child living in their household. Twenty percent of immigrants from the FSU lived with one or more children and Israeli immigrants reported the lowest rate of children in their household—only 11% of Israeli Jewish adults reported one or more children in their household.

Political Leanings

Jewish adults overwhelmingly skew Democrat. More than 58% of Jewish adults considered themselves a Democrat in 2012 and only 10% reported Republican leanings or identification. Foreign born Jewish adults were slightly less likely to consider themselves Democrats (45%) and more likely than the US Jewish population as whole to identify as Republican (13%). Immigrants from the FSU were the most likely to report a Republican political leaning (26%) than any other immigrant group. Jews from Latin America reported the lowest rates of Republican identity (2%); they also had Democratic leanings on par with the US populations as a whole. Israeli Jews had low levels of Republican affinity (8%) and 41% considered themselves Democrats.

DISCUSSION

Jewish identity

A key objective of this analysis is to understand how three groups of contemporary Jewish immigrants differ in their strength of Jewish identity across ethnic and religious lines. Using ordinary least square regression (OLS) analysis, I control for variables that influence the strength of Jewish identity and isolate the effect of immigrant status and region of origin. The model compares Jewish identity scales of immigrants from Latin America, Israel, FSU, Europe, the Middle East and Asia to native born US Jewish adults.

Assimilation

Overall, first- and second-generation immigrants show a statistical difference in the magnitude of religious and ethnic identity. Consistent with scholarship on the strength of Jewish identity on contemporary immigrants,[34] first-generation immigrants have deeper ethnic identities than both second-generation immigrants and native-born adults. While religion, as Robert Putnam puts it, ". . . is a bigger deal in America than in any other advanced nation on earth,"[35] public acts of faith and religious rites do not follow suit.[36] For example, US native-born Jews are more likely than their immigrant counterparts to state that believing in God is essential to being Jewish (74% versus 65%). Yet native-born adults are less likely to engage in religious rites such as fasting on Yom Kippur or attending a Passover Seder. Private religious rites are also more likely to be practiced among foreign-born Jewish adults. Almost 20% of immigrants report always lighting Shabbat candles, compared to 9% of second-generation immigrants and 7% of US born adults. A number of factors may account for tendency toward lower religiosity across immigrant generations. An important point for consideration is the role of religion and religious institutions in the migration trajectory of immigrants. Religion has a central role in the adaptation of immigrants—the institution is a link to familiar group and community, while religious practices provide an emotional connection to their pre-immigrant life.[37] The performance of religious rites reinforces in immigrants a sense of self and familiarity. Religion and religious doctrines are also useful instruments by which parents can transfer traditional (pre-migration) beliefs and customs to their US-born children.[38] And, religious organizations have always been central in providing immigrants with much needed information about schools, social services, medical assistance, jobs, and housing.

Jewish ethnic identity is also higher among first-generation immigrants than it is among second-generation immigrants or native-born Jewish adults with Jewish parents. Consistent with literature on ethnicity and ethno-religious identification, immigrants retain a strong sense of ethnic identity. This may be because ethnic identity is ascribed and inescapable as is the case with those who do not resemble the mainstream in appearance or behavior[39] or because it assures a sense of group belonging, particularly in the absence of complete acceptance by the host society.[40] In this study, the immigrants' generational differences points to a diminishing ethnic identity over time, a pattern that mimics the trajectory of Jewish assimilation into American life.[41]

Ethnic Identity among Jewish Immigrant Sub-groups

Controlling for variables such as age, income, region of residence, children and marital status, education and denomination, Israeli Jews have slightly stronger religious identities than their US native-born, FSU and Latin American Jewish adults with native born parents (for full regression results see appendix A). Qualitative studies of Israeli Jews in the Jewish Diaspora[42] find evidence that Israeli Jews continue to practice religious rites such as fasting on Yom Kippur and attending synagogue during the holidays as events that tie them to their Israeli homeland. While the Pew data show that Israelis in the United States are much less likely than native-born Jews to belong to a synagogue (90% of non-Orthodox Israeli Jews do not report synagogue membership), 44% attend synagogue at least a few times per year. Synagogue attendance may be tied to the institutional and social support that synagogues provide for immigrants, or outreach programs geared towards Israeli Jews that often take place in synagogues, such as an Israeli-style Shabbat or Israeli independence day celebrations. Israeli Jews are also more likely to abide by kosher dietary rules (in full or partially) and observe major holidays such as fasting on Yom Kippur or attending a Passover Seder. Again, these rites likely serve to preserve a link between Israeli holidays and culture, that in Israel are built into the social and national culture. At the same time, there is some evidence that Israelis become more religious in the Diaspora, as part of the process of identity construction.[43] Israeli Jews also have stronger Jewish ethnic identities in relation to immigrants and native-born Jews. The identity scale for Jewish ethnicity includes two variables related to Israel—importance of caring for Israel and strength of emotional tie to Israel, which likely bias the scale. Nonetheless, I include them because a relationship to Israel is one of the strongest indicators of an ethnic Jewish identity revolving around a "motherland" for all Jews.[44]

Jews from the FSU have stronger religious and ethnic identities than US native-born adults. All religious groups in the former Soviet Union faced strict restrictions in carrying out religious practices—leaving FSU Jews little room to partake in Jewish spiritual and traditional gatherings, rites and studies. Upon arrival in the United States, many FSU Jewish immigrants had little knowledge or prior practice of the religious aspects of Judaism. Jewish communal and religious institutions stepped in to offer FSU immigrants assistance with integration to Jewish life in the United States. The efforts on behalf of the US Jewish community were met with mixed results. Some FSU immigrants continued to identify as Jewish but did so beyond the confines of organized US Jewish community while others became more active in religious and communal organizations such as local Chabad centers or Jewish communal institutions. In examining the factors that comprise the religiosity scale, non-Orthodox Jewish immigrants from the FSU are slightly more likely to partake in rituals such as fasting on Yom Kippur, keeping kosher and lighting Shabbat candles. However, they are less likely than native-born Jews to state that believing in God is essential to being Jewish. Consistent with their pre-migration experience, FSU Jews also have stronger Jewish ethnic identities than their native-born peers. The strength of their Jewish identity stems is derived, in part, from a sense of Jewish peoplehood—almost 83% of non-Orthodox FSU immigrants reported a strong sense of belonging to the Jewish people compared to 71% of native-born Jewish adults. Jews from the FSU are also more likely to report a majority of close friends as Jewish (60%). These results suggest an increase in the religious identity of FSU Jews post-migration and a continuation of a strong sense Jewish ethnic identity tied to close social ties.

Overall Latino Jews arrive in the United States with a strong sense of Jewishness. Many Latino Jews report strong ties to organized cultural and educational Jewish institutions and a sense of belonging to their local Jewish community.[45] Levels of religiosity vary among Latin American Jews across countries, age groups, and Jewish sub-ethnic groups. Latin American Jews have historically placed more importance on the cultural, ethnic and political factors that comprise a Jewish identity, yet many Latin American Jews partake in spiritual rites such as lighting candles on Shabbat and/or attending Shabbat services. Latino Jews in the United States have the weakest religious and ethnic identities compared to their native-born and foreign-born peers. Latino Jews in the United States reported lower levels of ritual observances or practices associated with Jewish religiosity—such as fasting on Yom Kippur, lighting candles on Shabbat or attending a Passover Seder. Jewish immigrants from Latin America have slightly lower levels of Jewish ethnic identities than their native-born peers. Qualitative studies find strong levels of pre- and post-migration of Jewish identity,[46] stemming from a strong sense of communal interconnectedness in Latin America as well as an ethnic "othering" that occurs across the region. The lower levels of ethnic identity we find in this study are slight, and likely due to a combination of factors including loss of immediate ethnic group and lack of proximal host, defined as the category to which the immigrant would be assigned following immigration.[47] Latino Jews, as a group, diverge across regional backgrounds, levels of communal identification and religiosity. They also differ from existing Jewish communities around language, cultures and Jewish identity. As a result, members of this group are more likely to seek out alternative affiliations or construct new ethnic identities, which may differ in its composition. In other words, it is possible, and even likely, that Latino Jews in the United States have strong Jewish identities; what may differ are the factors that comprise these identities.

CONCLUSION

Immigrants differ in their levels of ethnic and religious identity compared to US native-born Jews. There are also clear differences across immigrant generations. As a whole, first-generation immigrants have stronger Jewish ethnic and religious identities than either second-generation immigrants or native-born adults. Second-generation immigrants have slightly higher ethnic and religious Jewish identities when compared to third-generation immigrants or higher. These trends indicate that, for immigrants, holding onto a sense of Jewish ethnicity and participating in some aspect of Jewish religious life, either in communal or private settings, are in line with past research on immigrant incorporation. Namely that the practice of ethno-religious rites, participation in ethno-religious organizations and a strong sense of ethno-religious social identity serve to both protect immigrants from a sense of loss during the process of migration and also aid in the integration process. The move towards lower levels of ethnic and religious identity across immigrant generations point to the eventual assimilation of Jewish immigrants into US Jewish life.

The diversity among immigrant groups in terms of Jewish identity also highlight the importance of understating pre-migration histories and post-migration trajectories across different groups. While this study is limited in its availability of data, what we can garner is that Jews from the FSU, Israel and Latin America diverge in their levels of Jewish religious and Jewish ethnic identity. These divergences are due to both the experiences in their home countries, including opportunities or lack thereof to partake in religious life, state or socially mandated ethnic "othering," and majority and minority status vis-à-vis the nation's civil religion. Upon migrating a number of factors influence the strengths of ethnic and religious identity—such as opportunities for integration into US Jewish life, accessibility to co-nationals, and acceptance into proximal host groups. When immigrants settle into life in the United States, the strength of their Jewish identity may weaken over time, or, perhaps, it merely changes and new Jewish identities are constructed. At the same time, as the current native-born Jewish population ages, new questions arise surrounding US Jewish life. Will the children of contemporary immigrants re-construct Jewish life and Jewish identity in the United States? Can we expect Jewish immigrants and their children to become active participants in and revitalize cultural Jewish institutions, Jewish schools and synagogues? Perhaps we can look forward towards a US Jewish identity that is more inclusive of all Jewish sub-ethnic groups and widens the current Ashkenazi-centric Jewish identity.

APPENDIX A

Table 1. Regression results for Jewish ethnicity across immigrant generation

Constant	.4698699 (.0043474)
Immigrant generation (Ref: first-generation)	
Second-generation	-.2459564*** (.0014044)
Native-born	-.2969077*** (.0012418)
Gender	
Female	.1073025*** (.0007181)
Annual household income (Ref: less than $20,000)	
$20,000 to less than $40,000	-.1677886*** (.002251)
$40,000 to less than $75,000	-.0257443*** (.0020368)
$75,000 to under $100,000	-.0545276*** (.0020637)
$100,000 to less than $150,000	-.1066563*** (.0020328)
More than $150,000	-.0158685*** (.0019865)
Has a one or more children	.0182178*** (.0008351)
Geographic region of residence (Ref: Northeast)	
Midwest	.1866055*** (.0012188)
South	.1166684*** (.0008912)

West	.023897*** (.0009267)
Age (squared)	.0000126*** (2.66e-07)
Race and ethnicity (Ref: White)	
Black	-.1264667*** (.0033197)
Hispanic	-.0674979*** (.0021463)
Other	.1846814*** (.0032723)
Education (Ref: less than high school)	
High school or equivalent	-.5430041*** (.0040698)
Some college	-.4362431*** (.0041175)
Associate's degree	-.4754976*** (.0041525)
BA or higher	-.4755232*** (.0040009)
Spouse Jewish in some capacity	.4769784*** (.0007413)
Denomination (Ref: Conservative)	
Orthodox	.0546801*** (.0015659)
Reform	-.1724774*** (.0008998)
None	-.4003696*** (.0011204)
Other	-.4336*** (.0011315)

Laura Limonic

R-squared	0.3117
Number of observations	2,254,352

Standard errors are reported in parentheses. *, **, *** indicates significance at the 90%, 95%, and 99% level, respectively.

Table 2. Regression results for Jewish religiosity across immigrant generation

Constant	.5885198 (.003826)
Immigrant generation (Ref: first-generation)	
Second-generation	-.0625898*** (.0013809)
Native-born	-.0802015*** (.0012093)
Gender	
Female	.0997598*** (.0007038)
Annual household income (Ref: less than $20,000)	
$20,000 to less than $40,000	-.1856579*** (.0022327)
$40,000 to less than $75,000	-.2004755*** (.0020501)
$75,000 to under $100,000	-.2231333*** (.0020567)
$100,000 to less than $150,000	-.2846418*** (.0020371)
More than $150,000	-.2626855*** (.0019914)
Has one or more children	.04014*** (.0008214)
Geographic region of residence (Ref: Northeast)	

Midwest	.1526584*** (.0011995)
South	.1391822*** (.0008762)
West	.0161017*** (.0009062)
Age (squared)	-.0000415*** (2.63e-07)
Race and ethnicity (Ref: White)	
Black	.7985836*** (.0031599)
Hispanic	-.1569076***
	(.0020918)
Other	.3064171*** (.0030915)
Education (Ref: less than high school)	
High school or equivalent	-.43972*** (.0035366)
Some college	-.3818444*** (.0035742)
Associate's degree	-.4090179*** (.003607)
BA or higher	-.403596*** (.0034477)
Spouse Jewish in some capacity	.5142995*** (.0007257)
Denomination (Ref: Conservative)	
Orthodox	.1184478*** (.0015163)
Reform	-.2246357*** (.0008834)

None	-.3978196*** (.0010991)
Other	-.3251413*** (.0011118)
R-squared	0.3425
Number of observations	(.0011118)

Standard errors are reported in parentheses. *, **, *** indicates significance at the 90%, 95%, and 99% level, respectively.

Table 3. Regression results for Jewish ethnicity by immigrant birth place

Constant	.5885198
Country of birth (Ref: United States)	(.003826)
Latin America	-.1132657*** (.0028262)
Asia	.0363681*** (.0047049)
Europe	.0581763*** (.0032431)
Middle East	.1812937*** (.0074443)
Africa	.2430184*** (.0041363)
FSU	.4397761*** (.0017986)
Israel	.5962849*** (.0031143)
Gender	
Female	.102737 ****** (.0007135)
Annual household income (Ref: less than $20,000)	
$20,000 to less than $40,000	-.1149636*** (.0022982)

$40,000 to less than $75,000	.0276867*** (.0020769)
$75,000 to under $100,000	-.005211*** (.0020998)
$100,000 to less than $150,000	-.0563502*** (.002078)
More than $150,000	.0471534*** (.002049)
Has one or more children	.0187848*** (.0008297)
Geographic region of residence (Ref: Northeast)	
Midwest	.1957573*** (.0012119)
South	.122822*** (.000888)
West	.0380907*** (.0009317)
Age (squared)	.0000166*** (2.58e-07)
Race and ethnicity (Ref: White)	
Black	.0945297*** (.003618)
Hispanic	.070332*** (.0022704)
Other	.1711674*** (.0033106)
Education (Ref: less than high school)	
High school or equivalent	-.5201063*** (.0040377)
Some college	-.4061612*** (.0040868)
Associate's degree	-.4440951*** (.0041213)

BA or higher	-.4495514*** (.0039701)
Spouse Jewish in some capacity	.4825238*** (.0007368)
Denomination (Ref: Conservative)	
Orthodox	.0401972*** (.0015753)
Reform	-.1884999*** (.0008886)
None	-.4382018*** (.0011312)
Other	-.4459475*** (.0011292)
R-squared	0.3247
Number of observations	2,252,372

Standard errors are reported in parentheses. *, **, *** indicates significance at the 90%, 95%, and 99% level, respectively.

Table 4. Regression results for Jewish religiosity by immigrant birth place

Constant	.5218998 (.0038407)
Country of birth (Ref: United States)	
Latin America	-.0348774*** (.0027337)
Asia	.3909379*** (.0048488)
Europe	-.1003404*** (.0029486)
Middle East	-.3497667*** (.0070677)
Africa	.1318604*** (.0039366)
FSU	.0620172*** (.0018329)

Israel	.3266001***
	(.0029784)
Gender	
Female	.0961901***
	(.000703)
Annual household income (Ref: less than $20,000)	
$20,000 to less than $40,000	-.2017007***
	(.0022837)
$40,000 to less than $75,000	-.2117945***
	(.0020858)
$75,000 to under $100,000	-.2351182***
	(.0020932)
$100,000 to less than $150,000	-.293301***
	(.0020793)
More than $150,000	-.2733731***
	(.0020533)
Has one or more children	.0187848***
	(.0008297)
Geographic region of residence (Ref: Northeast)	
Midwest	.1957573***
	(.0012119)
South	.122822***
	(.000888)
West	.0380907***
	(.0009317)
Age (squared)	.0000166***
	(2.58e-07)
Race and ethnicity (Ref: White)	
Black	.0945297***
	(.003618)

Hispanic	.070332*** (.0022704)
Other	.1711674*** (.0033106)
Education (Ref: less than high school)	
High school or equivalent	-.5201063*** (.0040377)
Some college	-.4061612*** (.0040868)
Associate's degree	-.4440951*** (.0041213)
BA or higher	-.4495514*** (.0039701)
Spouse Jewish in some capacity	.4825238*** (.0007368)
Denomination (Ref: Conservative)	
Orthodox	.0401972*** (.0015753)
Reform	-.1884999*** (.0008886)
None	-.4382018*** (.0011312)
Other	-.4459475*** (.0011292)
R-squared	0.3247
Number of observations	2,252,372

Standard errors are reported in parentheses. *, **, *** indicates significance at the 90%, 95%, and 99% level, respectively.

Notes

1. "A Portrait of Jewish Americans [Data File and Code Book]," Pew Research Center's Religion and Public Life Project (Washington, D.C.: Pew Research Center, 2013).
2. Nancy Foner and Richard Alba, "Immigrant Religion in the U.S. and Western Europe: Bridge or Barrier to Inclusion?" *International Migration Review* 42, no. 2 (2008): 374.
3. Oscar Handlin, *The Uprooted*, 2nd ed. (New York: Little, Brown and Company, 1973), 105–28; Will Herberg, *Protestant, Catholic, Jew* (Chicago: University of Chicago Press, 1983).
4. Hasia R. Diner, *The Jews of the United States, 1654 to 2000* (Berkeley: University of California Press, 2006), 41–70.
5. Richard Alba, *Blurring the Color Line: The New Chance for a More Integrated America* (Cambridge: Harvard University Press, 2009); K. Brodkin, *How Jews Became White Folks and What That Says about Race in America* (New Brunswick, NJ: Rutgers University Press, 1998); Alejandro Portes and Ruben G. Rumbaut, *Immigrant America: A Portrait* (Berkeley: University of California Press, 2006).
6. Richard Alba, "On the Sociological Significance of the American Jewish Experience: Boundary Blurring, Assimilation, and Pluralism," *Sociology of Religion* 67, no. 4 (2006): 347–58.
7. Steven J. Gold and Bruce A. Phillips, "Mobility and Continuity among Eastern European Jews," in *Origins and Destinies: Immigration, Race and Ethnicity in America*, ed. Silvia Pedraza and Rubén G. Rumbaut (Belmont, CA: Wadsworth Publishing Company, 1996).
8. Gerald Sorin, "Mutual Contempt, Mutual Benefit: The Strained Encounter Between German and Eastern European Jews in America, 1880–1920," *American Jewish History* 81, no. 1 (1993): 34.
9. Barry R. Chiswick, "Soviet Jews in the United States: Language and Labor Market Adjustments Revisited," in *Russian Jews on Three Continents: Migration and Resettlement*, ed. Noah Lewin-Epstein, Yaacov Ro'I, and Paul Ritterband (London: Frank Cass, 1996), 233.
10. Laura Limonic, *Kugel and Frijoles: Latino Jews in the United States* (Detroit, MI: Wayne State University Press, 2019), 25–44.
11. Gold and Phillips, "Mobility and Continuity among Eastern European Jews."
12. Miriam Pepper, Tim Jackson, and David Uzzell, "A Study of Multidimensional Religion Constructs and Values in the United Kingdom," *Journal for the Scientific Study of Religion* 49, no. 1 (2010): 127–46
13. Bethamie Horowitz, "Reframing the Study of Contemporary American Jewish Identity," *Contemporary Jewry* 23, no. 1 (2002): 24–26.
14. Adriana Brodsky, Beatrice Gurwitz, and Rachel Kranson, "Editors' Introduction: Jewish Youth in the Global 1960s," *Journal of Jewish Identities* 8, no. 2 (July 29, 2015): 1–11.

15. Limonic, *Kugel and Frijoles*, 25–44; Judit Bokser Liwerant, "Latin American Jewish Identities: Past and Present Challenges. The Mexican Case in a Comparative Perspective," *Identities in an Era of Globalization and Multiculturalism. Latin America in the Jewish World*, January 1, 2008, http://www.bjpa.org/publications/details.cfm?PublicationID=11703.

16. Larissa Remennick, "Identity Quest among Russian Jews of the 1990s: Before and after Emigration," in *Jewish Survival: The Identity Problem at the Close of the Twentieth Century*, ed. Ernest Krausz and Gitta Tulea (New Brunswick, NJ: Transaction Publishers, 1998).

17. Steven J. Gold, "From Nationality to Peoplehood: Adaptation and Identity Formation in the Israeli Diaspora," *Diaspora: A Journal of Transnational Studies* 13, no. 2 (2004): 337, https://doi.org/10.1353/dsp.2008.0007.

18. Tony Michels, "Is America 'Different'? A Critique of American Jewish Exceptionalism," *American Jewish History* 96, no. 3 (2010): 201–24; Eli Lederhendler, *American Jewry: A New History* (Cambridge: Cambridge University Press, 2016).

19. Richard D. Alba and Victor Nee, *Remaking the American Mainstream: Assimilation and Contemporary Immigration* (Cambridge, MA: Harvard University Press, 2003).

20. Alba, *Blurring the Color Line*, 21–50; V. C. Hattam, *In the Shadow of Race: Jews, Latinos, and Immigrant Politics in the United States* (Chicago: University of Chicago Press, 2007), 45–76; Brodkin, *How Jews Became White Folks and What That Says about Race in America*.

21. Eli Lederhendler, *New York Jews and the Decline of Urban Ethnicity: 1950–1970* (Syracuse, NY: Syracuse University Press, 2001), 105–16.

22. Phillip E. Hammond and Kee Warner, "Religion and Ethnicity in Late-Twentieth-Century America," *The Annals of the American Academy of Political and Social Science* 527 (May 1993): 55–56; Uzi Rebhun, "Jewish Identity in America: Structural Analyses of Attitudes and Behaviors," *Review of Religious Research* 46, no. 1 (September 2004): 60.

23. Herbert J. Gans, "Symbolic Ethnicity: The Future of Ethnic Groups and Cultures in America," *Ethnic & Racial Studies* 2, no. 1 (January 1979): 7, https://doi.org/Article.

24. Steven Sharot, *Comparative Perspectives on Judaisms and Jewish Identities* (Detroit, MI: Wayne State University Press, 2010).

25. "A Portrait of Jewish Americans: Findings from a Pew Research Center Survey of U.S. Jews," Pew Research Center's Religion and Public Life Project (Washington, D.C.: Pew Research Center, October 1, 2013), https://www.pewforum.org/2013/10/01/jewish-american-beliefs-attitudes-culture-survey/.

26. Limonic, *Kugel and Frijoles*, 25–44.

27. Annelise Orleck, "Soviet Jews: The City's Newest Immigrants Transform New York Jewish Life," in *New Immigrants in New York*, ed. Nancy Foner (New York: Columbia University Press, 2001), 111–40.

28. Steven J. Gold, "Patterns of Adaptation among Contemporary Jewish Immigrants

to the US," in *American Jewish Year Book 2015*, 12–14 (Springer, 2016), http://link.springer.com.ezproxy.gc.cuny.edu/chapter/10.1007/978-3-319-24505-8_1.

29. Gold, "From Nationality to Peoplehood," 335; Steven J. Gold, *The Israeli Diaspora* (London: Routledge, 2002), 181–216.

30. David Mittelberg and Mary C. Waters, "The Process of Ethnogenesis among Haitian and Israeli Immigrants in the United States," *Ethnic and Racial Studies* 15, no. 3 (July 1992): 420–25; Gold, "From Nationality to Peoplehood," 332.

31. "A Portrait of Jewish Americans [Data File and Code Book]."

32. Horowitz, "Reframing the Study of Contemporary American Jewish Identity"; Harriet Hartman and Moshe Hartman, "Jewish Identity and the Secular Achievements of American Jewish Men and Women," *Journal for the Scientific Study of Religion* 50, no. 1 (2011): 133–53.

33. US Census Bureau, "U.S. Census Bureau Releases New Educational Attainment Data," The United States Census Bureau, accessed June 19, 2020, https://www.census.gov/newsroom/press-releases/2020/educational-attainment.html.

34. Brodkin, *How Jews Became White Folks and What That Says about Race in America*; Gans, "Symbolic Ethnicity"; Alba, *Blurring the Color Line*.

35. Robert Putnam, "American Grace" (paper, The Tanner Lectures on Human Values, Princeton University, October 27–18, 2010).

36. Hartman and Hartman, "Jewish Identity and the Secular Achievements of American Jewish Men and Women."

37. Wendy Cadge and Elaine Howard Ecklund, "Immigration and Religion," *Annual Review of Sociology* 33 (2007): 366–68; Hammond and Warner, "Religion and Ethnicity in Late-Twentieth-Century America," 58; Charles Hirschman, "The Role of Religion in the Origins and Adaptation of Immigrant Groups in the United States," *The International Migration Review* 38, no. 3 (2004): 1206–33."

38. Mittelberg and Waters, "The Process of Ethnogenesis among Haitian and Israeli Immigrants in the United States," 431.

39. Joane Nagel, "Constructing Ethnicity: Creating and Recreating Ethnic Identity and Culture," *Social Problems* 41, no. 1 (February 1994): 155–57.

40. Mittelberg and Waters, "The Process of Ethnogenesis among Haitian and Israeli Immigrants in the United States," 430–32.

41. Alba, "On the Sociological Significance of the American Jewish Experience," 356–57.

42. Gold, *The Israeli Diaspora*; Lilach Lev Ari, "Multiple Ethnic Identities among Israeli Immigrants in Europe," *International Journal of Jewish Education Research* 5–6 (2013): 203–30; Gold, "From Nationality to Peoplehood."

43. Gold, "From Nationality to Peoplehood," 348–49.

44. Judit Bokser Liwerant, "Jewish Diaspora and Transnationalism: Awkward (Dance) Partners?" in *Reconsidering Israel-Diaspora Relations*, ed. Ben-Rafael Eliezer, Judit Bokser Liwerant, and Yosef Gorny (Leiden: Brill, 2014), 369–404.

45. Limonic, *Kugel and Frijoles*, 45–88.

46. Judit Bokser Liwerant, "Expansion and Interconnectedness of Jewish Life in Times (and Spaces) of Transnationalism: New Realities, New Analytical Perspectives," in *Jews and Jewish Identities in Latin America: Historical, Cultural and Literary Perspectives*, ed. Margalit Bejarano, Yaron Harel, Marta Topel F., and Margalit Yosifon (Brighton, MA: Academic Studies Press, 2017), 1–35; Judit Bokser Liwerant, "Latin American Jews in the United States: Community and Belonging in Times of Transnationalism," *Contemporary Jewry* 33, no. 1–2 (April 9, 2013): 121–43, https://doi.org/10.1007/s12397-013-9102-x; Limonic, *Kugel and Frijoles*.

47. Mittelberg and Waters, "The Process of Ethnogenesis among Haitian and Israeli Immigrants in the United States," 416.

Bibliography

"A Portrait of Jewish Americans (Data File and Code Book)." Pew Research Center's Religion and Public Life Project. Washington, D.C.: Pew Research Center, 2013.

"A Portrait of Jewish Americans: Findings from a Pew Research Center Survey of U.S. Jews." Pew Research Center's Religion and Public Life Project. Washington, D.C.: Pew Research Center, October 1, 2013. https://www.pewforum.org/2013/10/01/jewish-american-beliefs-attitudes-culture-survey/.

Alba, Richard. *Blurring the Color Line: The New Chance for a More Integrated America*. Cambridge: Harvard University Press, 2009.

————. "On the Sociological Significance of the American Jewish Experience: Boundary Blurring, Assimilation, and Pluralism." *Sociology of Religion* 67, no. 4 (2006): 347–58.

Alba, Richard D., and Victor Nee. *Remaking the American Mainstream: Assimilation and Contemporary Immigration*. Cambridge, MA: Harvard University Press, 2003.

Bokser Liwerant, Judit. "Expansion and Interconnectedness of Jewish Life in Times (and Spaces) of Transnationalism: New Realities, New Analytical Perspectives." In *Jews and Jewish Identities in Latin America: Historical, Cultural and Literary Perspectives*, edited by Margalit Bejarano, Yaron Harel, Marta Topel F., and Margalit Yosifon, 1–35. Brighton, MA: Academic Studies Press, 2017.

————. "Jewish Diaspora and Transnationalism: Awkward (Dance) Partners?" In *Reconsidering Israel-Diaspora Relations*, edited by Ben-Rafael Eliezer, Judit Bokser Liwerant, and Yosef Gorny, 369–404. Leiden: Brill, 2014.

————. "Latin American Jewish Identities: Past and Present Challenges. The Mexican Case in a Comparative Perspective." *Identities in an Era of Globalization and Multiculturalism. Latin America in the Jewish World*. January 1, 2008. http://www.bjpa.org/publications/details.cfm?PublicationID=11703.

————. "Latin American Jews in the United States: Community and Belonging in Times of Transnationalism." *Contemporary Jewry* 33, no. 1–2 (April 9, 2013): 121–43. https://doi.org/10.1007/s12397-013-9102-x.

Brodkin, K. *How Jews Became White Folks and What That Says about Race in America*. New Brunswick, NJ: Rutgers University Press, 1998.

Brodsky, Adriana, Beatrice Gurwitz, and Rachel Kranson. "Editors' Introduction: Jewish Youth in the Global 1960s." *Journal of Jewish Identities* 8, no. 2 (July 29, 2015): 1–11.

Bureau, US Census. "U.S. Census Bureau Releases New Educational Attainment Data." The United States Census Bureau. Accessed June 19, 2020. https://www.census.gov/newsroom/press-releases/2020/educational-attainment.html.

Cadge, Wendy, and Elaine Howard Ecklund. "Immigration and Religion." *Annual Review of Sociology* 33 (2007): 359–79.

Chiswick, Barry R. "Soviet Jews in the United States: Language and Labor Market Adjustments Revisited." In *Russian Jews on Three Continents: Migration and*

Resettlement, edited by Noah Lewin-Epstein, Yaacov Ro'I, and Paul Ritterband, 223–60. London: Frank Cass, 1996.

Diner, Hasia R. *The Jews of the United States, 1654 to 2000*. Berkeley: University of California Press, 2006.

Foner, Nancy, and Richard Alba. "Immigrant Religion in the U.S. and Western Europe: Bridge or Barrier to Inclusion?" *International Migration Review* 42, no. 2 (2008): 360–92.

Gans, Herbert J. "Symbolic Ethnicity: The Future of Ethnic Groups and Cultures in America." *Ethnic & Racial Studies* 2, no. 1 (January 1979): 1–20. https://doi.org/Article.

Gold, Steven J. "From Nationality to Peoplehood: Adaptation and Identity Formation in the Israeli Diaspora." *Diaspora: A Journal of Transnational Studies* 13, no. 2 (2004): 331–58. https://doi.org/10.1353/dsp.2008.0007.

———. *The Israeli Diaspora*. London: Routledge, 2002.

———. "Patterns of Adaptation among Contemporary Jewish Immigrants to the US." In *American Jewish Year Book 2015*, 3–43. Dordrecht: Springer, 2016. http://link.springer.com.ezproxy.gc.cuny.edu/chapter/10.1007/978-3-319-24505-8_1.

Gold, Steven J., and Bruce A. Phillips. "Mobility and Continuity among Eastern European Jews." In *Origins and Destinies: Immigration, Race and Ethnicity in America*, edited by Silvia Pedraza and Rubén G. Rumbaut, 182–94. Belmont, CA: Wadsworth Publishing Company, 1996.

Hammond, Phillip E., and Kee Warner. "Religion and Ethnicity in Late-Twentieth-Century America." *The Annals of the American Academy of Political and Social Science* 527 (May 1993): 55 66.

Handlin, Oscar. *The Uprooted*. 2nd ed. New York: Little, Brown and Company, 1973.

Hartman, Harriet, and Moshe Hartman. "Jewish Identity and the Secular Achievements of American Jewish Men and Women." *Journal for the Scientific Study of Religion* 50, no. 1 (2011): 133–53.

Hattam, V. C. *In the Shadow of Race: Jews, Latinos, and Immigrant Politics in the United States*. Chicago: University of Chicago Press, 2007.

Herberg, Will. *Protestant, Catholic, Jew*. Chicago: University of Chicago Press, 1983.

Hirschman, Charles. "The Role of Religion in the Origins and Adaptation of Immigrant Groups in the United States." *The International Migration Review* 38, no. 3 (2004): 1206–33.

Horowitz, Bethamie. "Reframing the Study of Contemporary American Jewish Identity." *Contemporary Jewry* 23, no. 1 (2002): 14–34.

Lederhendler, Eli. *American Jewry: A New History*. Cambridge: Cambridge University Press, 2016.

———. *New York Jews and the Decline of Urban Ethnicity: 1950-1970*. Syracuse, NY: Syracuse University Press, 2001.

Lev Ari, Lilach. "Multiple Ethnic Identities among Israeli Immigrants in Europe." *International Journal of Jewish Education Research* 5-6 (2013): 203–30.

Limonic, Laura. *Kugel and Frijoles: Latino Jews in the United States*. Detroit, MI: Wayne State University Press, 2019.

Michels, Tony. "Is America 'Different'?: A Critique of American Jewish Exceptionalism." *American Jewish History* 96, no. 3 (2010): 201–24.

Mittelberg, David, and Mary C. Waters. "The Process of Ethnogenesis among Haitian and Israeli Immigrants in the United States." *Ethnic and Racial Studies* 15, no. 3 (July 1992): 412–35.

Nagel, Joane. "Constructing Ethnicity: Creating and Recreating Ethnic Identity and Culture." *Social Problems* 41, no. 1 (February 1994): 152–76.

Orleck, Annelise. "Soviet Jews: The City's Newest Immigrants Transform New York Jewish Life." In *New Immigrants in New York*, edited by Nancy Foner, 111–40. New York: Columbia University Press, 2001.

Pepper, Miriam, Tim Jackson, and David Uzzell. "A Study of Multidimensional Religion Constructs and Values in the United Kingdom." *Journal for the Scientific Study of Religion* 49, no. 1 (2010): 127–46.

Portes, Alejandro, and Ruben G. Rumbaut. *Immigrant America: A Portrait*. Berkeley: University of California Press, 2006.

Putnam, Robert. "American Grace." Paper presented at The Tanner Lectures on Human Values. Princeton University, October 27–18, 2010.

Rebhun, Uzi. "Jewish Identity in America: Structural Analyses of Attitudes and Behaviors." *Review of Religious Research* 46, no. 1 (September 2004): 43–63.

Remennick, Larissa. "Identity Quest among Russian Jews of the 1990s: Before and after Emigration." In *Jewish Survival: The Identity Problem at the Close of the Twentieth Century*, edited by Ernest Krausz and Gitta Tulea. New Brunswick, NJ: Transaction Publishers, 1998.

Sharot, Steven. *Comparative Perspectives on Judaisms and Jewish Identities*. Detroit, MI: Wayne State University Press, 2010.

Sorin, Gerald. "Mutual Contempt, Mutual Benefit: The Strained Encounter Between German and Eastern European Jews in America, 1880–1920." *American Jewish History* 81, no. 1 (1993): 34–59.

The Process of Immigration to the United States and the Acculturation of Iranian Jews

by Nahid Pirnazar

T he story of Iranian Jewish immigration and subsequent acculturation in the United States is, truly, not so unique; in many respects, it resembles the experiences of other Jewish communities' moves to the United States. However, for Queen Esther's descendants, the move to this country, in many ways, was an end to nearly twenty-seven centuries of the unique culture of Iranian Jews. Without the Iranian homeland tying them to their mixed tradition, it seemed that all was lost. This exodus which climaxed with the Iranian Revolution of 1979, brought the unthinkable to life.

To understand the community's reactions to its own twentieth century mass immigration, it is necessary to look back at the history of the Iranian Jews in Iran. Iranian Jews are part of the greater Jewish subgroup of *Mizrachi* Jews. In large part, this distinction comes from the combination of Sephardic *halakhic* rules of the *Shulkhan Arukh* and ancient Iranian-Judaic traditions. Historically, Jews settled in the Persian Empire on four significant occasions. The first followed the fall of the Northern Kingdom of Israel, when the Assyrian Empire relocated parts of the ten Israelite tribes to Nineveh. The second came when Cyrus II of Persia—most commonly known as Cyrus the Great—freed Jewish captives of Babylonia. The third came after the destruction of the Second Temple. The fourth and final of these distinct occasions took place as a result of the Spanish Inquisition in the fifteenth century, when Sephardic Jews of the Ottoman Empire were relocated from Georgia to Farahabad, a city by the Caspian Sea, and later to other parts of Iran.

After the fall of the Northern Kingdom of Israel in 722 BCE, the Israelites gained the moniker of the "Ten Lost Tribes." They remained under Assyrian rule until the latter's defeat by an alliance of the Medes and Babylonians (ca. 609–05). After their joint victory, the Medes and Babylonians agreed to split the land; the Medes took the northern territories, including Nineveh, where the Israelites were located, while the Babylonians took the rest of Mesopotamia and western territories.[1] So, Jews were brought into the folds of Iranian society for the first time and under Median rule.

More Jews were drawn under Iranian rule with the rise of the Achaemenid dynasty in Iran. In 559 BCE, Cyrus II conquered the Medes and, in 539 BCE, Babylonia. He created a vast empire that encompassed all the previous civilized states of the ancient Near East and Southwest Asia. In Jewish history, the years between 538–331 BCE are known as the "Persian Period." It began in the reign of Cyrus the Great and his Edict in 538 BCE, which left a lasting legacy on Jewish history as well as the Jews of Iran. During this period, the Jews were granted considerable religious autonomy, resulting in opportunities for prosperity. Jews were offered the option to live in Babylonia or move back to Jerusalem. Regardless of where they resided, their religious practices were tolerated in all territories belonging to the Achaemenid dynasty. Those Jews who remained in Babylonia gradually moved eastward to Lar, Khuzestan, Shush, Pasargadae and finally Isfahan.[2]

Mordechai and Esther in the presence of King Xerses (486-465 BCE) in the Dura Europos synagogue in Syria.

Recognized as a liberator, Cyrus had high hopes of rebuilding the Temple for the Jews. Unfortunately, he did not live long enough to fulfill this plan. This mission was finally accomplished years later by his son-in-law and major general of his army, Dariush I (522–486 BCE). The Second Temple, built between the years of 520–16 BCE, became the symbol of Iranian presence in Jerusalem.[3]

The third occasion of Jewish migration to Iran following the destruction of the Second Temple in 70 CE by the Romans resulted in the expansion of Jewish Academies in Babylonia and lured many Jewish scholars who for centuries worked on the interpretation of *Mishnah*, the codified Jewish law, and made the compilation of the Babylonian Talmud in the Diaspora. In regard to this, Jacob Neusner, the scholar of the Sasanian era, states that Jews at the time of the Sasanians (226–642 CE) were living in different parts of Iran, from Armenia to the Persian Gulf and from the Caspian Sea to Fars.[4]

Also, as Habib Levy suggests, considering the facts that the Babylonian Talmud was composed on Iranian soil, and that the religious scholars compiling it had communication with the Sasanian court and entered into polemics with the Zoroastrian scholars, the "Babylonian Talmud could be considered the Iranian Talmud."[5]

In fact, some of the Jewish scholars, *Amoraim*, had never been to Jerusalem.[6]

Throughout the pre-Islamic era, Iranian Jews maintained dual allegiance to their Iranian and Jewish identities. The loyalty of Iranian Jews to both their religious ethnicity and their new self-selected homeland can be seen throughout the history of that era. Such relations date back to the influence of the prophets Daniel, Haggai and Zechariah in the Iranian courts as well as the mission of Zerubbabel for the rebuilding of the Second Temple from the Iranian treasury (520–15 BCE). Furthermore, the impact of the dual role of Ezra and Nehemiah as Jews and Iranian agents in the expansion and reconstruction of the City of Jerusalem speaks of the place of Jews in the royal court. In fact, it was a tradition during the Persian Period to make sacrifices for the health and prosperity of the Shahanshah of Iran and the royal family at the altar, in the Second Temple.[7] However, Iranian culture did not begin to permeate into the Jewish community until the early Sasanian era. Influenced by the friendly relationships maintained by the Jewish Academies and Shapur I and II, Rabbi Yossi (d. 323 CE), the religious leader of Jews in Diaspora, recommended that Jews learn to speak the language of the land.[8] Iranian Jews, who at the time spoke Eastern Aramaic, gradually began speaking Middle Persian, and continued to speak New Persian in Islamic Iran.

In the same era of the Sasanians, Iranian Jewish soldiers are reported to have fought against the Romans as a part of the Iranian army.[9] Rabbi Yossi's recommendation laid the foundation for the Iranian Jewish cultural identity, which would later give birth to the vast literary contributions of Judeo-Persian literature, something unique for Iranian Jews to identify themselves with. This gesture was another milestone in the development of Jewish identity in their respective lands. The impact of this policy is probably the main reason for the survival of Iranian Jews and the development of their unique characteristics. Thus, Iranian culture and language got imprinted into the soul of many Iranian Jews. However, such attachments did not diminish their ties to their Judaic heritage or Zionist hopes. From the time of Ezra and Nehemiah until the end of First World War and the Balfour Declaration, Zionism was seen mostly in a religious context among Iranian Jews and Political Zionism was a faraway dream.

With the arrival of Islam in Iran under the Pact of Omar, Jews, as second class citizens, were considered "People of the Book." Although protected by Islam, they were required to pay a "poll tax" and at some periods to wear patches or specific cloths. However, during a fifty-year period of the early Ilkhanid liberal rule in Iran (1258–96 CE), Jews again participated in the political and economic life and general affairs.[10] At no time in Islamic Iran were Iranian Jews so prominent in public life as they were during those fifty years. During that time Jews were given the opportunity of becoming court officials, court physicians, court astronomers, and, above all, political leaders and prime ministers, taking part in the history as well as the political and economic affairs of the country.[11]

Following that short period, with the conversion of Ilkhanid rulers to Islam, the regulations of the Omar Pact were enforced again. With the rise of Shi'ism in Iran during the early sixteenth century, except for some occasional protections offered by local clerics and scholars, Jews were once again humiliated, persecuted and discriminated against until the dawn of the twentieth century. It is worth noting that while in the seventeenth century whole communities were forced to convert, by the nineteenth century the conditions for Jews were so unbearable that large numbers voluntarily converted to Islam and other minority religions. Aside from economic and political reasons, such conversions were mainly to Christianity through the effort of British and American Christian missionaries, or into the Bahai faith through having contacts with followers of that religion. One major reason for their conversion to Christianity and Bahai faith, was that they were treated as equals with no stigma of "impurity."

Family of Hakim Nurmahmood the prominent physician of the court in the late 19th century. Courtesy of the House of Judeo-Persian Manuscripts.

Having gone through centuries of humiliation, the Jews were left with little pride in their social and religious identity. It was not until the emancipation of the Jews at the beginning of the twentieth century that some pride was restored to the Jewish Community. The emancipation first started with the Iranian constitution of 1906, which provided a national identity in place of religious identity for the Jews as citizens. The second element of emancipation was the educational opportunities provided for Jews by European Jewish organizations, such as the Alliance Israelite Universelle or other secular or Christian missionary schools.

Alliance Israelite Universelle, Girls school in Hamedan, 1926. Courtesy of Habib Levy Foundation.

These opportunities, especially in Tehran, allowed for a better life outside of the historical Jewish ghettoes. The third element of emancipation was the Balfour Declaration of 1917, relating to the establishment of a Jewish state in Palestine. As Iranian Jews were experiencing this rebirth of pride and identity in their religion, Jews worldwide were experiencing the birth of Zionism. The Balfour Declaration of 1917 gave Iranians the opportunity to express their Zionist passion and love of Jewish culture through the establishment of local Zionist associations and publications. By the 1920s, the first migrations to Israel had started. This migration was not successful due to the immigrants' maltreatment by Palestinians and the harsh opposition expressed by the Iranian media to such migration.[12] However, at that time many forced converts of Mashhad (1839) who lived for over eighty years under the pretense of Islam, were able to reveal their religious identity. Most of these Jews left Iran either for London, New York, or Australia, searching for a better life and freedom of religion.

From 1929 to the end of World War II, the flow of migration out of Iran slowed down due to its rapid modernization, and the desire of government officials not to inflame Muslim clerics in Iran and Arab countries with emigration to Palestine. According to the notes of the envoy of the National Jewish Agency to Iran in the 1940s, Iranian Jewish parliamentary representatives were reported to have been more concerned with the condition of Jewry in Iran than helping with immigration to Palestine.[13]

After the Second World War, either for Zionist ideologies, economic reasons or personal ambition, Iranian Jews emigrated primarily to Israel and a smaller number to Western European countries. Among those emigrants to Israel were the families of the past Israeli President Moshe Katsav from Yazd, and past Minister of Defense General Shaul Mofaz, from Isfahan.

Following the *de facto* recognition of the Jewish State of Israel by Iran in 1950, Iran allowed and encouraged mass emigration of Iranian Jews to Israel, mostly those living in poverty. Once again, the speed of emigration was later slowed down due to the impact of the liquidation of Jewish assets on the economy, the improvement of diplomatic relations between the two countries, and the sudden rise of the socio-economic status of Iranian Jews from the 1950s through the 1970s.

The religious crisis that arose during the World Soccer Cup, Asian Games, held in Tehran in 1968, was another turning point in the modern history of Iranian Jews. The competition between the two finalists, the Israeli Maccabees and their Iranian counterparts, aroused the expression of anti-Semitic feeling on the streets of Tehran, through demonstrations and chanting slogans. This incident served as a warning to Iranian Jews of hidden anti-Semitic feelings in the Iranian population. Coupled with other political, social and economic elements, that event was incentive enough for members of the Iranian Jewish community to contemplate alternative places to live, although not necessarily Israel. For the first time many intellectuals and affluent Jews, including the professionals and owners of large industries and trades, decided to either liquidate their assets or leave the country, moving to Europe, the United States and a marginal number to Israel.

By the time of the Islamic Revolution in 1979, the Iranian Jewish population was about 80,000 to 100,000, most of whom lived in Tehran and other major cities. The turmoil caused by the Revolution, once more brought out the radical anti-Semitic feelings of the clerical government, which cloaked its prejudice under the guise of anti-Zionism.

Represntatives of the Jewish Community received by Mohammad Reza Shah Pahlavi on his last birthday in Iran, October 26, 1978. Right to left: Massood Haroonian, Jewish Community Leader; Yousef Cohen, new representative to the parliament; Hakham Yedidia Shofet, Chief Rabbi of Iran; Hakham Ouriel Davidi, religious leader; Lotfollah Hay, former representative to the Parliament. Courtesy of Massood Haroonian family.

On May 14, 1979, during a visit paid by the Jewish religious and commu-
nal leaders to the Ayatollah Khomeini, he officially made a distinction between
Judaism and Zionism. His statement later became the slogan of the Iranian
Jewish community. Nevertheless, within the very first year of the establishment
of the Islamic Republic, some of the prominent members of the Iranian Jewish
Community were executed after being accused of being Zionists, including
Habib Elghanian (May 9, 1979), Albert Danialpour (June 5, 1980) and Ebrahim
Berookhim (July 31, 1980).

  Habib Elghanian   Albert Danialpour   Ebrahim Berookhim

Left to right: Habib Elghanian, excuted May 9, 1979, accused of being a Zionist, supporting Israel,
and encouraging Jews to export their assets. Courtesy of Iranian-American Jewish Federation;
Albert Danialpour, executed June 5, 1980, accused of supporting Zionism, suppressing the
Palestinian Revolution, spying for CIA, importing honey from Israel. Courtesy of Mr. Davar
Danialpour, son; Ebrahim Berookhim, executed July 31, 1980, accused of being a Zionist and a
spy for Israel and hosting Israeli and American spies at family-owned hotels. Courtesy of Mr. Jack
Berookhim, brother.

Front page of Ettelaat daily newspaper:
Habib Elghanian, pleading for his life in
court on May 8, 1979. He was executed the
day after. Photo provided by Mr. Karmel
Melamed, journalist.

Ever since then, the Jewish community, realizing the imminent threat to its well-being, has done everything in its power to express its disapproval of Zionism and Israel. Holocaust denial by President Mahmoud Ahmadinejad in 2006 was another manifestation of a broad fusion between Iran's anti-Zionist position and anti-Jewish messages. The current Jewish population in Iran is estimated at around 8,000–10,000 and surprisingly they are still the second largest Jewish community in the Middle East after Israel. Reports vary as to the condition and treatment of the small, tight-knit community of Iranian Jews, due to its isolation from world Jewry.

The history of mass migration out of Iran goes back to the Pre-Arab invasion, when Iranian Jews departed for India (Cochin) and China (Kaifung) due to the Zoroastrian suppression, and later in the seventeenth century to Bokhara and Herat in the north, due to the Shi'ite persecution.

As early as the 1930s, lower and middle class Iranian Jews left for Israel, while the upper class, intellectuals, and students went to Europe, the United States and Australia. With a few exceptions, it was not until the late 1940s that some Iranian Jews of a higher or upper middle socio-economic background began moving to California, mainly Los Angeles. Physicians and investors tended to go to the East Coast, settling in New York, New England, and some in midwestern Chicago. On the West Coast, immigrating students, at the beginning, landed in San Francisco, but later went to Southern California, attending the University of Southern California (USC), California Institute of Technology (Caltech) and University of California, Los Angeles (UCLA). Migrating professionals were primarily physicians and traders of antiques and carpets, living mostly in Los Feliz, North Hollywood, Hollywood Hills and the Pico-Robertson area; they also attended local American temples. It was not until 1958 that the very first Iranian Jewish family settled in Beverly Hills.[14]

The small, closely knit Iranian community of the fifties found it easier to acculturate by adopting a more American life-style. With such a small Iranian community, Iranian Jews primarily married American and European *Ashkenazi* Jews. Had it not been for the second and third waves of Iranian immigrants coming to Los Angeles in the early 1970s and post 1979, the first group would have completely assimilated into American Jewish society by now.

Due to an anti-Israel demonstration because of the World Soccer Cup Asian Games in Tehran, in 1968, many intellectuals and affluent Jews including the professionals and owners of large industries and trades, decided to either leave the country or liquidate their assets. Large sums of capital were sent abroad to be invested in cities such as Los Angeles and Beverly Hills. These investors often had two homes, one in Los Angeles and one in Tehran, where they still tried to enjoy the so-called economic benefits of the "Golden Era" of the Pahlavi Dynasty. 1976 saw the purchase of the Harold Lloyd Estate, in Beverly Hills, by Iranian investors, and the establishment of a boutique on Rodeo Drive, displaying the work of the late Iranian Muslim designer Bijan. A few years later, Iranian investments created the Rodeo-Collection and financed construction of the Peninsula Hotel. As for New York, most prominent Iranian Jews lived in Long Island and Forest Hills, while having businesses in the Garment District and Diamond District. Young students and physicians chose any location where they would be accepted for higher education or medical training at hospitals.

After September 1978, at the beginning of the Revolution, Jewish and non-Jewish Iranian families who could afford the expense were landing daily in JFK or Los Angeles International Airport, often believing they were coming for a temporary stay. As time went on, the dream of returning to Iran had to be abandoned. Even for those who could have returned, the fear of anti-Zionist threats and the absence of the rule of law did not allow those dreams to materialize.

The first time celebration of Thanksgiving in the United States, three generations, October 1979, Los Angeles. Back row left to right: Monir Pirnazar, Fakhri Pirnazar (Afari), Dr. Parviz Pirnazar, Nahid Pirnazar (Oberman), Jeffrey Oberman, Elyahou Pirnazar, Habib Afari; front row left to right: Shireen Oberman, Kambiz Pirnazar, Payman Pirnazar. Courtesy of the Pirnazar Family.

While the first to arrive were culturally sophisticated and affluent members of the community, by the early 1980s members of the middle and lower socio-economic class also moved to Los Angeles. Due to economic reasons, many Iranian Jewish families were forced to seek housing outside of Beverly Hills despite their desire to send their children to the city's prestigious public school system. In addition to the geographic divide, post Revolution immigrants took on a wider variety of professions including rabbis, shohets, bakers, butchers, educators and academics. These wandering Jews, filled with fear and anxiety of an unknown future, were in need of sharing their experiences with each other. On Friday nights during late 1978 and early 1979 many temples in Los Angeles and San Fernando Valley hosted the new immigrants who came to socialize and see familiar faces.[15] It was at this point that, upon the complaint of some of his temple members for allowing so many non-members to "disturb" their Shabbat Services, Rabbi Zvi Dershowitz of Sinai Temple on Wilshire Boulevard gave a particularly memorable sermon. He reminded his congregation of the role and responsibility of the "synagogue" towards fellow Jews who needed a place to worship and gather in times of crisis. Many of these temples are now the beneficiaries of both financial support and leadership from their Iranian congregants.

Once the difficulties of re-settlement had been somewhat resolved, the even more difficult process of acculturation began. For those who went to Israel at the time of its independence, the issue of acculturation has already been solved. The older generation of the 1950s, already retired, have put the difficult years of adjustment and language acquisition behind. They enjoy the product of their efforts, having their children as academicians, politicians, military officers, media operators, computer experts and medical researchers. By 1978 and the rise of the Islamic Revolution, El Al planes flew many lower- and middle-class Iranian Jews to Israel, almost daily, for free. Also, for the first time we find some affluent Iranian Jews who migrated to Israel or invested in Israel, while switching their residency between Israel and some Western countries.

Those who settled in Europe or Australia, found success more difficult due to religious and language challenges. As for those who came to the United States, there were wide cultural and religious differences between those who settled on the East Coast (New York) and those on the West Coast (Los Angeles).

In terms of religious observance, Iranian Jews of New York are more observant but divided in their religious identity. The descendants of the forced converts of Mashhad (1839) have established their own communities and temples, considering other Iranian Jews not sufficiently observant. However, immigrants from other Iranian cities belong to a different social and religious community in New York. Both groups are secluded in small neighborhoods such as Great Neck, Kings Point, Forest Hills, Queens and Roslyn based on their financial or professional status. At present, many hold medical and other professional positions, while others work in real estate, jewelry, clothing, carpet and antique businesses. Their cultural and philanthropic activities are mainly focused on Judaism and Israel, with very limited interaction with non-Jewish Iranians. The Iranian American Jewish Federation of New York, founded in 2002, has as its primary mission, "the establishment of unity among the large contingent of Iranian Jews in the greater New York metropolitan area and to act as a conduit between the community and other groups and organizations with respect to matters that affect their lives and matters pertaining to the State of Israel."[16] Among the very few Iranian restaurants or social halls, in the New York area, Kosher dietary laws are observed if they are owned by Jews. Their very conservative habits of life and style of life have affected the face of the city and their children's educational system.[17]

As for Iranian Jews of Los Angeles, the challenges of adapting to a new life in a new place varied depending on the age and socio-economic background of the individual. Those immigrants who came after the age of sixty-five had the most difficult acculturation experience. A great number of them could not speak English and were unable to pursue a new profession or business. Such obstacles seemed overwhelming, and rather than trying to adapt, they devoted their time and energy trying to recreate their Iranian life and facilities. Thus, they imported the Iranian Jewish traditions and characteristics to certain parts of Los Angeles, with all its advantages and disadvantages that prior immigrants had tried to leave behind. They started setting up their own temples to read prayers with their own Persian-Sephardic rituals and tones.

Thus, it fell upon the generation of those forty to sixty-five years old to carry the burden of dual identity in the process of acculturation. Whether professionals or tradesmen, this group tried to remain loyal to the traditions and values of Iran while adjusting themselves to fit into the American lifestyle. It is within this generation that women of the middle class, who had come to this country either as professionals or without any profession or language skills, played a significant role both at home and at work. In that same generation, there is another category of women, following the tradition in Iran, who mostly devoted their spare time to setting up charitable and philanthropic organizations. One can hardly find any American Jewish or Israeli charitable organization that does not have one or two active and supportive Iranian chapters.

Hannukah celebration 2019. Iranian Jewish Women's Organization honors generations of women. Right to left: Mahindokht Khorsandi, writer; Minoo Koutal, researcher and thematic peace artist; Gity Barkhor, philanathropic advocate, artist.

Hannukah celebration 2019. Right to left: Mrs. Aliza Halavi, a previous president and Mrs. Farrokh Maddahi, senior board member.

Hannukah, 2014. Iranian Haifa/ Malka Haddasah Chapter Honoring a pioneer immigrant couple to Los Angeles. Mansour and Mehri Sinai, by Mrs. Kathrine Merage, award for their philanthropic and communal services. Mrs.Merage herself is an active Zionist and philanthropist. Right to left: Kathrine Merage, Mehri and Mansour Sinai. Courtesy of the Sinai family.

The third and the youngest generation of immigrants, those who came under the age of forty, benefited the most from the mass migration of Iranian Jews to the United States. The land provided them with the incentive to re-alize the American Dream. The limited educational opportunity in Iranian universities, due to their difficult entrance exams, could not have given them the vast level of higher education available in their new homeland. In professional settings, they have been prominent lawyers, physicians as well as owners of medical centers. They have excelled as scholars, researchers in nuclear medicine, professors, directors of university departments and divisions at national and international levels. Also, successful business entrepreneurs have earned the recognition and respect from their fellow Americans, both Jews and non-Jews.

While some Iranian Jewish groups, such as the Iranian Jewish Women's Organization (1976) and the Iranian American Jewish Cultural Organization of California (1978), were established before the Islamic Revolution, many others were founded after the arrival of the larger cohort of immigrants. Among the first ones were SIAMAK, Iranian American Jewish Association of Southern California (1979), Eretz Synagogue & Cultural Center (1980), Nessah Educational and Cultural Center-Nessah Synagogue (1980) and Iranian-American Jewish Federation (1980). Most of them have continued for decades, maintaining their own synagogues and publications in Persian.

Furthermore, along with the other non-Jewish Iranians, they developed community and academic centers, restaurants, catering services, supermarkets, bookstores, yellow pages and media to preserve their cultural identity. Certain areas became so heavily Iranian, that councilmen have dedicated plaques designating them as "Little Teheran" or some similar Iranian marking.

Iranian Jews of Los Angeles have not forgotten their Iranian heritage and celebrate Persian New Year, Nowruz, with glory every year, as seen with the traditional display of Haft Seen.

Haft seen of Nowruz, prepared by Shahnaz Nassir at Iranian Jewish Women's Nowruz celebration, March 2007. Courtesy of Iranian Jewish Women's Organization.

Unlike the Jewish community of New York, there is much more interaction between Iranian immigrants of all different faiths in Los Angeles. In terms of their level of assimilation, Iranian Jews have assimilated with American Jews as well as to a high degree with non- Jews and non-Iranians.

Like all immigrant populations, Iranian Jews have witnessed accomplishments and challenges during the process of their acculturation. After four decades, most Iranians of any ethnic or religious background, having received their US citizenships, successfully adjusted and exceled within their new homeland. The older generation enjoys the medical and social benefits that the state and federal government provides. The middle-age generation of forty to sixty-five, has established itself comfortably in a wide range of small self-employed lines of work as well as growing industries such as textile, clothing, marble and furniture, doing business with Mexico, Latin America, Italy and the Far East. Iranian immigrants own industrial corporations, hotels and shopping centers, developments throughout California and the rest of the United States. As realtors and homeowners, they have had an impact on the architecture of certain areas of Beverly Hills and some other neighborhoods in which they live. Many houses built with columns and pretentious entries, are undoubtedly a reaction to centuries of being forced to live in Iranian ghettoes and poor homes with very low entrances, as enforced by the seventeenth century Shi'ite clerics.[18]

A new dimension to the acculturation of Iranian Jews has been in the political arena. This is an area that they did not have the opportunity to join in Iran. Their political involvement began through contacts with the federal government regarding issues of immigration, political asylum and social and medical benefits for their ethnic group. The American Israel Public Affairs Committee (AIPAC) and partisan activities have also drawn Iranian Jews into political forums. One such group, is Thirty Years After, a non-partisan organization for the Iranian-American Jewish community founded on the thirtieth anniversary of the Islamic Revolution. Its mission is to educate its members in the democratic processes of the United States. Its many activities include promoting civic action and voter registration drives.

Thirty Years After, May 2009, Tel Aviv University Conference, Iranian Studies. From left to right: Jason Massaband, Jonathan Yagoubzadeh, Sam Yebri, General Shaul Mofaz, Iranian born Israeli statesman, Debbie Farnoush, Nicole Farnoush, Jasmine Oberman, Michael Yadegaran, Natalie Kashefi, and Jasmin Niku. Courtesy of Jasmine Oberman.

Unlike most American Jewish communities, which are traditionally Democratic, the Iranian Jewish community is split between the two parties— affiliations often depending on the individual's level of wealth, social and political views as well as the current policies of each party towards the state of Israel. Iranian Jews have also won appointed positions at the state level and elected positions in the city councils including the office of the Mayor of the City of Beverly Hills.

In addition to their contribution to American politics, Iranian Jews have supported many academic programs not only at the University of California, Los Angeles; the University of California, Irvine and California State University, Northridge, but also out of state universities and colleges.

Los Angeles Iranians, Jews and non-Jews, actively support and participate in the areas of art, music, sports, entertainment, theatrical and motion picture production. Immigrants who lack language skills other than Persian, can access the outside world through Iranian radio and satellite television programs. Their entertainments include news about the Iranian National Soccer Team as well as tips for going to local Persian restaurants, theatrical performances or concerts by their favorite Persian musicians.

Having lived in a non-Jewish Middle Eastern country, the average Iranian Jewish level of religious observance and knowledge of Judaism, except for a small margin of religious leaders and scholars, has been very traditional and somewhat shallow, whereas, in the United States where all faiths are recognized, people are given the opportunity to practice their religion with pride and openly. Such privilege has given the Iranian Jews the liberty to celebrate their Jewish identity and holidays more openly. For example, many non-Jewish Iranians had not necessarily heard about Jewish holidays such as Hanukah, Rosh ha-Shanna or the terms Bar/Bat-Mitzvah. In addition, the wide range of Jewish life in the United States has given Iranian Jews a chance to re-assess their own religious attachments and level of their observance.

Nevertheless, the combination of the renewal of their Jewish identity, and financial prosperity have resulted a tendency towards extravagance. For some people, the pretentious celebration of solemn and joyous rituals has become a means to overcome and make up for the limitations they encountered in Iran.

The migration of Iranian Jews to Los Angeles after 1979 coincided with a worldwide swing towards more orthodox religiosity. Iranian Jews coming to America dealt both with this new trend as well as the cultural and generational gap that was growing among themselves. As a Jewish community steeped in tradition rather than religious textual knowledge, they were poorly equipped to deal with the variety of opportunities for the practice of Judaism. While the older generation kept to the traditions brought in from Iran, some of the middle aged were fascinated by the glory, adaptability and choral melodies in American conservative and reform temples. Thus, some of them, without really even understanding the language, attend the non-orthodox American temples, while sending their children to orthodox Jewish schools, unaware of the differences or consequences. Many of the children, not accepting their parents' level of observance, started to question the religious dedication of their families, thus widening generational and cultural gaps.

As family gaps have grown wider, some parents and members of the community have shown resentment and anger towards their orthodox religious mentors and leaders. Other *halakhic* and gender issues also divide the community between Iranian traditional synagogues and those who have tried to model themselves after conservative American, Sephardic or Ashkenazi houses of worship. While some of the Iranian temples still have debates over the use of a microphone on Shabbat or the wisdom of having a mixed congregation, the community of Iranian Jewish women still has to fight to appear on the pulpit for an *Aliya* in most Iranian temples or to demand the refutation of *Aguna* and men's right of Jewish divorce, named as *get*. In this respect, the joint effort of the Iranian Jewish Women's Organization in Los Angeles and the Ima Group of Iranian Women in New York should not be overlooked.

Conference on Jewish Divorce, November 2006. Right to left:
Rabbi Nissim Davidi Los Angeles; Rabi Yona Reiss, Director
of Beth Din of America, New York; Rabbi David Shofet,
Chief Rabbi, Los Angeles; Nahid Pirnazar, Ph.D., Moderator;
Parvaneh Sarraf, Ima Cultural Assoc, New York; Alexandra
Leichte, Esq., Family Law specialist, Los Angeles; Rabbi David
Akhamzadeh, Los Angeles. To the right is a publication of the
Iranian Jewish Women's Organization. Courtesy Iranian Jewish
Women's Organization.

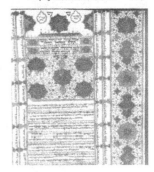

In the meantime, we notice a level of tolerance about the issue of intermarriage with non-Jews, same sex marriages and transgender individuals.
While thirty years ago such issues were a rarity, and still is by the older generation of immigrants, we see more tolerance from their offspring. For some
parents, even though it has not been easy, keeping the family together is pri-
oritized over keeping the faith or social norms. Marriage out of religion or
same sex marriage has become more or less an accepted matter among the
middle- and upper-class Iranian Jews, while the orthodox families have gone
in the opposite directions, having separate ceremonies for males and females.

In Los Angeles, while accepting many of the new norms in the community, immigrants have implanted some of the Iranian or Middle Eastern
customs and traditions into the larger non-Iranian Jewish community. For
example, in a Jewish temple on joyous occasions, often one hears the rabbi
requesting women to give a loud ritual thrilling cry, a *quell*, which is a symbol

of joy. There is almost no American, who having socialized with Persians, does not list Persian foods among favorite cuisines. Kosher Iranian restaurants are filled with non-Iranian Jews, and some Iranian Jewish markets are the busiest markets in town.

UCLA Hillel. Photo provided by Nahid Pirnazar.

Board Members of Iranian Jewish Women's Organization, donating towards the students' lounge of the UCLA Hillel Building: Left to right, sitting: Mehri Sinai, Mehry Tahery, Nahid Pirnazar, Shahla Javdan, Aliza Halavi, Louise Golshan, Jila Perry. Left to right, standing: Shimen Zakhor, Badieh Hakim, Zohreh Lalezari, Shahla Nikravesh, Shahin Eshaghpour, Farrokh Maddahi, Soraya Mobin, Minoo Koutal, Nizid Khalili, Shahnaz Nassir, Eshrat Soumekh, Gity Barkhordar, Soraya Bolour, and Vicotria Toubia. Photo taken by Abbas Hojatpanah, Studio.

Time to give to Academics. Photos provided by Nahid Pirnazar.

As part of the greater Jewish family, it seems likely that Iranian Jews will eventually acculturate into the American Jewish society. However, it seems more difficult to envision them giving up their Iranian identity, something they

Time to give to the community. Photos provided by Nahid Pirnazar.

have been acculturated to for more than twenty-seven centuries now. Iranians of Los Angeles, Jewish and other, maintain a unity embedded in their shared historical, cultural, and patriotic attachments. It is not clear whether the future generation of Iranian Jews, now Iranian Jewish Americans—in whichever order they prefer to place each aspect of their individual identities—will someday meld into the majority of American society, to become indistinguishable from their neighbors. Fortunately, whether assimilation is avoidable or not, an appreciation for multi-cultural societies seems to be gaining, slowly but surely, from the inside to the out. For now, it allows people of different backgrounds to be a part of American life and still maintain their individuality religion and ethnic background.

Notes

1. Siegfried H. Horn, "The Divided Monarchy: The Kingdoms of Judah and Israel," in *Ancient Israel: From Abraham to the Roman Destruction of the Temple*, ed. Hershel Shanks (Washington, DC: Biblical Archaeology Society, 1999), 192–93.

2. Jon L. Berquist, *Judaism in Persia's Shadow: A Social and Historical Approach* (Minneapolis: Fortress Press, 1995), 26; James D. Purvis, "Exile and Return: From the Babylonian Destruction to the Reconstruction of the Jewish State," in *Ancient Israel: From Abraham to the Roman Destruction of the Temple*, ed. Hershel Shanks (Washington, DC: Biblical Archaeology, 1999; Amnon Netzer, "Seyri Dar Tarikh-e Yahud-e Iran," in *Padyavand*, vol. I, ed. Amnon Netzer (Costa Mesa: Mazda Publishers, 1996), 13.

3. Purvis, "Exile and Return," 218–9.

4. Jacob Neusner, "Jews in Iran, p.2," in *The Cambridge History of Iran*, vol. III, ed. E. Yarshater (Cambridge: Cambridge University Press, 1983), 909.

5. Habib Levy, *Comprehensive History of Iranian Jews*, abridg. and ed, Hushang Ebrami, trans. George W. Maschke (Costa Mesa: Mazda Publishers, 1999), 133–38:

   The idea of having Middle Persian vocabulary, as well as non-Jewish concepts during the Sasanid period, suggest the name of "Iranian Talmud." Among such examples are: "proverbs and commentaries that run contrary to the teachings of the Torah and the prophets of Israel."

   Also see: Babylonian Talmud: Tractate Baba Kamma Folio 83a: "'[where] either the Holy Tongue or the Greek language [could be employed]?' And R. Jose said: 'Why use the Aramaic language in Babylon [where] the Holy Tongue or the Persian language [could be used]?'"

   For further details see: Shai Secunda, *The Iranian Talmud, Reading the Bavli in its Sasanian Context* (Philadelphia: University of Pennsylvania Press, 2014); Shai Secunda and Steven Fine, eds. *Shoshannat Yaakov: Jewish and Iranian Studies in Honor of Yaakov Elman* (Leiden: E.J. Brill, 2012).

6. Levy, *Comprehensive History*, 133.

7. Haim Tadmor, "The Period of the First Temple, the Babylonian Exile and the Restoration," in *A History of the Jewish People*, ed. H. H. Ben-Sasson (Cambridge: Harvard University Press, 1976), 172; Ezra 6:11).

8. Netzer, *Padyavand*, 1:42.

9. Netzer, *Padyavand*, 1:34–35.

10. Walter Fischel, "Under the Mongol Ilkhans," in *Jews in the Economic and Political Life of Mediaeval Islam* (New York: Ktav Publishing House, Inc, 1969), 93–94.

11. Walter Fischel, "Israel in Iran," in *The Jews: Their History, Culture, and Religion*, ed. Louis Finkelstein (Philadelphia: The Jewish Publication Society of America, 1949), 2:824–5.

12. Habib Levy, *Khatera-e Man* (Los Angeles: Ketab Co., 2002), 199; Levy, *Comprehensive History*, 521.

13. Moshe Yishy, "An Envoy Without Title," in *Padyavand*, ed. Amnon Netzer (Costa Mesa: Mazda Publishers, 1999), 3:127.

14. Interview with Cyrus Karubian, one of the early settlers in the United States in the early 1940s, first in New York and later in Los Angeles (2005).

15. Among those Jewish Temples who first opened their arms to Iranian Jews in Los Angeles were Temple Beth Jacob, on Pico Blvd and Temple Sinai, on Wilshire Blvd. As for the San Fernando Valley, Temple Valley Beth Shalom was among the first hosts. Up to the present time, they all have a large number of Iranian members.

16. "About Us," Iranian American Jewish Federation of New York, accessed March 14, 2020, https://www.iajfny.org/?page=about.

17. Interview with some non-Iranian citizens of Great Neck (2005).

18. See the list of the forty-five restrictions imposed on Jews during the seventeenth century: Levy, *Comprehensive History*, 293–95: "17. Jews may not build fancy houses. 18. Jews many not paint the rooms of their homes white, 18. The door of a Jew's House must be low and must be a single [not double] door."

Bibliography

Berquist, Jon L. *Judaism in Persia's Shadow: A Social and Historical Approach.* Minneapolis: Fortress Press, 1995.

Fischel, Walter. "Under the Mongol Ilkhans." In *Jews in the Economic and Political Life of Mediaeval Islam,* 159–94. New York: Ktav Publishing House, 1969.

———— "Israel in Iran." In *The Jews: Their History, Culture, and Religion,* edited by Louis Finkelstein, Vol. II, 817–58. Philadelphia: The Jewish Publication Society of America, 1949.

Horn, Siegfried H. "The Divided Monarchy: The Kingdoms of Judah and Israel." In *Ancient Israel: From Abraham to the Roman Destruction of the Temple,* edited by Hershel Shanks, 109–49. Washington, DC: Biblical Archaeology Society, 1999.

Iranian American Jewish Federation of New York. "About Us." Accessed March 14, 2020. https://www.iajfny.org/?page=about.

Levy, Habib. *Comprehensive History of Iranian Jews,* abridged and edited by Hushang Ebrami, translated by George W. Maschke. Costa Mesa: Mazda Publishers, 1999.

————. *Khatera-e Man.* Los Angeles: Ketab Co., 2002.

Netzer, Amnon. "Seyri Dar Tarikh-e Yahud-e Iran." Part 1. In *Padyavand,* Vol. I, edited by Amnon Netzer, 1–63. Costa Mesa: Mazda Publishers, 1996.

Neusner, Jacob. "Jews in Iran." Part 2. In *The Cambridge History of Iran,* Vol.3, edited by E. Yarshater, 909–23. Cambridge: Cambridge University Press, 1983.

New Oxford Annotated Bible with the Apocrypha, edited by Bruce M. Metzger and Ronald E. Merphy. New York: Oxford University Press, 1991.

Purvis, James D. "Exile and Return: From the Babylonian Destruction to the Reconstruction of the Jewish State." In *Ancient Israel: From Abraham to the Roman Destruction of the Temple,* edited by Hershel Shanks, 151–75. Washington, DC: Biblical Archaeology Society, 1999.

Tadmor, Haim. "The Period of the First Temple, the Babylonian Exile and the Restoration." In *A History of the Jewish People,* edited by H. H. Ben-Sasson, 91–182. Cambridge: Harvard University Press, 1976.

Yishay, Moshe. "An Envoy Without Title." In *Padyavand,* edited by Amnon Netzer, Vol. III, 109–39. Costa Mesa: Mazda Publishers, 1999.

Repatriating by Non-State Actors? The Emergence of (Skilled) Return Migration Industry in Israel

by Nir Cohen

INTRODUCTION

In 2014, speaking at a national human resource development conference, the Director of Israel's National Brain Gain Program (INBGP) introduced the government's program to repatriate highly skilled Israeli migrants by helping them find jobs in Israel.

> [T]he program directs great efforts towards employment assistance. These efforts include connecting between [Israeli] academics [abroad] and recruiters and linking them to organizations and [employment] networks. Our objective . . . is to be your employment agency that sends you, recruiters, only relevant and meticulously sorted CV's [of Israeli academics abroad].[1]

A couple of years later, at a news conference in Boston, American Jewish philanthropist Mortimer Zuckerman announced his $100M plan to reverse Israel's brain drain by attracting Israeli researchers in STEM disciplines from "Western" countries back to Israeli universities. In a video message to attendees, Israeli Prime Minister Benjamin Netanyahu thanked Mr. Zuckerman, proclaiming, "This project will help bring back some of Israel's most brilliant sons and daughters, allow them to advance their own careers here and . . . contribute to Israel's growing scientific excellence."[2]

Both messages attest to the changing institutional make-up of schemes of skilled return migration to Israel. Traditionally state-sponsored and implemented,[3] they have gradually come to draw upon human and material resources that are availed by non-state actors (hereafter NSAs). From wealthy donors to executive headhunting agencies, civic and private bodies are now full-fledged partners to Israel's repatriation initiatives. The growing reliance of the government upon NSAs as *inter alia* special advisors to programs, sponsors of recruitment fairs, or potential employers of returnees ought to be understood against the backdrop of two processes, which are linked to the neoliberalization of Israel's economy.[4] First, the gradual privatization of social and other services, which were historically provided by the Israeli state. Much like in the domain of Jewish in-migration,[5] the state has been gradually handing over some of its traditional financial, organizational and administrative functions in the domain of repatriation to NSAs.[6] Second, the multiplication of NSAs who specialize in the provision of services that are needed by returning migrants. Although their number remains fairly stable over time,[7] the economic potential of returnees, primarily those possessing higher levels of economic and cultural capital becomes clearer to civic and private organizations. Not only do skilled returnees make up a small, but growing market share in the country's insurance, shipping, and tax consulting markets, but their improved demographic profile makes them an important asset to a range of NSAs, from accountants and lawyers specializing in foreign tax and legal systems to employment agencies matching returnees to firms in Israel's thriving IT sector. Thus, for example, a study on returning scientists, estimates that in the first five years after repatriation, their overall contribution to Israel's economy is nearly $750 million.[8] While part of their contribution is reflected in obligatory payments to the government (e.g., income tax and social security), others may well benefit civic and private bodies (e.g., general spending and investments).

The chapter examines the rising engagement of NSAs with Israel's skilled return initiatives. It argues that the plurality of (not-) for profit groups and individuals who partake in Israel's hegemonic project of repatriation may be justifiably termed "return migration industry" (hereafter RMI). From private firms who gain financially from service-provision to returnees to non-governmental organizations who facilitate migrants' re-integration in Israel, actors of the industry are in/direct beneficiaries of the increasing commercialization of Israel's counter-migration regime. It further shows that NSAs who partake in the two phases of the return process, namely recruitment (or mobilization) and re-integration, differ considerably with respect to their engagement levels, functions, and mechanisms and scales of operation.

The chapter is divided to four sections. It first engages with the literature about the changing landscape of the governance of migration, focusing on the rising importance of NSAs in it. It then briefly explores repatriation programs in Israel, attending to their increasingly commercialized nature in recent years. It coins the term "Return Migration Industry" to refer to the multiple civic and private entities whose collaboration with the state at various scales—from the local to the transnational—facilitates the repatriation of (skilled) migrants. The third section classifies actors within the industry through their participation in the two stages within the process of repatriation, namely mobilization and re-integration. The concluding section outlines avenues of further research on the causes and effects of the return migration industry in Israel and beyond.

CHANGING LANDSCAPES OF MIGRATION GOVERNANCE

Recent years have witnessed a growing interest in the role of NSAs in the process of governing. From world politics to climate change, civic and private entities have taken an increasingly salient part in public policy-making.[9] Explanations for this shift from government to governmentality[10] center on statist aspirations to "govern at a distance." This new framework, it is argued, allows the state to transfer some of its exclusive responsibilities to an ensemble of loosely connected actors, while simultaneously continuing to shape their conduct and ensure their compliance with its own interests.[11] As E. Sørensen and J. Torfing argue,[12] "The mobilization of free action of resourceful and energetic actors within a framework of norms and rules that ensures a certain degree of conformity with the overall objectives of government can relieve the state from some of its regulatory burdens and help to reach various target groups with the deployment of less resources and less display of control from above." The art of governing also reflects a statist faith in the efficiency of markets and civil societies to mediate between state and citizens, lending itself to a new regime of "governing through networks."[13]

In the field of migration, the dislocation of state intervention presents opportunities for NSAs, thereby increasing their involvement in the provision of multiple related goods and services. Whether they detain the undocumented or recruit the highly skilled,[14] NSAs are now closely entangled in en/disabling international mobility. While states continue to retain high levels of control over migration procedures, scholarship has shown that many

NSAs are involved throughout its various phases, including admission and re(integration). G. Lahav,[15] for example, shows that in Europe, the regulatory "playing field" includes rent-seeking bodies like airlines, shipping carriers, transport companies, security services, and hotels, as well as not-for-profits like universities, churches and trade unions. The shift by which states delegate monitoring and execution powers upward (to intergovernmental agencies [e.g., EU]), downward (e.g., to cities) and outward (to non-state actors), creates "a vertical chain of policy making,"[16] which reflects statist efforts "to extend the burden of implementation *away* from central governments . . . and *towards* the source of control, thereby increasing national efficacy and decreasing costs in the process."[17]

Others also noted the facilitative role of migration intermediaries, namely those "key actors that facilitate, and sometimes drive, migration within and across borders,"[18] who work at the meso-level alongside macro- (e.g., state institutions) and micro-level (e.g., kinship networks) agents.[19] G. Menz,[20] for example, focusing on the role of trade unions and employer associations in the migration process, argues that on account of being delegated selective roles, both groups "are becoming involved in various forms of co-managing migration flows, ranging from a proactive role in setting annual migration quotas to representation in steering committees and active informal lobbying."[21] Yet, these *new regimes of migration governance*[22] do not necessarily signal the retreat of the state. In fact, they sometimes facilitate the expansion of repressive policies, as well as the shedding of functions and services long characteristic of the Keynesian state.[23]

The migration industry has recently emerged as a productive conceptual lens through which to explore the role of NSAs, or intermediaries, in migration policy-making. R. Hernández-León,[24] locates the migration-facilitating industry in the private and specialized services rendered by private, profit-seeking entrepreneurs. These include, for example, "trafficking and labor recruitment, the lending of funds to finance migration, passenger transportation and travel agencies, the sending of monetary and in kind remittances, application for and production of authentic and counterfeit documents, legal counseling, and telecommunications services for emigrants and their home communities."[25] Services provided to prospective migrants, including marketing of potential destination or housing opportunities within them, may also be considered part of the industry. While not dismissive of "the other engines of migration," including NGOs and migrant networks, he argues that in the absence of the purported pursuit of financial gain, their engagements with all migratory forms—from temporary to permanent and from unidirectional to cyclical—are fundamentally different.[26]

A more structural approach is advocated by M. P. Garapich, who defines the industry as "a sector of service markets that uses human mobility, adaptation in the host country and the sustenance of a transnational social field as its main resources."[27] Immigration advisors, tax refund offices, travel agents and ethnic media are all integral to the industry, which is is distinct from "the ethnic enclave" because of its "explicit and direct role [is] in stimulating further flows, . . . [which] lowers the risks of migrating."[28] A. Betts,[29] similarly suggests that the industry encompasses actors who play a salient role in facilitation, control and rescue in the domain of migration. Alongside smugglers, travel agents, airline companies, or recruitment organizations,[30] it includes those whose functions range from funding (e.g., philanthropists seeking to improve the rights of refugees) and lobbying (e.g., trade unions) to monitoring, enforcing (e.g., anti-immigrant vigilante groups) or supporting (e.g., refugee aid organizations) migration. Inasmuch as actors operate at various scales and engage differentially throughout the migratory process, they are not merely "economic actors" oriented exclusively towards a financial bottom line, but "are directly involved in agenda setting, negotiation, implementation, monitoring and enforcement activities."[31]

Actors operate along the three phases of Hernández-León's migration system's cycle, namely *initiation, takeoff,* and *stagnation and decline.*[32] *Initiation* sees the involvement of head hunters, recruiters and smugglers who search for, identify, stimulate, guide and move migrants from their point of origin. *Take off* does not see the disappearance of brokers, who change their chief function and location to become providers of services in destination points. It is in these new environments that "contractors and transporters can recruit immigrant labor, while immigrant banking, remittance and courier services provided thrive and operate intermingled with other ethnic and immigrant entrepreneurs."[33] Finally, as cross-border streams *decline,* some migration entrepreneurs go out of business while others shift attention to diasporic "nostalgia markets," satisfying increasing demands for ethnic food, music and other cultural good and services.

Yet, to date no studies have paid attention to the industry's role in facilitating return migration. This lacuna is surprising given both the quantitative surge in (in)voluntary migrant repatriation,[34] and the qualitative contribution of returnees to homeland development. Studies have long shown that returnees, especially skilled, exhibit high levels of business entrepreneurship, and possess higher than average economic, cultural (foreign language command) and professional (knowledge of new technologies) capital.[35] It is primarily for this reason that diaspora strategies of multiple countries currently include special incentive-oriented return migration schemes (known as SARPs, State-Assisted Repatriation Programs[36]). These initiatives have traditionally drawn on a range of non-state actors—from migrant organizations to relocation consultants who assist the (re)integration of returning households.[37] In Israel, economic neoliberalization of the 1990s has precipitated a change in the politics of diaspora strategies, return programs included. As N. Cohen shows,[38] one of the primary characteristics of the new politics has been the increasing involvement of NSAs in return schemes. In what follows I briefly attend to the changing landscape of skilled return in Israel, explaining how it brought about the emergence of RMI, namely private and civic actors partaking in state-sponsored repatriation schemes.

Returning Skilled Israelis: From Government to Governance

The repatriation of skilled Israelis began in the 1950s, when David Ben-Gurion's government offered (returning) academics teaching in American and British universities employment and housing benefits in Israel.[39] In the 1960s, different state institutions were established which sought to repatriate migrants, including the Bureau for the Academic Worker (1965) which courted highly educated Israelis living abroad. Later, the Ministry of Immigration and Absorption (1968), implemented a series of state-assisted return programs. In May 1968, for example, it oversaw an incentive-based program aimed at returning nationals residing abroad more than four years. It set a two-year "window of opportunities" for those wishing to return, and announced it would provide them with various tax, housing, and employment benefits.[40] A decade later (1978), it announced a nearly identical program, which offered returnees generous benefits, including a special bonus for those settling in peripheral areas. These—and most subsequent—programs, targeted primarily a narrow segment of highly skilled migrants, including researchers, scientists, (graduate) students and those with technical and technological skills. In the words of Yigal Alon, Israel's first Minister of Immigration and Absorption, "It is imperative that we create opportunities for those with talent and knowledge that wish to return."[41]

State-sanctioned programs continued in the 1980s. The appointment of Dov Shilanski as Deputy Minister for Emigration (1981) was a sign that repatriation had become a national priority.[42] As he declared, "Returning emigrants, our children, is a key role of this government."[43] The establishment of the Unit for Returning Residents in the MOIA and the Inter-Ministerial Committee to Streamline Anti-Emigration Policy were some key steps taken to consolidate state efforts in this domain.

Plummeting emigration rates in the 1990s also relieved state concerns over repatriation. As Israel's economy neo-liberalized quickly, skilled return budgets were significantly reduced. Outsourcing and privatization of project management ensued, as in other domains,[44] and state programs were subjected to principles of economic rationalism.[45] Consequently, state officials began conceiving leaner programs aimed at repatriating those whose expected contribution to the national economy was predicted to be the highest. The new approach was accompanied by two processes. First, a vigorous segmentation of the target group, namely emigrants. Traditional labels (e.g., "the academically educated") were replaced with a system of classification and, subsequently, repatriation initiatives aimed at them. By the end of the decade, smaller repatriation projects were tailored for specific sub-groups, including business owners, scientists, physicians, artists, and (post)-graduate researchers. Second, the state has increasingly drawn on a growing number of NSAs in the conception, implementation, monitoring and evaluation of repatriation projects. From policy-oriented think-tanks to emigrant organizations, the number and involvement of NSAs has increased considerably, evolving into what I call the "return migration industry." The next section describes some key actors, and identifies their main characteristics and tasks throughout the two phases of the return process, namely recruitment and (re)integration.

RMI between Recruitment and Reintegration

Following N. N. Sørensen and T. Gammeltoft-Hansen,[46] I define the return migration industry as an array of NSAs who, operating at scales ranging from local to transnational, provide services that facilitate, or assist international return migration along its two main phases—recruitment/mobilization and (re)-integration.[47]

Recruitment of skilled Israeli migrants is still primarily a state function.[48] Yet, increasingly NSAs take a more proactive approach, inducing return independently of official agencies. This is done, for example, by offering migrants different forms of direct material support, from reduced airfares to lucrative job offers. These actors may sometimes contribute indirectly to official repatriation programs, thereby brokering relations between state and migrants. Both forms are applicable in both sending and destination countries. Acts of indirect recruitment may include, for example, political lobbying for tax or labor market reform which specific segments of migrants would benefit from. This was the case several years ago when a number of key Israeli professional associations (e.g., The Manufacturers' Association, The Association of Banks, The Institute of Certified Public Accountants and The Bar Association) have rallied to support the legislation of *Section 168 of the Income Tax Ordinance*. The contested reform (aka *Milchan Law*, after the Billionaire Israeli-American film producer whose lawyers lobbied for it feverishly),[49] provides for an extensive tax exemption—including waiver of any reporting requirements of income and gains of new and returning migrants for up to ten years—was approved by the Israeli parliament (Knesset) in August 2008.[50] Other acts, which prompt skilled return indirectly may take place in destination countries and include, for example, hosting or sponsoring of state-led repatriation events.

Key actors in this phase include, for example, international recruitment agencies. These agencies offer various services in the field of human resources and have recently "discovered" the potential of Israeli migrants who wish to return. Corporate Resource Group and HR Global Services are examples of human resource agencies specializing in talent acquisition management. They identify and recruit Israeli talents overseas for their corporate clients in Israel, including Amdocs, Nice Systems and Siemens. Their transnational connections enable them to repatriate "[Q]uality Israeli workers in the fields of high-tech, bio-tech and finance who reside in the US."[51] Their clients are both long-time Israeli migrants as well as former expatriates whose "mother companies relocated . . . but forgot to return."[52]

Other recruitment agents are Israel-based branches of multinational corporations who scan the global job market in search for Israeli migrants in senior positions who wish to return. Their transnational reach allows them direct access to a global pool of return-interested skilled migrants. In contrast to external recruitment agencies, their engagement with returnees (and their household members) does not stop at the recruitment stage. Multinational corporations like Intel and Siemens, for example, provide skilled migrants hired by their subsidiaries in Israel, assistance in a range of areas, including *inter alia* home-finding, children's schooling, tax benefits, health insurance, and shipment. While some corporations deliver such services in-house by their respective departments of human resources, others prefer to outsource them to specialized agencies who constitute "one-stop-shop" for relocation services.

The latter is more common among very large corporations who often use the same agencies to handle all their intra-corporate relocations.[53]

Recruitment of skilled returnees is not limited to large corporations. Smaller firms, like Bell Labs Israel, have occasionally utilized their cross-border professional networks to develop limited "brain return" programs.[54] These small-scale initiatives, which typically lead to the repatriation of a handful of skilled workers, are nonetheless important, because they indicate the still dominant position of the Zionist Ideology in Israel, and its repatriation discourse specifically. As Teva's VP for Human Resources argued in this respect, "One cannot depend on the government all the time [to combat brain drain]. Any mid-size to large firm can repatriate [skilled] academics."[55]

In some cases, NSAs have been collaborating with each other on self-sponsored repatriation initiatives. A case in point is a series of roundtables hosted by Motorola during the 2008 global financial crisis. Under the heading of "Talent flow/return to Israel," local firms in the fields of InfoTech, BioTech and Finance sectors have deliberated how "[T]o return quality and excellent workers living in the US to Israel's labor marker." Participants deliberated best recruitment practices of workers, "[W]ho accumulated extensive experience in the international market and may be strategic assets to any . . . [Israeli] firm."[56]

Civic organizations, including non-governmental, migrant, and diasporic organizations also partake in recruitment efforts. On account of their limited resource, they typically take auxiliary roles, including compilation and maintenance of skilled migrants' online databases, organizing, sponsoring and hosting of repatriation events abroad, and lobbying for and marketing state-led campaigns among relevant constituencies. The Organization of Israeli Scientists Abroad (aka Science Abroad) is by far the most salient civic actor. With its three thousand members and twenty-five branches in North America and Europe, it aims "[T]o harness the power of senior Israeli scientists abroad . . . [and] facilitate the return of great minds to Israel."[57]

To do so, it (co)-organizes recruitment fairs in Israel and overseas, circulates job listings among its members, and provides financial support to those travelling to Israel for job interviews. It is funded by the Government of Israel (through the MOIA), The Israeli American Council (IAC), public Israeli universities and multiple commercial and philanthropic bodies. Thanks to these ties, Science Abroad has recently obtained an "exclusive supplier"[58] status, for different services pertaining to skilled migrants. This privileged status has allowed it to forge strong partnerships with civic, public and private agencies to recruit skilled migrants. A recent example is its partnering with Bar Ilan

University in its $150 million plan to repatriate in the next decade 150 Israeli STEM researchers who live abroad.[59] According to the plan, the university will use the organization's branches (located at university campuses abroad) to hold a series of career fairs. Vice President for Research at Bar Ilan thanked the organization for its role in the plan, saying it would help the university "become the ideal academic home of returnees."[60]

IAC, mentioned above, is another key player in Israel's RMI. It was established in 2007 in Los Angeles and has since become the most powerful Israeli diasporic organization in the world. With generous donations from Jewish philanthropists, notably Sheldon Adelson, it aims "to build an engaged and united Israeli-American community."[61] Although most of its projects were set to institutionalize Israeli migrant communities in the US, in recent years it has become increasingly involved in nation-wide enterprises to promote Israel-related causes, repatriation included. For example, in each of its recent annual conferences, special panels on brain return to Israel were held, as well as informational sessions on InfoTech job opportunities in Israel.

The IAC also promotes brain return indirectly by supporting other organizations, which contribute—administratively or financially—to Israeli state-sponsored repatriation initiatives. These include, for example, Jewish federations and community centers who typically operate at the metropolitan scale (e.g., The Jewish Federation of the Greater Atlanta), as well as smaller 501c organizations like Tarbuton, which supports grassroots projects in San Diego or *Dor Chadash* (Hebrew for New Generation), a network of young Jewish professionals who set up Israel-related educational and social projects. The latter organizations fulfilled different auxiliary roles in Israel's NBGP, including the sponsoring of info-sessions at university campuses across the US. The American Friends of Tel Aviv University (AFTAU), another beneficiary of the AIC, recently kicked-off a repatriation fund raising campaign, pleading its members "to turn brain drain into brain gain" by helping Tel Aviv University "bring . . . [Israeli] academic all-stars home."[62]

Organizations are also involved in the second phase of the return migration process, namely (re)-integration. Re-integration, "the re-inclusion or re-incorporation of . . . a migrant into the society of their country of return,"[63] spans social, economic and cultural domains, which allow migrants to brace for—and accomplish—a successful re-adaptation to their countries of origin. While some preparatory measures of re-integration are typically applied in destination countries, before physical departure, the majority occur after one's arrival in her country of origin. However, both types of measures, from acquiring information about employment and housing opportunities to applying for children's educational institutions back home, require considerable investment by (prospective) returnees, aim to reduce levels of uncertainty and diminish the costs, material and psychological, associated with return.

Traditionally, the literature on re-integration focused on the experience of migrants from developing countries, many of whom have had irregular legal status in destination countries.[64] For those, re-integration was often mediated by state personnel in countries of destination and/or origin, specialized agencies (e.g., United States Agency for International Development), or multilateral organizations like the International Labor Organization. In contrast, most Israeli returnees receive little—or no—assistance from state agencies.[65] Indeed, public assistance to returning migrants has been quite limited, and typically included minor measures like subsidized air travel or customs-free (sea) shipping.[66] For different reasons, Israeli migrants have traditionally relied on their Israel-based social networks, including family, friends, and former colleagues in preparing for—and following—return.[67] These patterns are consistent with a recent study showing that compared with skilled Israelis who opted to stay abroad, skilled returnees enjoy significantly higher levels of homeland-based social—but also economic and cultural—capital.[68]

In recent years, a growing number of returnees have been seeking assistance beyond their social networks.[69] This tendency is undoubtedly related to the surge in the "basket of services" offered by the Israeli state in the context of SARPs.[70] However, it is also attributed to the transformation (from government to governance) described earlier, by which non-state return-supporting agents have proliferated. Both processes have made the provision of return-oriented services, like tax consulting or talent recruitment, more efficient, facilitating (potential) returnees' access to them and smoothening their overall re-integration process. In the context of the NBGP, for example, a range of placement agencies and mostly private employers—from small Israeli startup firms to multinational corporations like Intel, Teva Pharmaceuticals, and Citibank—were mobilized by the state, forming a pool of job listings for returning migrants. Vacancies were listed using online platforms, thus allowing returnees to browse through them, contact employers and interview for specific positions before physically returning to Israel. It is estimated that between August 2013 and December 2016 more than 600 Israelis received *at least* one job offer from employers associated with the program. In 2016 alone, employers brokered nearly three hundred migrants' (and families) way back home.[71]

In recent years, the domain of employment services has gradually been outsourced to NSAs. The MOIA, for example, increasingly subcontracts not-for-profit organizations, private firms, and individual advisors to provide returnees with an array of products and services. Using Request for Tenders (RTFs) suppliers are invited to place bids on the establishment and operation of national call centers for returning entrepreneurs (Business-IL), provision of consulting services to returnees on how to improve their skills in using social media (e.g., LinkedIn), leads on job-search workshops, and organization of preparation courses for certification tests in legal and financial professions (MOIA Website). These initiatives facilitate labor market reintegration of returnees by allowing them better access to employment services, prior to and in the aftermath of their physical return.

Tax planning and consulting is another domain in which NSAs have become progressively salient. According to Israel Tax Authority, between 2008 and 2014 the total volume of tax planning in the country has reached $21 billion.[72] The surge is attributed in part to the growing number of relocated employees in the InfoTech—and other—industries,[73] as well as the aforementioned Amendment 168 to the country's Income Tax Code. The legislation, which has turned Israel into "the world's best tax haven,"[74] exempts returning migrants (but also *Olim Chadashim*, new immigrants) from tax payments on their passive foreign-earned income (e.g., capital gains, business revenue) for a maximum of ten years. The amendment is part of the government's plan to incentivize in-migration of wealthy Diasporic Jews and return migration of skilled Israelis. Its enactment has led to a surge in the number of (prospective) returnees who sought tax consulting and planning. As a result, international taxation, specifically for returning migrants has become a significant market niche for certified accountants, many of whom devised marketing campaigns tailored for the needs of this growing segment.[75]

Finally, children's education is another dimension of re-integration, which NSAs are slowly becoming more engaged with. Since the 1990s, the Israeli government has introduced a series of de-regulatory measures to the once exclusively public education system.[76] One of the results is that Israel currently has multiple (semi)-private educational streams (e.g., Democratic, Waldorf, and Montessori). Each of these streams, or movements, oversee dozens of primary, middle, and high schools throughout the country that are managed and operated by either private or not-for-profit groups.[77] Although they must conform with national educational standards set by the Ministry of Education, they often enjoy a certain degree of flexibility in designing their own curricula. Importantly, they charge significantly higher tuition than public schools and, as a result, are biased towards students from privileged socioeconomic backgrounds. Prospective returnees, especially those possessing high cultural and economic capital, whose children seek admission to (semi)-private schools, engage with their staff ahead of their return. Engagements—either electronically or physically (e.g., during visits to Israel)—typically begin months before the family's return date and may involve intense negotiation (for instance, when mid-year admission is sought). The outcomes of negotiations are key not just to the process of children's re-integration in Israel, but to their parents' return *and* destination selection decisions.[78]

CONCLUSIONS

NSAs have been increasingly involved in migration governance. However, studies have thus far focused primarily on flows of incoming (mostly non-citizen) migrants, paying little attention to their brokering role in return migration of nationals. This chapter sought to begin filling this gap by attending to the ways in which NSAs mediate Israeli skilled repatriation. From individual philanthropists who fund—almost single-handedly—repatriation projects to migrant organizations who broker between returnees and Israeli InfoTech firms, these civic and private bodies form Israel's return migration industry.

Israel's return migration industry is a fairly new phenomenon, and most of the agencies mentioned in this chapter have only been established in the last two decades. However, it has since grown considerably, in both size and reach. Small increments in emigration and—at times—return, the economic potential of (skilled) returnees, and the intensifying shedding of responsibilities by the Israeli state, have created multiple opportunities for the engagement of non-state actors in the repatriation process. Insurance, shipping, tax and legal consulting, children's education, talent management and real estate are some of the fields in which new opportunities have been presented for the involvement of non-state actors. Importantly, some actors do not operate in a single location (e.g., country), but develop transnational and, sometimes, global strategies, to court (returning) migrants and/or offer them their services prior to or in the aftermath of repatriation. Lessons from Israel could be useful for scholars working in other contexts. Three are worth mentioning in brief; first, although NSAs are instrumental in en/discouraging migration flows, their involvement varies with different types of migration. Aid organizations are justifiably more engaged with inflows of asylum seekers, whereas recruitment agencies often spearhead efforts to mobilize skilled migrants. Indeed, the desirability of specific migrant groups is a decisive factor not only in state policy, but also in the extent to which its agents may choose to delegate responsibility to NSAs for their mobilization and (re)-integration. Students of migration should further map out and study these *migration sub-industries* and, where possible, assess—both qualitatively and quantitatively—the variegated strategies employed by actors in them, as well as their impact on repatriation of skilled Israelis.

Secondly, examining industries at both origin and destination countries is imminent in order understand the transnational reach of actors in migration industries, links between them and the extent to which they benefit from (often the very same) migration flows. Future studies should explore their links and mutual functioning across national borders in order to better understand how they conjointly (re)produce distinct trajectories of migration and return.

Finally, despite the growing size and reach of the industry, it should be clear that the state still dominates the legal, institutional and regulatory frameworks necessary for repatriation. As such, relations between the state and the industry are best characterized as complementary (rather than mutually exclusive). Yet, complementarity does not always eliminate differences with respect to organizational positions or motivations. Indeed, in some instances, the "ideological" stance advocated by the state—or parts thereof, may clash with the financial interests that drive at least some private actors. A more critical approach is therefore needed to examine the effects of these differences on (return) migration policymaking, and the mechanisms through which conflicting interests are aligned. In light of the increasing involvement of both state and non-state actors in migration governance globally, such an approach may prove particularly useful to deciphering the power relations between the main forces that continue to "oil the wheels" of international mobility.

Notes

1. Human Resource Portal, *Placement of Quality Workers and Zionism*, 2014, http://www.hrus.co.il/.
2. A. S. Clark, "$100M to Fight Israeli Brain Drain," *The Jewish Week*, January 26, 2016.
3. N. Toren, "Return Migration to Israel," *International Migration Review* 12, no. 1 (1978): 39–54.
4. A. Krampf, *The Israeli Path to Neoliberalism: The State, Continuity and Change* (London: Routledge, 2018).
5. *Aliya*; see I. Shpaizman, "Load-shedding and Reloading: Changes in Government Responsibility—the Case of Israeli Immigration and Integration Policy 2004–10," *Social Policy Review* 25 (2013): 183–202.
6. See N. Cohen, "A Web of Repatriation: The Changing Politics of Israel's Diaspora Strategy," *Population, Space and Place* 22, no. 3 (2016): 288–300.
7. Between 8,000 to 10,000 migrants, defined as those who had been away for a minimum of one year, returned annually to Israel in the period 2004–17 (Central Bureau of Statistics, 2019). These are slightly lower annual figures than the 12,000 quoted by S. J. Gold, *The Israeli Diaspora* (Seattle: University of Washington Press, 2002), 217 for the mid-1990s.
8. Nova, *Examination of the Economic Benefit of Returning Scientists to Israel and Possible Measures to Encourage Return* (Tel Aviv: Nova Publications, 2018), https://drive.google.com/file/d/1Q7c4tLuCsIfJWGOzVCFI-jBQTSpU527T/view.
9. H. Bulkeley and P. Newell, *Governing Climate Change* (London: Routledge, 2015); T. Risse, "Transnational Actors and World Politics," in *Corporate Ethics and Corporate Governance* (Heidelberg: Springer, 2007): 251–86.
10. M. Foucault, *Discipline and Punish: The Birth of the Prison* (London: Penguin Books, 1991).
11. N. Rose and P. Miller, "Political Power beyond the State: Problematics of Government," *British Journal of Sociology* (1992): 173–205; M. Dean, *Governmentality: Power and Rule in Modern Society* (Thousand Oaks: Sage Publications, 2010).
12. E. Sørensen and J. Torfing, eds., "Governance Network Research: Towards a Second Generation," in *Theories of Democratic Network Governance* (Basingstoke: Palgrave MacMillan, 2016), 6.
13. R. A. W. Rhodes, "The New Governance: Governing without Government," *Political Studies*, 44, no. 4 (1996): 652–67.
14. M. Flynn and C. J. Cannon, *The Privatization of Immigration Detention: Towards a Global View* (Geneva: Global Detention Project Working Paper, 2009); D. Van den Broek, W. Harvey, and D. Groutsis, "Commercial Migration Intermediaries and the Segmentation of Skilled Migrant Employment," *Work, Employment and Society* 30, no. 3 (2016): 523–34.

15. G. Lahav, "Immigration and the State: The Devolution and Privatization of Immigration Control in the EU," *Journal of Ethnic and Migration Studies* 24, no. 4 (1998): 675–94.

16. V. Guiraudon and G. Lahav, "A Reappraisal of the State Sovereignty Debate: The Case of Migration Control," *Comparative Political Studies* 33, no. 2 (2000): 177.

17. Lahav, "Immigration and the State," 686.

18. D. Agunias, "Guiding the Invisible Hand: Making Migration Intermediaries Work for Development," *Human Development Research Paper* 22 (2009): 2.

19. D. Groutsis, D. van den Broek, and W. S. Harvey, "Transformations in Network Governance: The Case of Migration Intermediaries," *Journal of Ethnic and Migration Studies* 41, no. 10 (2015): 1558–76.

20. G. Menz, "The Neoliberalized State and Migration Control: The Rise of Private Actors in the Enforcement and Design of Migration Policy, *Debatte* 17, no. 3 (2009): 315–32.

21. Ibid., 323.

22. G. Menz, "Neo-liberalism, Privatization and the Outsourcing of Migration Management: A Five-Country Comparison," *Competition and Change* 15, no. 2 (2011): 116–35.

23. G. Menz, "The Governance of Migration beyond the State," in *Handbook of the International Political Economy of Governance*, ed. A. Payne and N. Phillips (Cheltenham, UK: Edward Elgar Publishing, 2014): 379–94.

24. R. Hernández-León, "The Migration Industry in the Mexico-US Migratory System," *California Center for Population Research*, 2005.

25. Ibid., 10.

26. Ibid., 12–17.

27. M. P. Garapich, "The Migration Industry and Civil Society: Polish Immigrants in the United Kingdom before and after EU Enlargement," *Journal of Ethnic and Migration Studies* 34, no. 5 (2008): 738.

28. Ibid.

29. A. Betts, "The Migration Industry in Global Migration Governance," in *The Migration Industry and the Commercialization of International Migration* (London: Routledge, 2013), 63–81.

30. J. L. Hennebry, "Bienvenidos a Canadá? Globalization and the Migration Industry surrounding Temporary Agricultural Migration in Canada," *Canadian Studies in Population* 35, no. 2 (2008): 339–56; J. Lindquist, "Labour Recruitment, Circuits of Capital and Gendered Mobility: Reconceptualizing the Indonesian Migration Industry," *Pacific Affairs* 83, no. 1 (2010): 115–32.

31. Betts, "The Migration Industry," 58

32. R. Hernández-León, "Conceptualizing the Migration Industry," in *The Migration Industry and the Commercialization of International Migration*, ed. T. Gammeltoft-Hansen and N. N. Sørenson (London: Routledge, 2013), 26–32.

33. Hernández-León, "Conceptualizing the Migration Industry, 29.

34. International Organization for Migration, *World Migration Report* (Geneva: IOM Publications, 2020).

35. S. Ammassari, "From Nation-building to Entrepreneurship: The Impact of Élite Return Migrants in Côte d'Ivoire and Ghana," *Population, Space and Place* 10, no. 2 (2004): 133–54; J. Wahba, "Who Benefits from Return Migration to Developing Countries?" *IZA World of Labor* (2015).

36. See N. Cohen and D. Kranz, "State-assisted Highly Skilled Return Programmes, National Identity and the Risk(s) of Homecoming: Israel and Germany Compared," *Journal of Ethnic and Migration Studies*, 41, no. 5 (2015): 795–812.

37. S. L. Chang, "Causes of Brain Drain and Solutions: The Taiwan Experience," *Studies in Comparative International Development* 27, no. 1 (1992): 27–43; H. Song, "From Brain Drain to Reverse Brain Drain: Three Decades of Korean Experience," *Science, Technology and Society* 2, no. 2 (1997): 317–45; D. Zweig, "Competing for Talent: China's Strategies to Reverse the Brain Drain," *International Labour Review* 145 (2006): 65–90.

38. Cohen, "A Web of Repatriation."

39. N. Cohen, "From Nation to Profession: Israeli State Strategy toward Highly-skilled Return Migration, 1949–2012," *Journal of Historical Geography* 42 (2013): 1–11.

40. Toren, "Return Migration to Israel."

41. Cited in N. Cohen, "Come Home, Be Professional: Ethno-nationalism and Economic Rationalism in Israel's Return Migration Strategy," *Immigrants & Minorities* 27, no. 1 (2009): 11.

42. The portfolio was a governmental response to rising emigration rates after the 1973 War. Between 1978 and 1983, nearly 100,000 Israelis left the country.

43. Committee on Immigration and Absorption, *Protocol #23* (Jerusalem: Knesset Publications, 1982), 4.

44. Israel's (Jewish) immigration (*Aliya*) and integration policies had undergone similar processes at that time. Non-state organizations like *Nefesh B'Nefesh* (Hebrew "soul to soul") and *AMI* (My People) have assumed exclusive responsibility over the recruitment and integration of Jewish migrants from North America and France, respectively. For an excellent discussion of these processes, which are beyond the scope of this article, see Shpaizman, "Load-shedding and Reloading."

45. Cohen, "Come Home, Be Professional."

46. N. N. Sørensen and T. Gammeltoft-Hansen, "Introduction," in *The Migration Industry and the Commercialization of International Migration*, ed. T. Gammeltoft-Hansen and N. N. Sorensen (London: Routledge, 2013), 6–7.

47. Hernández-León, "Conceptualizing the Migration Industry."

48. Cohen, "From Nation to Profession."

49. S. Sade and H. Amit, "The Bad Movie of Arnon Milchan," *The Marker* Online, February 3, 2017.

50. Recent reports showed that the reform failed completely. Although it managed to attract some high-profile Israeli migrants, including business-owners in media and telecommunication, most re-migrated shortly before exemptions expired (E. Neuman, "We Came, Abused, Left: How Israel Became a Tax Haven for the Rich, Thanks to Milchan Law," *The Marker* Online, December 3, 2019).

51. D. Neev, "Brain Flow: Returning Israeli Talents from the US," *Human Resource Management* (September 2, 2009), http://www.hrm.co.il/default.asp?topic=article&id=454.

52. Ibid.

53. A case is point is the Netanya-based O.R.I. Relocation, to which corporations like Teva, Strauss and ECI have outsourced all their relocation services.

54. *Globes*. "The Challenge of Bell Labs—Brain Return to Israel," *Globes* Online, June 11, 2015.

55. N. Darom, "What Have We Done to Return You? Nothing," *Ha'Aretz* Online, October 7, 2010.

56. Jobs Today [Hebrew}, https://www.jobstoday.co.il.

57. Science Abroad: The Organization of Israeli Scientists Abroad, https://www.scienceabroad.org.il

58. In Israel, an Exclusive Supplier (Hebrew *Sapak Yachid*) is a local firm or organization which is designated by the state as the sole provider of certain goods or services. Those obtaining the desired status are exempted from tendering for public sector contracts.

59. G. Weinrab, "Bar Ilan's Ambitious Plan to Return 150 Scientists," *Globes*, July 31, 2018, https://www.globes.co.il/news/article.aspx?did=1001248132.

60. "Bar Ilan University and the Organization of Israeli Scientists Abroad in a Campaign to Return and Recruit 150 Israeli Scientists," Bar Ilan University Spokesman's Office, August 5, 2018.

61. "About the IAC," Israeli American Council, https://www.israeliamerican.org.

62. "Make a Donation to the Brain Gain Campaign," American Friends of Tel Aviv University, https://www.aftau.org/page.aspx?pid=377.

63. M. Haase and P. Honerath, *Return Migration and Reintegration Policies: A Primer* (German Marshall Fund of the United States, 2016): 5.

64. L. Hammond, "'Voluntary' Repatriation and Reintegration," in *The Oxford Handbook of Refugee and Forced Migration Studies*, ed. E. Fiddian-Qasmiyeh et al. (Oxford: Oxford University Press, 2014), 499–511.

65. Dr. Nurit Eyal estimates that less than a quarter of migrants who returned to Israel during the duration of the program have sought state assistance (Interview, July 15, 2016).

66. Cohen, "Come Home, Be Professional."

67. Gold, *The Israeli Diaspora*.

68. E. Israel, N. Cohen, and D. Czamanski, "Return on Capital? Determinants of Counter-migration among Early Career Israeli STEM Researchers," *PloS one* 14, no. 8 (2019): e0221882.

69. Eyal, Interview, July 15, 2016.

70. Cohen & Kranz, "State-assisted Highly Skilled Return Programmes."

71. Midgam Consulting and Research, "Determinants of Migration and Return of Israeli Academics," Research Report Prepared for the National Brain Gain Program [in Hebrew] (Jerusalem: Ministry of the Economy, 2016).

72. A. Barkat, "The Volume of Tax Planning in Israel in Five Years: 21 Billion NIS," *Globes* Online, December 14, 2014, https://www.globes.co.il/news/article.aspx?did=1000993357.

73. E. Levi-Vinriv, "The Relocation and Its Rupture," *Globes* Online, August 25, 2013.

74. A. Nov, "The World's Best Tax Haven," *Globes* Online, October 13, 2009.

75. Levi-Vinriv, "The Relocation and Its Rupture."

76. Some measures were aimed at the tertiary (academic) system and included, for example, the opening up of private colleges, which have since been competing with the more established, public universities in Israel (A. Volansky, *Academia in a Changing Environment: Israel's Policy of Higher Education, 1952–2004* [Tel Aviv: Hakibbutz Ha-me'uchad and the Shmuel Nee-man Institute, 2005]).

77. N. Dagan-Buzaglo, *Privatization in the Israeli School System: Selected Issues* [in Hebrew] (Tel Aviv: Adva Center, 2010), https://adva.org/wp-content/up-loads/2014/09/Edu2010eng.pdf.

78. A study conducted among skilled migrants who returned to Israel found that children's education was the second most important factor in their return decision (Midgam Consulting and Research, "Determinants of Migration").

Bibliography

Agunias, D. "Guiding the Invisible Hand: Making Migration Intermediaries Work for Development." *Human Development Research Paper* 22 (2009): 1–95.

American Friends of Tel Aviv University. "Make a Donation to the Brain Gain Campaign." https://www.aftau.org/page.aspx?pid=377.

Ammassari, S. "From Nation-building to Entrepreneurship: The Impact of Élite Return Migrants in Côte d'Ivoire and Ghana." *Population, Space and Place* 10, no. 2 (2004): 133–54.

Bar Ilan University Spokesman's Office. "Bar Ilan University and the Organization of Israeli Scientists Abroad in a Campaign to Return and Recruit 150 Israeli Scientists." August 5, 2018.

Barkat, A. "The Volume of Tax Planning in Israel in Five Years: 21 Billion NIS." *Globes* Online, December 14, 2014. https://www.globes.co.il/news/article.aspx?did=1000993357.

Betts, A. "The Migration Industry in Global Migration Governance." In *The Migration Industry and the Commercialization of International Migration*, 63–81. London: Routledge, 2013.

Bulkeley, H., and P. Newell. *Governing Climate Change*. London: Routledge, 2015.

Chang, S. L. "Causes of Brain Drain and Solutions: The Taiwan Experience." *Studies in Comparative International Development* 27, no. 1 (1992): 27–43.

Clark, A. S. "$100M to Fight Israeli Brain Drain." *The Jewish Week*, January 26, 2016.

Cohen, N. "A Web of Repatriation: The Changing Politics of Israel's Diaspora Strategy." *Population, Space and Place* 22, no. 3 (2016): 288–300.

———. "Come Home, Be Professional: Ethno-nationalism and Economic Rationalism in Israel's Return Migration Strategy." *Immigrants & Minorities* 27, no. 1 (2009): 1–28.

———. "From Nation to Profession: Israeli State Strategy toward Highly-skilled Return Migration, 1949–2012." *Journal of Historical Geography* 42 (2013): 1–11.

Cohen, N., and D. Kranz. "State-assisted Highly Skilled Return Programmes, National Identity and the Risk(s) of Homecoming: Israel and Germany Compared." *Journal of Ethnic and Migration Studies* 41, no. 5 (2015): 795–812.

Committee on Immigration and Absorption. *Protocol #23*. Jerusalem: Knesset Publications, 1982.

Dagan-Buzaglo, N. *Privatization in the Israeli School System: Selected Issues* [in Hebrew]. Tel Aviv: Adva Center, 2010. https://adva.org/wp-content/uploads/2014/09/Edu2010eng.pdf.

Darom, N. "What Have We Done to Return You? Nothing." *Ha'Aretz* Online, October 7, 2010.

Dean, M. *Governmentality: Power and Rule in Modern Society*. Thousand Oaks: Sage Publications, 2010.

Flynn, M., and C. J. Cannon. *The Privatization of Immigration Detention: Towards a Global View.* Geneva: Global Detention Project Working Paper, 2009.

Foucault, M. *Discipline and Punish: The Birth of the Prison.* London: Penguin Books, 1991.

Gammeltoft-Hansen, T., and N. N. Sorensen, eds. (2013). *The Migration Industry and the Commercialization of International Migration.* London: Routledge, 2013.

Garapich, M. P. "The Migration Industry and Civil Society: Polish Immigrants in the United Kingdom before and after EU Enlargement." *Journal of Ethnic and Migration Studies* 34, no. 5 (2008): 735–52.

Globes. "The Challenge of Bell Labs—Brain Return to Israel." *Globes* Online, June 11, 2015.

Gold, S. J. *The Israeli Diaspora.* Seattle: University of Washington Press, 2002.

Groutsis, D., D. van den Broek, and W. S. Harvey. "Transformations in Network Governance: The Case of Migration Intermediaries." *Journal of Ethnic and Migration Studies* 41, no. 10 (2015): 1558–76.

Guiraudon, V., and G. Lahav. "A Reappraisal of the State Sovereignty Debate: The Case of Migration Control." *Comparative Political Studies* 33, no. 2 (2000): 163–95.

Haase, M., and P. Honerath. *Return Migration and Reintegration Policies: A Primer.* German Marshall Fund of the United States, 2016.

Hammond, L. "'Voluntary' Repatriation and Reintegration." In *The Oxford Handbook of Refugee and Forced Migration Studies*, edited by E. Fiddian-Qasmiyeh et al., 499–511. Oxford: Oxford University Press, 2014.

Hennebry, J. L. "Bienvenidos a Canadá? Globalization and the Migration Industry surrounding Temporary Agricultural Migration in Canada." *Canadian Studies in Population* 35, no. 2 (2008): 339–56.

Hernández-León, R. "Conceptualizing the Migration Industry." In *The Migration Industry and the Commercialization of International Migration*, edited by T. Gammeltoft-Hansen and N. N. Sørenson, 24–44 (London: Routledge, 2013).

———. "The Migration Industry in the Mexico-US Migratory System." *California Center for Population Research*, 2005.

Human Resource Portal. *Placement of quality workers and Zionism.* 2014. http://www.hrus.co.il/.

International Organization for Migration. *World Migration Report.* Geneva: IOM Publications, 2020.

Israel, E., N. Cohen, and D. Czamanski. "Return on Capital? Determinants of Counter-migration among Early Career Israeli STEM Researchers." *PloS one* 14, no. 8 (2019).

Krampf, A. *The Israeli Path to Neoliberalism: The State, Continuity and Change.* London: Routledge, 2018.

Lahav, G. "Immigration and the State: The Devolution and Privatization of Immigration Control in the EU." *Journal of Ethnic and Migration Studies* 24, no. 4 (1998): 675–94.

Levi-Vinriv, E. "The Relocation and Its Rupture." *Globes* Online, August 25, 2013.

Lindquist, J. "Labour Recruitment, Circuits of Capital and Gendered Mobility: Reconceptualizing the Indonesian Migration Industry." *Pacific Affairs* 83, vol. 1 (2010): 115–32.

Menz, G. "The Governance of Migration beyond the State." In *Handbook of the International Political Economy of Governance*, edited by A. Payne and N. Phillips, 379–94. Edward Elgar Publishing, 2014.

———. "Neo-liberalism, Privatization and the Outsourcing of Migration Management: A Five-Country Comparison." *Competition and Change* 15, no. 2 (2011): 116–35.

———. "The Neoliberalized State and Migration Control: The Rise of Private Actors in the Enforcement and Design of Migration Policy." *Debatte* 17, no. 3 (2009): 315–32.

Midgam Consulting and Research. "Determinants of Migration and Return of Israeli Academics." Research Report Prepared for the National Brain Gain Program [in Hebrew]. Jerusalem: Ministry of the Economy, 2016.

Neev, D. "Brain Flow: Returning Israeli Talents from the US." *Human Resource Management*, September 2, 2009. http://www.hrm.co.il/default. asp?topic=article&id=454.

Neuman, E. "We Came, Abused, Left: How Israel Became a Tax Haven for the Rich, Thanks to Milchan Law." *The Marker* Online, December 3, 2019.

Nov, A. "The World's Best Tax Haven." *Globes* Online, October 13, 2009.

Nova. *Examination of the Economic Benefit of Returning Scientists to Israel and Possible Measures to Encourage Return.* Tel Aviv: Nova Publications, 2018. https://drive. google.com/file/d/1Q7c4tLuCsIfJWGOzVCFI-jBQTSpU527T/view.

Rhodes, R. A. W. "The New Governance: Governing without Government." *Political Studies*, 44, no. 4 (1996): 652–67.

Risse, T. "Transnational Actors and World Politics." In *Corporate Ethics and Corporate Governance*, 251–86. Heidelberg: Springer, 2007.

Rose, N., and P. Miller. "Political Power beyond the State: Problematics of Government." *British Journal of Sociology* (1992): 173–205.

Sade, S., and H. Amit. "The Bad Movie of Arnon Milchan." *The Marker* Online, February 3, 2017.

Shpaizman, I. "Load-shedding and Reloading: Changes in Government Responsibility— the Case of Israeli Immigration and Integration Policy 2004–10." *Social Policy Review* 25 (2013): 183–202.

Song, H. "From Brain Drain to Reverse Brain Drain: Three Decades of Korean Experience." *Science, Technology and Society* 2, no. 2 (1997): 317–45.

Sørensen, E., and J. Torfing, eds. "Governance Network Research: Towards a Second Generation" In *Theories of Democratic Network Governance.* Basingstoke: Palgrave MacMillan, 2016.

Sørensen, N. N., and T. Gammeltoft-Hansen. "Introduction." In *The Migration Industry and the Commercialization of International Migration*, edited by T. Gammeltoft-Hansen and N. N. Sorensen, 1–23. London: Routledge, 2013.

Toren, N. "Return Migration to Israel." *International Migration Review* 12, no. 1 (1978): 39–54.

Van den Broek, D., W. Harvey, and D. Groutsis. "Commercial Migration Intermediaries and the Segmentation of Skilled Migrant Employment." *Work, Employment and Society* 30, no. 3 (2016): 523–34.

Volansky, A. *Academia in a Changing Environment: Israel's Policy of Higher Education, 1952–2004.* Tel Aviv: Hakibbutz Ha-me'uchad and the Shmuel Nee-man Institute, 2005.

Wahba, J. "Who Benefits from Return Migration to Developing Countries?" *IZA World of Labor*, 2015.

Weinrab, G. "Bar Ilan's Ambitious Plan to Return 150 Scientists." *Globes*, July 31, 2018. https://www.globes.co.il/news/article.aspx?did=1001248132.

Zweig, D. "Competing for Talent: China's Strategies to Reverse the Brain Drain." *International Labour Review* 145 (2006): 65–90.

Jews Residing in Three Cities in France and Belgium: Patterns of Ethnic Identity and Identification

by Lilach Lev Ari

INTRODUCTION

The present study focuses on immigrant Jews who reside in three cities in Europe: Paris, Brussels and Antwerp. I analyze various dimensions of ethnic identity and identification, such as Jewish identity, transnational (with country of origin) and local (assimilative). The main research questions refer to possible explanations which influence the participants' ethnic identity and identification, primarily their city of residence and its socio-cultural atmosphere which enables (or not) vivid overt Jewish life. Other questions refer to the effects of country of origin, particularly Israel versus Maghreb countries, being part of the majority versus the minority there; belonging to a Sephardic or Ashkenazi ethnic group; and migration cohort, namely year of immigration—on the construction of ethnic identity and identification among immigrant Jews in three cities in Europe.

The three cities in Western Europe were chosen for this study since they are geographically adjacent and are characterized by their ethnically diverse Jewish communities: secular, religious, ultra-orthodox, Ashkenazi, Sephardi, native-born and migrants. In addition, Paris is a metropolis and a "world city," Brussels is the center of the European Union, whereas Antwerp is unique due to its changing variety of Jewish population, including the growing ultra-orthodox population. The three cities are somewhat similar in their culture (the usage of French is common, particularly in two of them), but also unique, as they belong to different nation states. The three cities are characterized by a long-standing Jewish history of dynamic interaction with local non-Jewish populations, both native-born and migrant, until the present day.

In addition, Paris is a global city that has attracted many migrants from the Middle East for decades, while Brussels is the center of the European Union and attracts many migrants from all over the world. All three cities, including Antwerp, have large and vibrant Jewish communities.

Whereas numerous studies focus upon Jewish immigrants in the United States,[1] very few studies have examined Jewish-ethnic identity among immigrant Jews in Western Europe. Furthermore, studies regarding ethnic identity and identification among immigrant Jews in France and Belgium, which are based on mixed methods, are rare as well.[2]

The need for research on the Jews of Western Europe has become even more warranted today in view of the current wave of antisemitism accompanied by numerous violent incidents, including barbaric murders. Jews in France, Belgium and other European countries are increasingly expressing interest in emigrating to Israel or to other destinations. Europe is facing an overall rise in racism and xenophobia: growing racism and violence against minorities, fed by ultra-nationalism, antisemitism, and anti-Muslim hate. The Coronavirus-inspired antisemitic expressions constitute forms of traditional Jew hatred and of conspiracy theories. So far, these accusations appear to be promoted mainly by extreme rightists, ultra conservative Christian circles, Islamists, and to a minor extent by the far-left, each group according to its narrative and beliefs—such as different conspiracy theories as well as the image of the Jew as a producer of diseases.[3]

Thus the findings of the present study expands migration studies by analyzing ethno-religious identity and identification among immigrants in the city context. In addition, the usage of mixed methods elaborates the complex and dynamic meaning of theoretical terms such as ethnic identity and identification, transnational, religious or assimilative, among migrants and their various attitudinal and behavioral components. Particularly, the main contribution of this study is in focusing on particular Jewish immigrants, in different cities, from different countries of origin and migration cohorts and their unique ethnic identity characteristics, vis-à-vis their host societies and homelands.

ETHNIC IDENTITY AND IDENTIFICATION AMONG MIGRANTS

In recent decades, international migration has been referred to as "transnational migration." This approach places emphasis on the differences between migration in the past and contemporary migration. Transnational migration is a process in which migrants maintain ties with their past and forge new ties that connect their society of origin and their host society, namely with more than one country.[4] The social space of transnational migrants is fluid and changes frequently by means of a set of connections and commitments to more than one place.[5] Through constant interaction with the host society and country of origin, immigrants and their descendants dynamically re-construct their multiple ethnic identities.[6]

A major component of migrant experience in the host society is the construction of migrants' ethnic identity and identification.[7] Ethnic identity has a number of components: inner beliefs, attitudes and emotions toward the ethnic group, identification as a member of the group, a sense of belonging and commitment to the group, a sense of shared attitudes and values.[8] In an era in which people live in the global village, ethnic identity is anchored in a variety of geographic spaces situated beyond national borders. Indeed, ethnic identity has become transnational identity.[9]

Migrants undergo dynamic processes that develop and enhance their identity and ethnic identification. Ethnic identity is constructed dynamically and continues to develop, following changes in the location of the group and the individual as well as changes in the social structure of the destination country or community. Ethnic boundaries are defined and redefined by constant negotiation and are restructured through the reciprocal relations between various groups. Unlike ethnic identity, which has almost no external manifestation, ethnic identification represents a willful, conscious act on the part of the individual.[10]

Ethnic identification is the behavioral expression of identity, the genuine expression of a connection to an ethnic or religious group, through religious practice and community involvement, affiliation and customs—among other components.[11]

Another possible construction of ethnic identity and identification among migrants is one that can be described as "assimilative," namely in convergence with classical assimilation linear models: migrants are becoming more similar over time (particularly their descendants) in their values, norms, behaviors and characteristics to the host society. However, new models of assimilation, particularly that of transnationalism, focus on various dynamic forms of identity, according to personal socio-demographic characteristics,

ethnic communities' sources and host society policy towards migrants' assimilation, and others.[12]

A specific group of immigrants may also exhibit "subethnicity": even
though all the subgroups share ethnic characteristics, each may have its own national identity and particular traditions. These subgroups may also be marked
by socioeconomic differences. A case in point is the Iranian community in the
US, which is composed of Moslems, Jews, Baha'is and Armenian Christians.[13]

In addition, in a globalized world, "identity and community often serve
as a focus of resistance to centralizing and homogenizing forces."[14] Some migrant groups, after their initial integration in host country or city, develop their
own sub-communities and social, cultural and economic organizations: places
of worship, formal and informal educational institutions for their children,
media channels and other services. These sub-communities and institutions
reflect on their ethnic identity and identification. Migrants also play a significant role in communities' structure, by establishing their own neighborhoods
and distinctive use of private and public places.[15]

The following section describes Jewish identity among Jews in general,
and those among Jews in Europe in particular.

ETHNIC IDENTITY AND IDENTIFICATION
AMONG JEWS IN EUROPE

In general, Jewish identity and identification find expression in various contexts: religious, ethnic, cultural, communal, social, historical and folklorist.
Some Diaspora Jews see their identity and identification in the context of being
part of Jewish history, while others see it in belonging to Jewish organizations.
In an attempt to simplify this complexity, S. DellaPergola describes four possible patterns of Jewish identity and identification.[16] The first is the *normative-
traditional* pattern. Jews who follow this pattern express their identity openly
and maintain Jewish beliefs, values and norms while conforming to Jewish customs and ceremonies. Another mode of Jewish identity and identification is
ethno-communal. Jews belonging to this group maintain associative networks
that are predominantly Jewish but in which in-group communication entails
spontaneous and not necessarily Jewish content. Jews in this group may refer
to themselves as secular and use many symbols deriving from the non-Jewish
environment while preserving several traditional Jewish customs. The next

pattern of Jewish identity and identification is of *cultural residue*. Jews conforming to this pattern express interest in Jewish tradition, history and culture and are even to some extent involved in Jewish cultural activity, yet, in general, they are not affiliated with any of the religious streams of Judaism or with Jewish organizations. Their Jewish identity is relatively weak and manifested in occasionally expressed intellectual or emotional interest. The fourth mode of Jewish identity and identification is termed as *dual or none*. This group includes individuals that cannot be assigned to any of the above three categories. The group is characterized by weakened Jewish identification alongside identity and identification with other religions, ethnic groups or communities that are not Jewish.[17]

Among the Jews of Europe, observance of religious commandments and signs of Jewish identification have been on the decline since the 1970s. Synagogue attendance began to wane, as did observance of the kosher dietary laws and other Jewish commandments. The State of Israel became an important source of identification for Jews in many communities in Europe, and support for Israel increased. Nonetheless, in the wake of the wave of terrorism that washed across Europe in the 1970s and 1980s, Israel became a burden and a source of suspicion and fear in the lives of European Jewish communities, due to the link between Israel and the Jews.[18] A recent survey published by D. Graham regarding Jewish identity and identification among Jews who reside in eight European nations (France, Belgium, UK, Italy, Germany, Hungary, Latvia and Sweden) indicates that Jewish societies are more heterogeneous than homogeneous.[19] Unlike the world's two largest Jewish populations, in Israel and in the United States, Europe's Jewish population is scattered across various nation states and lacks a singular historical commonality. The few common components of Jewish identity emerging from the report are a strong sense of importance attached to remembering the Holocaust and a feeling of being part of the Jewish people. The local culture in each country has a significant impact on the construction of ethnic identity, as does local policy toward ethnic minorities and the size of the local Jewish community, which allows (or not) the provision of religious services, including Jewish day schools. Regarding Jewish practices, only 30% of European Jews preserve the laws of Kashrut [dietary laws] in their homes, and this differs according to country of residence as well as socioeconomic status.[20] Following Graham,[21] I specifically discuss the question of homogeneity versus heterogeneity with respect to ethnic identity and identification among the three groups of immigrants.

In the next sections, I refer specifically to the characteristics of the Jewish communities in France and Belgium and previous findings regarding their Jewish identity and identification, including Israelis, who constitute part of the local migrant groups.

JEWISH IMMIGRATION TO FRANCE AND BELGIUM: CHARACTERISTICS AND COUNTRIES OF ORIGIN

Migration is usually perceived as movement from one country to another. However, it is primarily in cities that migrants and non-migrants interact, be it through working, studying, living or raising their families.[22] As J. Darling claimed, "Cities have come to be seen as key mediators in global politics, the global economy and in the social and cultural tensions of living with diversity."[23] Hence, migration has become the driving force behind increased urbanization, making some cities much more diverse places to live in. Nearly one-fifth of all migrants live in the world's twenty largest cities. In many of these global cities, migrants represent over a third of the population.[24] Thus, new forms of global organizations lead to the construction of "global cities" which attract immigrants from various socio-economic statuses.[25]

Europe is the third most important demographic and socio-political center of world Jewry: 9.2% of all Jews (1.35 million) reside in the whole of Europe, west and east.[26] Immigrants comprise more than a quarter (27%) of the Jewish population in Europe.[27] Jewish immigrants studied here reside in three cities in France and Belgium: Paris, Brussels and Antwerp.

The largest Jewish population in Europe lives in France, which is the third largest Jewish community in the world. In 2018 the total number of Jews in France was estimated at 453,000.[28] A third (34%) of the Jewish population in France was born outside the country; most of these (75%) were born in the Maghreb countries (Algeria, Morocco and Tunisia) and immigrated mainly from the mid-1950s to the mid-1960s and even to some extent during the 1970s.[29] Migration from Algeria was regulated by bilateral agreements, which accorded Algerian migrants, including Jews, a unique status. Moroccans and Tunisians, by contrast, were regulated through the Office National d'Immigration (ONI), which was established by France in order to recruit workers from Southern Europe beginning in 1945. The policy was implemented to solve postwar labor shortages.[30] Due to the new political and social order, as well as the Israeli-Arab conflict after 1948 and its effect on the rise of anti-Jewish hostility, Maghreb Jews decided, at that time, to emigrate from their countries of origin. These Jews had strong links to the former colonial regimes and an attachment to Israel.[31]

Thus, most of Maghreb Jews came from Algeria, due to their unique status (130,000). Others emigrated from Tunisia (50,000) and Morocco (30,000).[32] A total number of 250,000 Jews emigrated from North Africa to France between 1948 and 1968.[33] More than half (277,000) of the Jews in France live in Paris.[34] Most of the Jews living in Paris are Sephardi Jews (originating from MENA countries). A minority are Ashkenazi Jews (Jews of European origin).[35]

Furthermore, compared with previous Jewish immigration from Eastern Europe (after WWII), those who came from North Africa were acquainted with the French socio-cultural structure and could be integrated to a larger degree in the host society. North African Jews who arrived in France in the seventies enjoyed an era of individualism and upward mobility which characterized the French society at that time. Since then, Jews in France were part of the general economic prosperity and political stability and benefited from Catholics who accepted the Jews.[36]

Among the Israelis living in France, 6,600 are native-born Israelis and another 10,000 were born elsewhere and immigrated first to Israel and then to France. Israelis constitute two to three percent of the Jewish population of France.[37]

Similar to France, in the aftermath of the Second World War, Belgium was facing serious difficulties in recruiting labor for coal production. Domestic recruitment dried up, forcing authorities to look to foreign labor. Beginning with Italy in 1946, Spain (1956), Greece (1957), Morocco (1964), Turkey (1964), Tunisia (1969), Algeria (1970), and Yugoslavia (1970), the government pursued several bilateral agreements. When a crisis struck in the 1960s, these immigrant workers left to find employment in other industries. In the early 1960s, when the demand for labor was still strong, the Ministry of Justice stopped strictly applying the legislation governing immigration. New laws were passed to control the granting of work permits in order to regulate the flow of immigrants into the country in line with economic needs. Immigration since 1974 has simply changed, especially with regard to the types of immigration and the national origins of the migrants. Since the early 1980s, the major social fact of migration has become increasingly politicized. The fear of the invasion of Europe by citizens from poorer countries has rapidly spread.[38]

The number of Jews in Belgium in 2018 was estimated at 29,200, making it the sixteenth largest Jewish community in the world. Twenty-seven percent

(27%) of the Jewish population in Belgium are immigrants. The community is relatively stable in size and is based upon the traditional Orthodox community in Antwerp and on the European Union headquarters in Brussels, which also attracts Jews from other countries.[39] Jews from North Africa came to Belgium in small numbers during the 1960s, after the French decolonization.[40] Most members of the Belgian Jewish community (74%) today are Ashkenazi Jews born in Belgium, the descendants of former immigrants from Eastern Europe and Holocaust survivors. The majority reside in Brussels, the French-speaking capital.[41] According to Y. Cohen, there are 2,281 Israelis in the country.[42]

JEWS IN FRANCE AND BELGIUM: PREVIOUS STUDIES REGARDING SOCIAL INTEGRATION PATTERNS AND ETHNIC IDENTITY

Studies examining French Jewry found that these Jews present themselves as traditional and maintain strong ties with Israel, as manifested, for example, in their many trips to Israel.[43] The massive immigration of Maghreb Jews to France (see details in the introduction) did not affect the religious structure of the Jewish French community. The newcomers joined the existing Orthodox leadership. Those who were more prone to assimilation did not create alternative religious institutions. Since the 1990s, the French Jewish community has become more religious, inclining towards Ultra-Orthodox streams.[44]

Many French Jews express their Jewish identity and identification by representing themselves as Jews and expressing their affiliation with traditional streams in Judaism (51%). French Jews feel a strong attachment to Israel and more than half have visited Israel at least once.[45] In more recent studies similar findings were reported: a comparison among eight European nations found that in France, where Jews reported the strongest feelings of being part of the Jewish People, they also have the strongest level of emotional attachment to Israel. However, since Jewish schools in France charge fees, only 24% send their children to these schools.[46]

Algerian Jews in France (mainly those residing in Paris), who constitute the majority of Maghreb Jews in France, are unique in having some transnational cultural and ethnical attachment to Algeria, due to its exclusionary citizenship laws.[47] The Jewish population in France is constantly decreasing primarily due to emigration, mainly to Israel, but also to Canada, the US, and other countries. Migration to Israel, after surpassing 2,000 annually for several years, actually increased to a historical peak of 6,627 in 2015, and lowered to 3,160 in 2017, for a total of over 45,000 between 2001 and 2017. Jewish emigration was directed as well toward other western countries and reflected the continuing sense of uneasiness in the face of antisemitism. Based on estimations that Israel attracted two-thirds of the total who emigrated from France, about 70,000 Jews and family members have done so since 2001. Some of these may have returned to France in the meantime, thus reducing the impact of net migration.[48]

Since the beginning of the millennium and to a larger extent, recently, French Jews must cope with antisemitic and anti-Israeli statements and acts. While they want to demonstrate support for Israel and for their communities, they fear being perceived as having dual loyalty.[49] A recent survey which was conducted by Kantor Center[50] reports that during 2019 there was a rise of 18% in major violent cases compared to 2018 (456 cases in 2019 compared to 387 in 2018). Seven Jews and non-Jews were killed during antisemitic attacks, and there was a rise in most other manifestations, in most countries. At least fifty-three synagogues (12%) and twenty-eight community centers and schools (six percent) were attacked. There was an increase in life-endangering threats (47%) and in attacks on private properties (24%).[51] In France alone, thirty-five incidents of violent antisemitism were reported.[52]

Jews in Belgium are socially and economically assimilated into Belgian society and are no longer considered migrants. The Consistoire Central Israelite de Belgique is the main Jewish institution serving Belgian Jews. With respect to identity and ethnic identification among the Jews of Belgium, 40% consider themselves secular, 15% define themselves as liberal, over a quarter perceive themselves as traditional and a sixth define themselves as Orthodox.[53] Jews in Belgium are most likely to send their children to Jewish schools (out of eight European countries): 46% send their children to these institutions. The Jews in Belgium are also characterized by a polarization between the observant and non-observant.[54]

Except for France, Jews do not experience anywhere in the EU as much hostility on the streets as they do in Belgium. Since 2001, Belgium has seen an increase in the number of cases related to antisemitism. Nineteen violent incidents were reported in Belgium in 2019.[55] These Jews do not consider Belgium antisemitic, but they have experienced antisemitism from a number of perspectives, some related to the Israeli-Palestinian conflict, and they feel more vulnerable in this regard than in the past. Despite their criticism of Israeli policy, they do express solidarity with Israel. At the same time, Belgian Jews

feel a sense of belonging in Belgium and support their country as they usually belong to the prosperous segments of the Belgian population. Moreover,
the Jewish community in Belgium is strong and pluralistic, and its character
emerges in an excellent school system alongside cultural components such as
the press, the radio, synagogues and clubs that provide Belgian Jews with tools
to cope with antisemitism. The two main Belgian communities differ in that
the community in Antwerp consists of almost 50% ultra-Orthodox Jews who
speak mainly Yiddish, while those who reside in Brussels define themselves
as liberal or not religious.[56] Significant emigration since 2000 reflected growing concerns about Islamization, terrorism, and antisemitism, similarly to the
situation in Paris:[57] Around 224 Belgian Jews immigrated to Israel in 2014 and
242 in 2015.[58]

Jewish emigration from Israel, particularly in recent decades, should
be seen as part of voluntary Jewish migration movements. Despite temporary
fluctuations, the percentage of Israeli-born Jews who migrate away from their
homeland has declined over time. More than half a million Israelis, including first-generation migrants and their descendants, live abroad and most of
them emigrated from Israel since the eighties.[59] Most of the Israelis who moved
abroad (84%) live in English-speaking countries: the United States—66%,
Canada—9%, Britain—6% and Australia—3%. Most of these countries, and
primarily the United States, have a policy of multiculturalism that eases migrant assimilation. Most Israelis live close to Jewish communities, mainly in
the large cities, and these communities provide them some degree of assistance in integrating into the host societies.[60] Only 15% of Israeli migrants live
in Europe and most of them have arrived there since the nineties.[61]

Israelis who had defined themselves as secular prior to migrating to cities such as Paris, London, Sydney, Los Angeles and New York, began feeling
the need to become more involved in Jewish communities in the course of
their lives in the Diaspora, in order to reinforce their Jewish and Israeli identity. First-generation migrants felt that their Israeli identity was central to their
identity as migrants. They reported this identity in terms of their military service, the climate in Israel, speaking Hebrew, ceremonies and rituals, shared
history and food. While their Israeli identity was familiar and central to them,
their Jewish identity was acquired during their time spent abroad.[62]

Another study conducted among Israelis who live in twenty-seven
European countries characterized them as engaging mainly with Hebrew-
speaking and Israeli networks. They also moderately engaged with local Jewish
communities for specific events and services but not as active members of

these communities. Israelis identify themselves mostly as secular. Their main ethnic identity is Israeli.[63]

A study that focused on Israelis living in Paris and London found that Israelis residing in London were more connected to the organized Jewish community than were Israelis in Paris.[64] Israelis in both cities perceived their Israeli national identity as central to their ethnic identity as migrants and represented themselves as Israelis in many opportunities. A fifth of the young people in these cities, most of them Israeli-born and particularly those who reside in Paris, date and spend their leisure time with non-Jewish local young people.

Israeli migrants reside also in Brussels and Antwerp. These migrants do not integrate into the local community and fail to establish their own organizations due to their small numbers (2,281, see the introduction) and frequent turnover. For several years (2008–10) there was an "Israel house" in the Israeli consulate which supplied some cultural activities for the Israeli community. It seems, similar to findings in other European cities,[65] that Israeli migrants in Belgium mix among themselves, as in a "bubble" and, to some extent, integrate into the local Jewish communities, particularly through sending their children to Jewish educational institutes.[66]

THE STUDY AND PARTICIPANTS

As mentioned in the introduction, this study employed two research methods: the correlative-quantitative method, using survey questionnaires and the qualitative semi-structured interview method. The questionnaires were completed by telephone, face-to-face or via the internet. A total of 454 questionnaires were filled by native-born and immigrant Jews during 2017 and 2018. For this manuscript, I included data on 155 respondents who are immigrants from various countries, particularly from North Africa and Israel.

In addition, I interviewed twenty-two people (native-born and immigrants) through semi-structured interviews. In this manuscript I included citations of immigrants, according to city of residence (four from Paris, four from Antwerp and two from Brussels) and content, to supplement the quantitative data.

The respondents were selected using purposive convenience sampling. In the course of the research, I received assistance in contacting the research population from the Israel Ministry of Absorption and from its representative organization (the Israeli House) in each city, as well as from local Jewish organizations. The main connections that facilitated acquisition of research respondents were obtained through the snowball method. I asked local people involved in the community to distribute questionnaires to their relatives, friends and people in their social networks. The in-depth interviews were conducted by me. Three key themes were included in the interviews: 1) Ethnic identity and identification among the respondents: Jewish identity and the place of Israel; Trans-national identity with country of origin and local-assimilative identity; 2) Ethnic identification (Jewish practice) and 3) Community involvement and children's education.

RESPONDENTS

Analysis of the quantitative data included descriptive and inferential statistics. Interviews were transcribed verbatim, and content was analyzed by grouping main themes into common topics that were meaningful for the research questions.[67]

The sample included 155 Jewish immigrants, residing in Paris (56%), Brussels (28%) and Antwerp (17%). The immigrants constitute 36% of the total sample (N=454); wherein 37% of the Parisians are immigrants, 30% of those in Brussels and 47% in Antwerp. On average, the percentages of immigrants in Paris and Brussels are almost similar to those found in previous and more representative studies, while those in Antwerp are over-represented (34% in Paris; 27% in Belgium in general, see Graham[68]).

When analyzed by city of residence, various background characteristics were found to be significantly different. Although 97% of the sample were born Jewish, 7% among those residing in Brussels and 4% in Antwerp were converted to Judaism (very few belong to another religion—1–2 percent).

The Parisians are the oldest (Mean 55; SD 16 years), compared with those residing in Antwerp (M 46; SD 12 years) and Brussels (M 44; SD 10 years). Accordingly, the number of years the respondents have lived in their cities since migration (migration cohort) are as follows: in Paris 34 years (SD 19 years; 44% arrived between 1951–79, 31% between 1980–99 and 25% are new migrants from 2000–2017); in Brussels and Antwerp—19 years each (SD 13; 10 years accordingly). In both Belgian cities about 60% are new migrants who immigrated between 2000 and 2017, about a third between 1980 and 1999 and only 7% before 1979. These findings are similar to those regarding emigration to France which mainly occurred from the fifties through the early seventies of the twentieth century, while those from Israel (who constitute a large portion of the immigrants in the two Belgian cities) arrived in Europe mainly in the twenty-first century.[69] Those from Paris immigrated when they were in their adolescent years (Mean 15 years; SD 10 years), while those residing in Brussels and Antwerp immigrated as young adults (Mean 23 years, SD 14; 24, SD 10 years, accordingly).

Although most of the respondents are married (74%), there is a significant difference according to city of residence: while almost all of those residing in Antwerp (96%) are married, and 81% in Brussels (9% bachelors and 10% divorced), the rate of married people in Paris is lower (63%) and there are larger percentages of divorced (15%), bachelors (12%) and widowed (9%).

Cities of residence also differ significantly according to countries of origin: Israelis reside mainly in Belgium (81% from those residing in Antwerp, 65% in Brussels and only 16% in Paris). North Africans constitute two third of Jewish immigrants in Paris, 23% in Brussels and none in Antwerp.[70] Those from other countries constitute less than a fifth in each city: 19% in Antwerp, 16% in Paris and 12% in Brussels. As noted by Graham,[71] at least half of Belgian Jews send their children to Jewish school—thus the over-representation of young Israeli immigrants in Belgium who serve as educational staff and emissaries in both communities. Other Jewish immigrants in Belgian were attracted to the two Belgian cities mainly due to their unique status: Brussels as the capital of the EU, and Antwerp, as a diamond business center.

As for ethnic affiliation, the Parisians define themselves mainly as "Sephardim" (95%) and only 5% as "Ashkenazim." Two thirds of those residing in the Belgian cities define themselves as "Ashkenazim" (65% in Brussels and 64% in Antwerp).

Regarding higher education attainment, those from Brussels have the highest rates of academic achievements: 92% have a BA, MA or PhD. Antwerp residents come second, with 59% having academic degrees and the Parisians having gained academic degrees at much lesser rates (32%). About half of the sample own dwellings, but those residing in the Belgian cities have higher rates (75% in Antwerp and 70% in Brussels) compared with those residing in Paris (42%).

The differences in socio-economic status "in favor" of those residing in the Belgian cities, of whom above two thirds are immigrants from Israel, confirm other studies on Israelis abroad in general,[72] and those residing in Europe in particular.[73] Israeli immigrants are characterized by arriving in their twenties

(mainly from the late 1990s and the beginning of the millennium) after having acquired academic qualifications, and enjoying particularly high socio-
economic status wherever they reside.[74] However, contrary to other studies,
wherein Jews in Paris have high socio-economic status,[75] those in the current
study have much lower socio-economic status. A possible explanation might
stem from the fact that most of them came from Maghreb countries, during
the fifties through the early seventies and mostly during their adolescent years.
Maybe at that time some of them had fewer opportunities to complete higher
education diplomas. In comparison, those who are *Jewish native-born* residing in Paris (who consist the rest of the sample but were not included in this
analysis) have much higher educational achievement: more than two thirds
have higher education.

The following background components were found not significantly different according to city of residence: gender (58% women), occupational status
(self-employed 25%, paid employees 57% and 18% are not employed) and civic
status. Sixty-nine percent (69%) are citizens, 21% are permanent residents and
10% have other status).

Since the sample was built through "snow ball" sampling, it is not statis-
tically representative. However, the rates of immigrants are almost similar to
larger samples[76] and some of the socio-demographic characteristics indicate
similarities with larger samples as well. For example, the high percentage of
"Sephardim" among the Parisians and "Ashkenazim" in both Belgian cities, as
well as years of arrival to host countries are similar to the findings of E. Ben
Rafael, E. H. Cohen, Graham, and DellaPergola.[77]

ETHNIC IDENTITY

The three groups of migrants appear to differ on various components of their
ethnic identity (Table 1). The differences in the summary indices are significant
for all identity components: identification with Judaism and Israel, identification with origin and host countries.

Jewish Identity and the Place of Israel

Those who reside in Paris and Antwerp have higher Jewish identity than the
ones who reside in Brussels and their spiritual and emotional attachment to

Israel is higher as well (although not significant), even though some of them were not born in Israel. A possible explanation stems from the findings that these two communities are more religious or traditionally inclined, compared with those from Brussels, and thus Israel serves as part of their spiritual identity.

The main differences are in their feeling as Jews, presenting themselves as such and showing pride in being Jewish. The Parisian group is the most homogenous (according to standard deviations), while the Belgian groups are more heterogeneous in this identity component, which indicates that some of them have high Jewish identity while others have much lower identity.

The findings from the interviews support the quantitative results regarding Jewish identity and the place of Israel in the respondents' lives. For example, A. from Brussels who emigrated eleven years ago from Israel with her husband, defines herself as a secular Jew and does not understand what is wrong with intermarriage between Jews and non-Jews:

> It was very difficult for me to understand. What's the big deal here? I always said that if my son or daughter brings home a non-Jewish girl or boy I would never consider it as an issue because what is really important is a person's soul.

A. seems to have very liberal and fluid Jewish ethnic identity; she perceives intermarriage as an unimportant component even though this might lead to future assimilation of her children into non-Jewish society.

Contrary to that, M., who also immigrated to Antwerp from Israel, defines himself as a religious-Zionist Jew, refers to the Jewish religion as an important part in his present life in Antwerp, compared with that in Israel. He perceives religion as the most significant component regarding ethnic identity among Jews in the Diaspora:

> In Israel you don't have to define yourself as Jewish all day long. You are a Jew, you live in Israel [. . .] so you find other definitions such as "I am a religious Jew, I am a secular Jew, I am a Zionist Jew, I am a Haredi [Ultra-Orthodox]." Here the only thing that distinguishes you from the wide population is your Jewishness. Thus, the significance of Jewishness here is stronger than the Israeli or the Belgian.

Israel plays an important role in the respondents' ethnic identity. Although the statistical differences among the three cities are not significant, those who reside in Paris have the highest emotional attachment to Israel and perceive it as the spiritual center for the Jewish people (see Table 1). Rabbi Y. who was born in Morocco and emigrated to Paris decades ago, describes his strong feelings of attachment to Israel as part of his and his wife's Jewish identity, which was transferred to his children:

> So the first time I came to Israel was for my Bar-Mitzva at the age of
> 13 [. . .] and I did not have any connection with Israel then [. . .]. All
> I did as a Rabbi was to support Israel, which is not only a country
> but also a necessary place for the Jewish people. [. . .] My wife is very
> Zionist [. . .] she insisted that our children will love Israel [. . .] that is
> why six out of seven of our children live here in Jerusalem.

Trans-national and Local Identity

Regarding feelings of identity with their countries of origin—emotional attachment and affiliation, as well as feeling "at home" there—those residing in Antwerp and Brussels reported a much stronger transnational ethnic identity, compared with those residing in Paris. Those residing in Antwerp are the most homogenous group in their identification with their country of origin, while immigrants residing in Paris and Brussels are similar in their heterogeneity. However, Parisians have the strongest and relatively homogeneous feelings of identity with their host society: they feel "at home" there, are emotionally attached to it, and feel French—compared to those residing in the Belgian cities, who still feel more alienated from their host societies (Table 1).

Table 1. Ethnic identity: A comparison among migrants in three cities (ANOVA analysis, means and SD, 1=not at all, 5=to a very large extent). Summary indices calculated on the basis of principal component analysis, rotation method: Varimax with Kaiser normalization; KMO=0.76, sig.=0.00)

Variables	Paris N=86		Brussels N=41		Antwerp N=26		Sig. (2-tailed)
	Mean	SD	Mean	SD	Mean	SD	
Identity with Judaism and Israel							
Feel Jewish	4.78	0.58	4.26	0.99	4.72	0.70	**
Present yourself as a Jew	4.40	0.95	3.69	1.30	4.34	1.02	**
Emotionally attached to Israel	4.58	0.66	4.31	1.05	4.16	1.43	n.s
Proud to be Jewish	4.67	0.75	4.21	0.96	4.69	0.83	**

Israel serves as a spiritual center for the Jewish people	4.19	1.15	3.69	1.21	4.08	1.31	n.s
Having a clear sense of being Jewish	4.27	0.90	4.07	0.99	4.58	0.88	n.s
Summary index (Cronbach's alpha=0.88	4.49	0.58	4.02	0.81	4.43	.81	**
Identity with country of origin (transnational)							
Emotionally attached to country of origin	2.96	1.42	3.79	1.49	3.80	1.47	**
Feel mostly belonging to country of origin	2.93	1.51	3.67	1.45	4.04	1.16	**
Feel 'at home' in country of origin	2.72	1.57	3.78	1.42	4.22	1.02	**
Present oneself as native-born from country of origin	3.20	1.40	3.48	1.46	3.87	1.07	n.s
Summary index (Cronbach's alpha=0.84)	2.97	1.21	3.62	1.20	4.03	.90	**
Identity with host society							
Feel 'at home' in host country	3.52	1.05	3.28	1.03	3.44	1.22	n.s
Emotionally attached to host country	3.50	1.08	2.48	1.12	2.45	1.25	**
Feel Belgian or French	3.59	1.23	2.48	1.46	2.47	1.37	**
Summary index (Cronbach's alpha=0.82)	3.53	0.94	2.73	1.02	2.86	.99	**

*P<.05; **P<.01; n.s=not significant

Regarding their countries of origin versus current host societies, the respondents expressed differences in their ethnic identity in the interviews as well. For example, Y. from Antwerp, who emigrated from Libya to Israel with her parents at the age of fourteen and then moved to Antwerp with her husband thirty-eight years ago, feels more "at home" in Antwerp than in Israel. Libya was not even mentioned as a country which is relevant to her ethnic identity today. Israel is important to her but not as a concrete "home," namely family-wise, civilian status, work and familiarity with the city:

> My children live here, my grandchildren live here, my work is here. I have built a life for myself here, my husband is here. [. . .] I bought a house here, I feel at home. I am familiar with everything here. Now when I visit Israel I actually feel like a guest there. [. . .] I am Belgian, but I also feel Israeli. [. . .] If something happens in Israel, it hurts as if it happened to me. [. . .] Israel is very important to me.

S., an immigrant from Morocco to France, feels "at home" in France but defines "home" in different ways, compared with Y.; this also emphasizes the quantitative findings regarding Israel as a spiritual "home":

> One can feel at home living in France as a democratic state: Open, tolerant, beautiful culture, you can enjoy everything, and then you feel at home [. . .]. But from the more Jewish-spiritual-religious dimension and even from a practical point of view, [home, L. L.] is in Israel.

However D., an Israeli immigrant in Paris describes typical transnational identity between two cities: "I am totally at home in two places, I am totally split." When I asked him between which places? He answered: "Between Tel Aviv and Paris."

Summary

It is obvious that the Parisians are the most homogenous group, while the Belgians, in both cities, are much more heterogeneous in their Jewish identity, which means that some of them have strong Jewish identity while others are more secular in their attitudes or even assimilative. Furthermore, two thirds of the immigrants in the two Belgian cities are from Israel, some of them (particularly in Brussels) are characterized in previous studies as secular,[78] as are other Jewish residents of Brussels.[79]

As for ethnic identification with the country of origin, namely having *transnational identity*, those residing in Antwerp and Brussels reported a much stronger transnational ethnic identity, compared with those residing in Paris. This identity is different compared to the spiritual and emotional part of Israel in their Jewish identity since it reflects a sense of concrete attachment to the homeland and part of their history, memories, friends and family. Regarding those residing in Paris, these findings are different than those of S. S. Everett's,[80] who claimed that Algerian Jews in Paris, who constitute the majority of

Maghreb Jews there, are unique in having some transnational cultural and ethnical attachment to Algeria. A possible explanation for that contradiction is the fact that many years have passed since emigration from Algeria and thus transnational attachment fades. On the other hand, those who reside in the Belgian cities are mostly Israelis who emigrated in later decades and their transnational identity is much stronger, as was found in a previous study in Europe[81] and in the United States.[82]

It is important to note that the Antwerp group is the most homogeneous with regard to its transnational identity when compared to Paris and Brussels, which indicates the finding that the respondents in the last two groups can be characterized as being split in their local versus transnational identity.

Finally, those residing in Paris, identify to a greater extent with their *local host society* and feel "at home" there, compared with most of the respondents who reside in the Belgian cities. Both E. H. Cohen[83] and Graham[84] reached the same conclusions, and discussed them in light of the French Republic 'demands' of loyalty to the French State alone; thus, French-Jewish identity (identification with Israel) could be construed as dual loyalty.[85] As I argued earlier in the discussion, the component of Israeli attachment is part of this group's Jewish spiritual and emotional identity, and thus does not contradict their civilian national identity. Thus, Parisian immigrant Jews have local identity without assimilating, due to their strong and homogeneous Jewish identity.

ETHNIC IDENTIFICATION

Jewish Practice

One of the components of ethnic identification is religious practice. Since almost all the respondents in this study are Jewish, they were asked whether they practice Jewish customs. As Table 2 indicates, all components of Jewish practice, except for Rosh Hashanah [New Year] celebration, are stronger and more homogeneous among those from Antwerp and Paris, particularly with respect to lighting Shabbat candles, eating kosher meat, fasting on Yom Kippur and synagogue affiliation. With respect to Jewish practices on high holidays such as Rosh Hashanah and Passover, the three groups are more similar. In sum, Jewish immigrants residing in Antwerp and Paris have higher Jewish identification compared with those residing in Brussels. This finding is coherent with that of their Jewish identity which reported earlier.

Table 2. Jewish practice: A comparison among migrants in three cities (ANOVA analysis for independent samples, means and SD, 1=not at all, 5=to a very large degree)

	Paris N=83		Brussels N=40		Antwerp N=25		Sig. (2-tailed)
	Mean	SD	Mean	SD	Mean	SD	
Light Shabbat candles	3.84	1.41	2.95	1.56	3.72	1.54	**
Participate in Passover Seder	4.38	0.78	4.31	1.17	4.84	0.47	*
Eat kosher meat	3.98	1.25	2.35	1.68	3.96	1.51	**
Fast on Yom Kippur	4.44	0.90	3.62	1.74	4.24	1.47	**
Celebrate Rosh Hashanah	4.37	0.91	4.29	1.14	4.76	0.52	n.s
Synagogue affiliation	3.66	1.51	2.87	1.63	4.04	1.45	**
Summary index (Cronbach's alpha=0.88)	4.11	.95	3.34	1.21	4.26	1.02	**

*P<.05; **P<.01; n.s=not significant

S., an immigrant from Morocco who came to Paris more than thirty years ago, perceives religion and Jewish practice as an important cultural construct that unites the Jewish community:

> [Religion] gives meaning to the Jewish society to be together. It also protects people socially: Communication, love, attachment among them. [. . .] There is also communality, shared history, shared identity [. . .] shared religion, shared folklore, meeting together.

He also describes the revival and renewal of the Parisian Jewish community during the seventies and eighties regarding Jewish community organizations such as synagogues, books in Hebrew, Hebrew knowledge and Jewish prayers:

> Me, as an education person, I saw the phenomenon, the revolution during the seventies and eighties. The synagogues were empty, really empty [. . .]. Lots of people who came to pray did not know how, did not know Hebrew [. . .]. Today everybody knows how to read,

everybody reads Hebrew, sings in Hebrew and their children did not attend synagogues [. . .]. Today the synagogues are full with children, adults and youth.

J., an immigrant from England to Antwerp claimed that the Jewish religion is important to her personally. She practices some Jewish customs, such as celebrating Passover and visiting the synagogue on Jewish events, but she did so for her children when they were young. She has some Jewish identification, without defining herself religious and she resents any form of religious enforcement:

> I will go to my parents in Pesach and when the children were smaller I would do Shabbat, our own version of Shabbat and I always did our version of Hanukah. But for the rest, no. I, if I go to synagogue it will only be if someone I know and I'm friends with, if there's a wedding, if there's a bar mitzvah I will go for that and [. . .] but socially if people would just ask me to do, I won't [. . .] I'm not religious, I feel very very Jewish, it's something very important to me not in a religious way [. . .] I would say that when I was young I was anti-religious but now I'm not at all anti-religious, that's what changed [. . .] as long as no one tries to force it on me.

Community Involvement and Children's Education

Another component of ethnic identification referred to communal activities and involvement, as well as formal and informal education for the respondents' children. When compared by city of residence, all the components analyzed and included in Table 3, are significantly different. The respondents' children receive formal and informal Jewish education particularly in the Belgian cities. Participating in activities which support Israel characterizes again mainly those residing in the Belgian cities, probably since a large portion of them are Israelis. Volunteering and belonging to the Jewish community and organizations characterizes particularly those residing in Antwerp. The rates of those who belong to non-Jewish organizations are very low among all respondents, but those from the two Belgian cities, primarily from Brussels, have still greater affiliation with these organizations.

The summary index (which does not include participation in non-Jewish organizations) indicates that although the Parisians have strong Jewish identity, and high degree of religious practice (see Tables 1 and 2), their communal

Jewish activities are low. Most of them do not send their children to formal Jewish education institutions and informal Jewish and Zionist youth movements. Those from Brussels, who have much lesser Jewish identity, do send their children to Jewish schools and youth movements—which, in that respect, expresses high Jewish identification—although they have some affiliation with non-Jewish organizations as well. Jewish immigrants residing in Antwerp have the highest Jewish identification regarding communal activities and Jewish education for their children. The Brussels group is the most homogenous regarding these components of Jewish identification (Table 3).

Table 3. Jewish education, communal activities and involvement: A comparison among migrants in three cities (ANOVA analysis for independent samples, means and SD, 1=not at all, 5=to a very large degree)

	Paris N=80		Brussels N=41		Antwerp N=26		Sig. (2-tailed)
	Mean	SD	Mean	SD	Mean	SD	
Children participate in Jewish or Zionist youth movement	2.19	1.46	3.81	1.59	3.41	1.88	**
Children enroll in a Jewish school	2.91	1.84	4.30	1.36	4.20	1.58	**
Participation in activities which support Israel	2.93	1.28	3.87	1.19	3.52	1.32	**
Volunteering in the Jewish community	2.20	1.26	3.12	1.50	3.76	1.45	**
Belonging to a Jewish community organization	2.68	1.48	2.82	1.63	3.92	1.32	**
Summary index (Cronbach's alpha=0.82)	2.63	1.16	3.51	1.08	3.78	1.18	**
Belonging to a non-Jewish community organization	1.21	.71	1.56	0.99	1.46	1.04	**

**P<.01

In the interviews communal activities and solidarity differences are evident as well. For example, Rabbi M., who heads one of the largest synagogues in Paris, immigrated to France from Israel almost two decades ago. He describes the Jewish community in Paris as united, dynamic, multi-ethnic and multi-denominational:

> The Jewish community here is very unique [. . .]. They tried to break the walls between Sephardim and Ashkenazim, Liberal and Conservative [. . .]. The community went through changes since the establishment of the "Consistoire" [the Jewish council].

G., a teacher-emissary from Israel, who has resided in Antwerp for more than a year, admires the strong local Jewish formal and informal education institutions. However, as a Zionist-religious person she describes the expansion of the Ultra-Orthodox community in the city and the constant attrition of people of her kind:

> I think that one of the experiences here surprised me. We knew that there is a very strong Jewish community here [. . .] but I was surprised that the religious community is so small [. . .]. They immigrate and then leave or go to more religious frames [. . .]. This affects my children and my experience [. . .]. It is impressing and amazing to see how they make it here and despite that able to supply Jewish education [. . .]. They have here Bnei Akiva as a youth movement [. . .]. They have a clear knowledge of the Israeli flag and Hebrew [. . .]. Sometimes they are even more Zionist than what we are able to do in Israel.

T., an Israeli immigrant who has resided in Brussels for over ten years, describes a very organized Jewish community as well, having many socio-cultural events:

> There are many organizations in the Jewish community and we have many activities that include every one: They call it "Lag Ba'omer" [Jewish holiday], but it is actually a sports day which includes all youth movements, organizations and Keren Kayemeth Le'Israel [Jewish National Fund].

Summary

As for Jewish identification, Jewish immigrants residing in Antwerp and Paris reported a more intensive *Jewish practice*, compared with those residing in Brussels. The Parisian group is again the most homogeneous in this regard, compared with the two Belgian cities, whereas some of the respondents hardly practice the religion and might be even considered assimilative.

All three communities are organized and vivid. In all of them *Jewish communal involvement* seems to be intense and quietly inclusive (according to the interviewees). However, the Parisian community is more united and homogeneous, due to religious community activities, which include mainly those who attend synagogue, while those in Antwerp and Brussels (mainly Israelis) have other focuses which are more educational, Zionist and even secular, which characterizes Israelis who immigrated to the United States as well.[86]

Some possible explanations could be offered here. The first is that Jewish education in both countries costs money,[87] and thus another explanation is embedded in the affordability aspect: those residing in both Belgian cities, particularly in Brussels, have much higher socio-economic status, compared with the Parisians, which also enables more than half of them to send their children to Jewish educational formal and informal institutions.

Regarding Paris, since the respondents immigrated decades ago, perhaps they sent their children to the public educational system during the sixties through the eighties, when Jewish educational institutions were not as developed as contemporary institutions (also according to the interviews). Sending their children to public schools in Paris might also be a statement of civic loyalty to the French republic by the Jews who reside there, as discussed earlier here. Another explanation is associated with the fact that Paris offers many more religious activities and institutions than those existing in both Belgian cities; thus, sending children to Jewish educational institutes, particularly in Brussels, might mean offering the children some Jewish content.

Summary Model

In light of previous findings, the summary model (Table 4) includes an analysis which indicates the independent variables that explain the five dependent variables (indices) of ethnic identity and identification. City of residence is one of the independent variables in this model, along with others.

As for Jewish identity and the spiritual and emotional place of Israel within it, Sephardi respondents have stronger Jewish identity compared with Ashkenazi respondents. Also, those residing in Antwerp have a stronger Jewish identity, compared with that of Brussels respondents. The longer the years of residence in the host city, the stronger Jewish and Israeli identity become. The total explanation of the independent variables is 19%.

Transnational identity with country of origin is very high among immigrants from Israel, compared with that of North Africa, and to a lesser extent, compared with immigrants from other countries. In addition, those who arrived in later years are obviously still more attached to their country of origin, compared with those who have resided in the host city for longer periods. The total explanation of the variance in the dependent variable is the highest among the five equations and equals 30%.

Local-host society identity is higher among immigrants from North Africa, compared with those who immigrated from Israel and to a lesser degree (not significant) from other countries. The total explanation of the independent variables in this equation is the lowest and equals 17%.

Regarding ethnic identification, Jewish practice is higher among Sephardic Jews, and among those who reside in Antwerp (compared with Brussels). Jewish practice is also more intensive among those who emigrated from North Africa, compared with the Israeli immigrants. The total explanation of the independent variables is 22%. Finally, community activities and involvement, as well as children's Jewish education—other components of Jewish identification—are explained mainly by city of residence: those residing in Brussels have higher Jewish identification, regarding communal and educational Jewish activities, than those residing in Paris. Sephardic respondents and those who emigrated from Israel are more active in the Jewish community and send their children to Jewish educational institutes—compared with Ashkenazi Jews and those who emigrated from other countries. The total explanation is 24% of the dependent variable.

In summary, the city of residence explains Jewish and Israeli identity as well as Jewish practice and communal activities: mainly, while those residing in Antwerp have stronger Jewish identity and more intensive Jewish practice compared with those residing in Brussels, the last group is very active regarding communal Jewish activities and sending their children to Jewish educational institutions, particularly in comparison with the Parisians.

Israeli immigrants are much more transnational in their identification with their country of origin, while those who emigrated from North Africa have higher local identification and are more active in Jewish practice. Sephardic respondents have higher Jewish identity and also Jewish identification. Since most of the Parisians are "Sephardim" it has "double impact" on their strong Jewish identity. Those residing in the two Belgian cities are mostly "Ashkenazi" Jews and their ethnic sub-ethnicity[88] does not affect their Jewish identity and identification. Furthermore, Israeli immigrants, particularly the Ashkenazim, are mostly secular, as found in previous studies.[89]

It is interesting to note that years of residency in a host city have similar but opposite impacts on different dimensions of ethnic identity among the respondents; the longer they reside the stronger Jewish their identity becomes, while the shorter the period since immigration is, the more they are transnational.

Table 4. *Summary model: Predictors of the dependent variables (Standardized coefficients—Beta, and the percentage of explained variance based on multiple regression analysis)*

Dependent variables	Identity with Judaism and Israel (N=134)	Identity with country of origin (N=130)	Identity with host society (N=132)	Jewish practice (N=129)	Communal activities and children's education (N=129)
Independent variables					
Ethnic affiliation (0=Sephardi; 1=Ashkenazi)	-.32**	-.02	-.08	-.31**	-.33**
City of residence Antwerp (Brussels=0; Antwerp=1)	.23*	.01	.06	.29**	.02
City of residence Paris (Brussels=0; Paris=1)	-.02	-.05	.12	.00	-.65**
Years of residence in the city (in years)	.18*	-.18*	.11	.01	.12
Countries of origin Other countries (Israel=0; Other countries=1)	.08	-.22*	.15	.13	.18*
Countries of origin North Africa (Israel=0; North Africa=1)	.12	-.45**	.24*	.27*	-.00
R^2	.19	.30	.17	.22	.24

*P<.05; **P<.01

CONCLUSIONS

The present study focused on immigrant Jews, who reside in three cities in Europe (Paris, Brussels and Antwerp). Using mixed methods (quantitative and qualitative), I analyze various dimensions of ethnic identity and identification, such as Jewish identity, transnational (with country of origin) and local. Ethnic identification included Jewish practice, community involvement and children's Jewish education. Following Graham,[90] the results of the present study, both quantitative and qualitative, point to many differences and very few similarities between the three groups in their ethnic identity and identification.

The major contribution of the present findings is their elaboration regarding contemporary Jewish communities in Europe: their ethnic identity and identification construction in their daily interactions with the host cities. Each group of immigrants developed a unique pattern of Jewish identity and identification, based primarily on city of residence, but also on country of origin, ethnic affiliation as Sephardim or Ashkenazim and cohort of migration.

Furthermore, based on DellaPergola's model,[91] the socio-political context in each city and the size of the local Jewish community and its construction, I offer Jewish identity and identification typologies for each group of immigrants.

The Parisians could be characterized as belonging to the *normative-traditional* group, who have strong ethnic identity, while conforming to Jewish customs and ceremonies. This community is large and has many types of Jewish religion-based activities. Thus, Jews can send their children to non-Jewish educational systems without risking their assimilation and segregating them from the host society.

Jewish immigrants residing in Brussels are more heterogeneous in their Jewish identity and thus part of them are secular, more pluralistic and liberal in their ethnic identity. The city of residence and its attitudes towards immigrants is also important: Brussels is more pluralistic and multicultural than Paris, being the capital of the European Union. The formal and informal educational activities in Brussels derive their contents from Jewish religion but also from secular pluralistic and not entirely Jewish contents. This group can be assigned to the *ethno-communal* type.

Those residing in Antwerp can be assigned to both groups, with a bias towards the first; their Jewish ethnic identity and identification is very strong, and thus they could be characterized as *normative-traditional*. At the same time, their Jewish communal activity and children's education are also strong and thus they can be considered as belonging to the *ethno-communal* type. In their case, the educational Jewish system is part of their unique Israel Zionist-religious or traditional affiliation that distinguishes them from the Ultra-Orthodox in the city, who constitute 50% of the Jewish community in the city.

Despite some limitations of the present study, including its partial representativeness, it has various contributions, based on rich and original data, both on the macro and the micro level—especially concerning migration and contemporary Jewish studies. The findings elaborate migration studies by analyzing ethno-religious identity and identification among immigrants in the city context. The local culture in each city has a significant impact on the construction of ethnic identity and identification (in addition to other variables), as does local policy toward ethnic minorities and the size of the community, which makes it possible (or not) to provide religious services.

In addition, the usage of mixed methods elaborates the complex and dynamic meaning of theoretical terms such as ethnic identity and identification, transnational, religious or assimilative, among migrants and their various attitudinal and behavioral components.

While some studies have been conducted regarding French and Parisian Jewry, studies regarding Brussels and Antwerp are scarce. It seems that the present study elaborates findings regarding the three cities in general, and those residing in Antwerp in particular. More than 80% of the Jewish immigrants in Antwerp are Israelis who are much more traditionally inclined than those residing in Brussels or elsewhere, whereas some tend to assimilate in the host societies.[92] Most of them, however, are not part of the Ultra-Orthodox community. They have very strong Jewish identity and identification which is similar to that of the Parisian respondents. Thus, the current study actually indicates ethnic identity and identification of another Israeli migrant group and expounds on knowledge regarding Israelis who reside in Europe.

Finally, in light of the recent rise of antisemitism in France and Belgium, ethnic identity and identification is dynamically reconstructed through daily inner-group interactions with Jewish as well as non-Jewish host societies, in different cities' socio-cultural and political atmosphere. Transnational connections, primarily with Israel, are also crucial in that regard.

The three Jewish migrant communities which were studied here, have unique patterns of Jewish identity and identification, as well as different strategies in making their communities vivid and vibrant. Despite the rising antisemitism, particularly in Paris and Brussels, and out migration, the three communities seems to overcome these difficulties.

The Jewish community in Paris maintains its Jewish vitality by keeping Jewish practice and Jewish institutions as a dynamic center, which is relevant and appeals to members from various age groups (although mainly Sephardim). The community in Brussels, although it seems to be less attached to Judaism and more liberal and assimilative, keeps its vitality through the young generation, their children, by sending them to Jewish schools and youth movements. These formal and informal educational institutions serves as a vibrant core for Jewish ethnic identification both for children and their parents. However, these communal activities do not necessarily use traditional Jewish contents, but more secular-Israeli-Zionist. Antwerp has a large Ultra-Orthodox community which, of course, contributes to the demographic and cultural-religious vitality. However, in the present study, I focused on immigrants, which in Antwerp are mostly Israelis, who are more religious or traditionally inclined, compared with those in Brussels. These immigrants have strong Jewish identity and as part of the educational stuff in Antwerp serve as a bridge between identity and community among Jews in Antwerp. Thus, in this critical era it is important to study Jewish identity and identification, as a mirror to Jewish communities' boundaries, resilience and continuity in contemporary European cities.

Acknowledgment
This work was supported by Oranim Academic College of Education and Kantor Center for the Study of Contemporary European Jewry at Tel Aviv University.

Notes

1. E.g., S. DellaPergola, "World Jewish Population, 2018," in *The American Jewish Year Book, 2018*, ed. A. Dashefsky and I. M. Sheskin (vol. 118; NewYork: Berman, Jewish Databank, 2019), 361–452; L. Lev Ari, *The American Dream: For Men Only? Gender, Immigration and the Assimilation of Israelis in the United States* (El Paso, TX: LFB Scholarly, 2008); L. Lev Ari, "North Americans, Israelis, or Jews? The Ethnic Identity of Immigrants' Offspring," *Contemporary Jewry* 32, no. 3 (2012): 285–308; U. Rebhun and L. Lev Ari, *American Israelis: Migration, Transnationalism, and Diasporic Identity* (Leiden: Brill, 2010).

2. But see L. Lev Ari, "Multiple Identities among Israeli Immigrants in Europe," *International Journal of Jewish Education Research* 6 (2013): 29–67; U. Rebhun, "Immigrant Acculturation and Transnationalism: Israelis in the United States and Europe Compared," *Journal for the Scientific Study of Religion* 53, no. 3 (2014): 613–35.

3. Kantor Center, *Antisemitism Worldwide 2019 and the beginning of 2020* (Tel Aviv University: Kantor Center for the Study of Contemporary European Jewry, 2020), General Analysis Draft, https://en-humanities.tau.ac.il/sites/humanities_en.tau. ac.il/files/media_server/humanities/kantor/Kantor%20Center%20Worldwide%20 Antisemitism%20in%202019%20-%20Main%20findings.pdf.

4. L. Basch, G. N. Glick-Schiller, and C. B. Szanton, *Nation Unbound: Transnational Projects, Postcolonial Predicaments and Deterritorialized Nation States* (New York: Gordon & Breach, 1994).

5. C. B. Brettell and J. F. Hollifield, eds., "Migration Theory: Talking across Disciplines," in *Migration Theory: Talking across Disciplines*, ed. C. B. Brettell and J. F. Hollifield (New York: Routledge, 2015), 1–21; P. Levitt and B. N. Jaworsky, "Transnational Migration Studies: Past Developments and Future Trends," *The Annual Review of Sociology* 33 (2007): 129–56.

6. S. Castles and M. J. Miller, *The Age of Migration: International Population Movements in the Modern World* (United Kingdom: Palgrave Macmillan, 2009); S. Castles, H. de Haas, and M. J. Miller, *The Age of Migration: International Population Movements in the Modern World* (United Kingdom: Palgrave Macmillan, 2014).

7. A. Portes and R. G. Rumbaut, *Legacies: The Story of the Immigrant Second Generation* (Berkeley: University of California Press, 2001).

8. Lev Ari, "North Americans, Israelis, or Jews"; Lev Ari, "Multiple Identities."

9. G. N. Glick-Schiller, N. L. Basch, and C. B. Szanton, "Transnationalism: A New Analytic Dramework for Understanding Migration," *Annal of the New York Academy of Sciences* 645 (1992): 1–24.

10. Lev Ari, "Multiple Identities."

11. S. DellaPergola, *Jewish Demographic Policies: Population Trends and Options in Israel and in the Diaspora* (Jerusalem: The Jewish People Policy Institute, 2011); Lev Ari, "North Americans, Israelis, or Jews."

12. F. D. Bean and S. K. Brown, "Demographic Analysis of Immigration," in *Migration Theory: Talking across Disciplines*, ed. C. B. Brettell and J. F. Hollifield (New York: Routledge, 2015), 67–89.

13. C. Der-Martirosian, G. Sabagh, and M. Bozorgmehr, "Subethnicity: Americans in Los Angeles," in *Immigration and Entrepreneurship*, ed. I. Light and P. Bhachu (New Jersey: Transaction Publishers, 1993), 243–58.

14. Castles and Miller, *The Age of Migration*, 40.

15. Castles and Miller, *The Age of Migration*; Castles, de Haas and Miller, *The Age of Migration*; S. J. Gold, "Patterns of Adaptation among Contemporary Jewish Immigrants to the US," in *American Jewish Year Book*, ed. A. Dashefsky and I. Sheskin (vol. 116; Switzerland: Springer, 2016), 3–43.

16. DellaPergola, *Jewish Demographic Policies*.

17. DellaPergola, *Jewish Demographic Policies*.

18. B. Wasserstein, *Vanishing Diaspora: The Jews in Europe since 1945* (London: Penguin Books, 1996).

19. D. Graham, *European Jewish Identity: Mosaic or Monolith? An Empirical Assessment of Eight European Countries* (JPR/Report. Institute for Jewish Policy Research, 2018), http://archive.jpr.org.uk/object-eur183.

20. Graham, *European Jewish Identity*, 39.

21. Graham, *European Jewish Identity*.

22. A. Singer, "Migration and the Metropolis," in *Practice to Policy: Lessons from Local Leadership on Immigrant Integration*, ed. Bonnie Mah (Toronto: Maytree Foundation, 2012), 9–10, http://citiesofmigration.ca/wp-content/uploads/2012/03/Practice-to-Policy.pdf.

23. J. Darling, "Forced Migration and the City: Irregularity, Informality, and Politics of Presence," *Progress in Human Geography*, 41, no. 2 (2017): 178.

24. International Organization for Migration (IOM) World Migration Report 2015—Migrants and Cities: New Partnerships to Manage Mobility, 2015, http://publications.iom.int/books/world-migration-report-2015-migrants-and-cities-new-partnerships-manage-mobility#sthash.OFstnNsn.dpuf.

25. Castles and Miller, *The Age of Migration*; Castles, de Haas and Miller, *The Age of Migration*.

26. L. D. Staetsky and S. DellaPergola, *Why European Jewish Demography?* (London: Institute for Jewish Policy Research [JPR], 2019), 3.

27. Graham, *European Jewish Identity*. 13.

28. DellaPergola, "World Jewish Population, 2018," 380.

29. E. H. Cohen, *The Jews of France at the Turn of the Third Millennium. A Sociological and Cultural Analysis* (The Rappaport Center for Assimilation Research and Strenghtening Jewish Vivality. Ramat Gan: Bar Ilan University, 2009), 20; Graham, *European Jewish Identity*, 14; DellaPergola, "World Jewish Population, 2018," 404.

30. Castles and Miller, *The Age of Migration*.

31. M. Abitbol and A. Astro, "The Integration of North African Jews in France," *Yale French Studies* 85 (1994): 248–61; S. DellaPergola, "Jews in Europe: Demographic Trends Contexts and Outlooks," in *A Road to Nowhere? Jewish Experiences in Unifying Europe*, ed. J. H. Schoeps and O. Glockner (Leiden: Brill, 2011b), 3–34.

32. D. Bensimon and S. DellaPergola, *La Population Juive de France: Socio-demographie et identite* (Jerusalem: Hebrew University, 1984).

33. DellaPergola, "Jews in Europe," 9.

34. DellaPergola, "World Jewish Population, 2018," 404.

35. E. H. Cohen, *The Jews of France*; DellaPergola, "World Jewish Population, 2018."

36. M. Cohen, "Les Juifs de France. Modernité et identité," *Vingitème siècle, revu d'histoire religions d'Eroupe* 66 (2000): 91–106.

37. Y. Cohen, "Israeli-Born Emigrants: Size, Destinations and Selectivity," *IJCS: International Journal of Comparative Sociology* 52, nos. 1–2 (2011): 49–50.

38. E. Florence and M. Martiniello, "The Links between Academic Research and Public Policies in the Field of Migration and Ethnic Relations: Selected National Case Studies," *International Journal on Multicultural Societies* 7, no. 1 (2005): 3–10.

39. DellaPergola, "World Jewish Population, 2018," 363; Graham, *European Jewish Identity*, 57.

40. See also Florence and Martiniello, "The Links between Academic Research."

41. E. Ben Rafael, "Religion Jews and Neo Antisemitism," *Contemporary Jewry* 37, no. 2 (2017): 275–93.

42. Y. Cohen, "Israeli-Born Emigrants," 49.

43. E. H. Cohen, *The Jews of France*.

44. I. Dahan, "The Role of Spiritual Leadership in Shaping Collective Identity: The Case of the French Immigrant Community in Israel" [in Hebrew], *Hed Haulpan Hachadash* 104 (2015): 65–78.

45. E. H. Cohen, *Non-Jewish Jews, Jewish-Israeli Ethnic Identity and the Challenge of Expansion of the Jewish Nationality* [in Hebrew], (Jerusalem: Hartman Institute, Ramat-Gan: Bar-Ilan University and Tel Aviv: Keter, 2006).

46. Graham, *European Jewish Identity*, 41; L. D. Staetsky and J. Boyd, *Will My Child Get a Place? An Assessment of Supply and Demand of Jewish Secondary School Places in London and Surrounding Areas* (London: Institute for Jewish Policy Research, 2017), 4.

47. S. S. Everett, "The Many (Im)possibilities of Contemporary Algerian Judaites," in *Algeria: Nation, Culture and Transnationalism 1988–2015*, ed. P. Crowley (Liverpool: Liverpool University Press, 2017), 63–80.

48. DellaPergola, "World Jewish Population, 2018," 404.

49. E. H. Cohen, *Non-Jewish Jews.*"

50. Kantor Center, *Antisemitism Worldwide 2019*, 14–15.

51. Kantor Center, *Antisemitism Worldwide 2019*, 27.

52. Kantor Center, *Antisemitism Worldwide 2018*.

53. Ben Rafael, "Religion Jews and Neo Antisemitism," 1.

54. Graham, *European Jewish Identity*, 41.

55. Kantor Center, *Antisemitism Worldwide 2018*, 5.

56. Ben Rafael, "Religion Jews and Neo Antisemitism."

57. Ben Rafael, "Religion Jews and Neo Antisemitism"; S. DellaPergola, "World Jewish population, 2016," in *The American Jewish Year Book, 2016*, ed. A. Dashefsky, S. DellaPergola and I. M. Sheskin (vol. 116; Dordrecht: Springer, 2017), 253–332.

58. DellaPergola, "World Jewish population, 2016."

59. Y. Cohen, "Israeli-Born Emigrants"; Rebhun and Lev Ari, *American Israelis*.

60. Y. Cohen, "Israeli-Born Emigrants," 48; Rebhun and Lev Ari, *American Israelis*.

61. Y. Cohen, "Israeli-Born Emigrants," 48; Lev Ari, "Multiple Identities."

62. S. J. Gold, *The Israeli Diaspora* (London and New York: Routledge, 2002); Gold, "Patterns of Adaptation"; Lev Ari, *The American Dream*.

63. M. Dimentstein and R. Kaplan, *The Israeli-European Diaspora: A Survey about Israelis Living in Europe*. United Kingdom: JDC International Center for Community Development and Machon Kehilot, 2017, https://scholar.google.co.il/scholar?q=The+Israeli-European+Diaspora:+A+survey+about+Israelis+living+in+Europe&hl=iw&as_sdt=0&as_vis=1&oi=scholart.

64. Lev Ari, "Multiple Identities."

65. Lev Ari, "Multiple Identities."

66. E. Tzadik, "Israeli Somen in Brussels: To Live in an Israeli 'Bubble'" [in Hebrew], *Hagira* 2 (2013): 121–46; E. Tzadik, "Between Bubbles and Enclaves: Discussing a New Working Term to Inter-culturalism and Meaning via the Case Study of Women in Brussels," in "Cultural Encounters in Multi-cultured Societies: Towards Multicultural Education?," special issue, *Malta Review of Educational Search* 10, no. 1 (2016): 51–67.

67. J. W. Creswell, *Research Design: Qualitative, Quantitative, and Mixed Methods Approaches* (Thousand Oaks, CA: SAGE, 2014).

68. Graham, *European Jewish Identity*.

69. See also E. H. Cohen, *The Jews of France*; Lev Ari, "Multiple Identities."

70. See also E. H. Cohen, *The Jews of France*; DellaPergola, "World Jewish Population, 2018."

71. Graham, *European Jewish Identity*.

72. Lev Ari, *The American Dream*; Rebhun, "Immigrant Acculturation"; Rebhun and Lev Ari, *American Israelis*.

73. Lev Ari, "Multiple Identities."

74. Lev Ari, *The American Dream*; Rebhun, "Immigrant Acculturation"; Rebhun and Lev Ari, *American Israelis*; Lev Ari, "Multiple Identities."

75. See for example: E. H. Cohen, *The Jews of France*.

76. Graham, *European Jewish Identity*.

77. Ben Rafael, "Religion Jews and Neo Antisemitism"; E. H. Cohen, *The Jews of France*;

Graham, *European Jewish Identity*; and DellaPergola, "World Jewish Population, 2018."

78. See, for example, Gold, *The Israeli Diaspora*; Lev Ari, "Multiple Identities."
79. Ben Rafael, "Religion Jews and Neo Antisemitism."
80. Everett, "The Many (Im)possibilities."
81. Lev Ari, "Multiple Identities."
82. Gold, "Patterns of Adaptation."
83. E. H. Cohen, *The Jews of France.*
84. Graham, *European Jewish Identity.*
85. See also E. H. Cohen, *The Jews of France.*
86. See Gold, "Patterns of Adaptation"; Lev Ari, "North Americans, Israelis, or Jews?"
87. Graham, *European Jewish Identity*; Tzadik, "Between Bubbles and Enclaves."
88. See also Der-Martirosian, Sabagh, and Bozorgmehr, "Subethnicity."
89. See for example: Lev Ari, *The American Dream*; Lev Ari, "Multiple Identities."
90. Graham, *European Jewish Identity.*
91. DellaPergola, *Jewish Demographic Policies.*
92. See also Gold, *The Israeli Diaspora*; Gold, "Patterns of Adaptation"; Dimentstein and Kaplan, *The Israeli-European Diaspora*; Lev Ari, "Multiple Identities"; Rebhun and Lev Ari, *American Israelis.*

Bibliography

Abitbol, M., and A. Astro. "The Integration of North African Jews in France." *Yale French Studies* 85 (1994): 248–61.

Avenarius, C. B. "Migrant Networks in New Urban Spaces: Gender and Social Integration." *International Migration* 50, no. 5 (2012): 25–55.

Basch, L., G. N. Glick-Schiller, and C. B. Szanton. *Nation Unbound: Transnational Projects, Postcolonial Predicaments and Deterritorialized Nation States.* New York: Gordon & Breach, 1994.

Bean, F. D., and S. K. Brown. "Demographic Analysis of Immigration." In *Migration Theory: Talking across Disciplines*, edited by C. B. Brettell and J. F. Hollifield, 67–89. New York: Routledge, 2015.

Ben Rafael, E. "Religion Jews and Neo Antisemitism." *Contemporary Jewry* 37, no. 2 (2017): 275–93.

Bensimon, D., and S. DellaPergola. *La Population Juive de France: Socio-demographie et identite.* Jerusalem: Hebrew University, 1984.

Brettell C. B., and J. F. Hollifield, eds. "Migration Theory: Talking across Disciplines." In *Migration Theory: Talking across Disciplines*, edited by C. B. Brettell and J. F. Hollifield, 1–21. New York: Routledge, 2015.

Castles, S., H. de Haas, and M. J. Miller. *The Age of Migration: International Population Movements in the Modern World.* United Kingdom: Palgrave Macmillan, 2014.

Castles, S., and M. J. Miller. *The Age of Migration: International Population Movements in the Modern World.* United Kingdom: Palgrave Macmillan, 2009.

Cohen, E. H. *The Jews of France at the Turn of the Third Millennium. A Sociological and Cultural Analysis.* The Rappaport Center for Assimilation Research and Strenghtening Jewish Vivality. Ramat Gan: Bar Ilan University, 2009.

———. *Non-Jewish Jews, Jewish-Israeli Ethnic Identity and the Challenge of Expansion of the Jewish Nationality* [in Hebrew]. Jerusalem: Hartman Institute, Ramat-Gan: Bar-Ilan University and Tel Aviv: Keter, 2006.

Cohen, M. "Les Juifs de France. Modernité et identité." *Vingitème siècle, revu d'histoire religions d'Eroupe* 66 (2000): 91–106.

Cohen, Y. "Israeli-Born Emigrants: Size, Destinations and Selectivity." *IJCS: International Journal of Comparative Sociology* 52, nos. 1–2 (2011): 45–62.

Creswell, J. W. *Research Design: Qualitative, Quantitative, and Mixed Methods Approaches.* Thousand Oaks, CA: SAGE, 2014.

Dahan, I. "The Role of Spiritual Leadership in Shaping Collective Identity: The Case of the French Immigrant Community in Israel" [in Hebrew]. *Hed Haulpan Hachadash* 104 (2015): 65–78.

Darling, J. "Forced Migration and the City: Irregularity, Informality, and Politics of Presence." *Progress in Human Geography* 41, no. 2 (2017): 178–98.

DellaPergola, S. *Jewish Demographic Policies: Population Trends and Options in Israel and in the Diaspora.* Jerusalem: The Jewish People Policy Institute, 2011.

———. "Jews in Europe: Demographic Trends Contexts and Outlooks." In *A Road to Nowhere? Jewish Experiences in Unifying Europe,* edited by J. H. Schoeps and O. Glockner, 3–34. Leiden: Brill, 2011b.

———. "World Jewish population, 2016." In *The American Jewish Year Book, 2016,* edited by A. Dashefsky, S. DellaPergola and I. M. Sheskin, 253–332. Vol. 116. Dordrecht: Springer, 2017.

———. "World Jewish Population, 2018." In *The American Jewish Year Book, 2018,* edited by A. Dashefsky and I. M. Sheskin, 361–452. Vol. 118. NewYork: Berman, Jewish Databank, 2019.

———. "World Jewish Population, 2019." In *The American Jewish Year Book, 2019,* edited by A. Dashefsky and I. M. Sheskin, 263–356. Vol. 119. New York: Berman, Jewish Databank, 2020 (in printing).

Der-Martirosian, C., G. Sabagh, and M. Bozorgmehr. "Subethnicity: Americans in Los Angeles." In Immigration and Entrepreneurship, edited by I. Light and P. Bhachu, 243–58. New Jersey: Transaction Publishers, 1993.

Dimentstein, M., and R. Kaplan. *The Israeli-European Diaspora: A Survey about Israelis Living in Europe.* United Kingdom: JDC International Center for Community Development and Machon Kehilot, 2017. https://scholar.google.co.il/scholar?q=The+Israeli-European+Diaspora:+A+survey+about+Israelis+living+in+Europe&hl=iw&as_sdt=0&as_vis=1&oi=scholart.

Everett, S. S. "The Many (Im)possibilities of Contemporary Algerian Judaites." In *Algeria: Nation, Culture and Transnationalism 1988–2015,* edited by P. Crowley, 63–80. Liverpool: Liverpool University Press, 2017.

Florence, E., and M. Martiniello. "The Links between Academic Research and Public Policies in the Field of Migration and Ethnic Relations: Selected National Case Studies." *International Journal on Multicultural Societies* 7, no. 1 (2005): 3–10.

Glick-Schiller, G. N., N. L. Basch, and C. B. Szanton. "Transnationalism: A New Analytic Dramework for Understanding Migration." *Annal of the New York Academy of Sciences* 645 (1992): 1–24.

Gold, S. J. *The Israeli Diaspora.* London and New York: Routledge, 2002.

———. "Patterns of Adaptation among Contemporary Jewish Immigrants to the US." In *American Jewish Year Book,* edited by A. Dashefsky and I. Sheskin, 3–43. Dordrecht: Springer, 2016.

Graham, D. *European Jewish Identity: Mosaic or Monolith? An Empirical Assessment of Eight European Countries.* JPR/Report. Institute for Jewish Policy Research, 2018. http://archive.jpr.org.uk/object-eur183.

International Organization for Migration (IOM) World Migration Report 2015—Migrants and Cities: New Partnerships to Manage Mobility, 2015. http://publications.iom.int/books/world-migration-report-2015-migrants-and-cities-new-partnerships-manage-mobility#sthash.OFstnNsn.dpuf.

Kantor Center. *Antisemitism Worldwide 2018*. Tel Aviv University: Kantor Center for the Study of Contemporary European Jewry, 2019. General Analysis Draft. http://kantorcenter.tau.ac.il/sites/default/files/Doch_full_2018_220418.pdf.

————. *Antisemitism Worldwide 2019 and the beginning of 2020*. Tel Aviv University: Kantor Center for the Study of Contemporary European Jewry, 2020. General Analysis Draft. https://en-humanities.tau.ac.il/sites/humanities_en.tau.ac.il/files/media_server/humanities/kantor/Kantor%20Center%20Worldwide%20Antisemitism%20in%202019%20-%20Main%20findings.pdf.

Lev Ari, L. *The American Dream: For Men Only? Gender, Immigration and the Assimilation of Israelis in the United States*. El Paso, TX: LFB Scholarly, 2008.

————. "Multiple Identities among Israeli Immigrants in Europe." *International Journal of Jewish Education Research* 6 (2013): 29–67.

————. "North Americans, Israelis, or Jews? The Ethnic Identity of Immigrants' Offspring." *Contemporary Jewry* 32, no. 3 (2012): 285–308.

Levitt, P, and B. N. Jaworsky. "Transnational Migration Studies: Past Developments and Future Trends." *The Annual Review of Sociology* 33 (2007): 129–56.

Portes, A., and R. G. Rumbaut. *Legacies: The Story of the Immigrant Second Generation*. Berkeley: University of California Press, 2001.

Rebhun, U. "Immigrant Acculturation and Transnationalism: Israelis in the United States and Europe Compared." *Journal for the Scientific Study of Religion* 53, no. 3 (2014): 613–35.

Rebhun U., and L. Lev Ari. *American Israelis: Migration, Transnationalism, and Diasporic Identity*. Leiden: Brill, 2010.

Singer, A. "Migration and the Metropolis." In *Practice to Policy: Lessons from Local Leadership on Immigrant Integration*, edited by Bonnie Mah, 9–10. Toronto: Maytree Foundation, 2012. http://citiesofmigration.ca/wp-content/uploads/2012/03/Practice-to-Policy.pdf.

Staetsky, L. D., and J. Boyd. *Will My Child Get a Place? An Assessment of Supply and Demand of Jewish Secondary School Places in London and Surrounding Areas*. London: Institute for Jewish Policy Research, 2017.

Staetsky, L. D., and S. DellaPergola. *Why European Jewish Demography?* London: Institute for Jewish Policy Research (JPR), 2019.

Tzadik, E. "Between Bubbles and Enclaves: Discussing a New Working Term to Interculturalism and Meaning via the Case Study of Women in Brussels." In "Cultural Encounters in Multi-cultured Societies: Towards Multicultural Education?" Special issue, *Malta Review of Educational Search* 10, no. 1 (2016): 51–67.

————. "Israeli Somen in Brussels: To Live in an Israeli 'Bubble'" [in Hebrew]. *Hagira* 2 (2013): 121–46.

Wasserstein, B. *Vanishing Diaspora: The Jews in Europe since 1945*. London: Penguin Books, 1996.

"Cleanliness Like That of the Germans": Eastern European Jews' Views of Germans and the Dynamics of Migration and Disillusionment

by Gil Ribak

Stopping in Berlin in 1882 on his way to America, future radical Yisroel Kopelov was deeply impressed by the Germans' fine manners and "smooth, fresh" faces, especially in comparison to the people in his native Bobroysk, with their "gloomy, yellow faces" and embarrassing gestures. But soon after a corpulent German shouted at him "Goddamn Jew!" Kopelov begged "Bobroysk's forgiveness." More than twenty years later (1908), seventy-five Jewish immigrants in America signed a letter that was published in a Yiddish newspaper in Russia, advising Jews to boycott German ships: on their way from Bremen to New York, German crewmen "raised their hands against" Jewish passengers, and when a passenger asked for a clean glass, the German buffet worker answered, "Why do you want a clean glass when you stink, Jew."[1]

The relationship between German and German Jews at the time of immigration to the United States has been at the center of several studies. Several scholars, such as Hasia Diner, have suggested that many of the Central European Jewish immigrants, who arrived in America between the 1820s and 1870s, should not be characterized as German, as they did not hail from Germany proper, but rather from areas to its east; or they were still Yiddish-speaking rural Jews, and in any case Germany did not exist as an independent country before 1871. On the other hand, other historians, such as Avraham Barkai and Stanley Nadel, have emphasized the attachment of those Jewish immigrants to German Culture and identity even decades after their arrival in America.[2]

Much less scholarly attention, however, has been given to the relationship between Germans and Eastern European Jews. Whereas some 150,000 to 180,000 Jews emigrated from Central Europe to the United States between the 1820s and 1870s, nearly 2.5 million Jewish immigrants from Eastern Europe (Tsarist Russia, Habsburg-ruled Galicia, and Romania) came to America between 1881 and 1924. Smaller numbers had arrived from Eastern Europe already beforehand: when famine and a cholera epidemic in the Pale of Settlement happened in the late 1860s and early 1870s, those years witnessed the beginning of more substantial immigration from Russia to America. Most of Eastern European Jewish immigrants had made their way through Germany, heading to one of the major European ports of Amsterdam, Rotterdam, Antwerp, Bremen, and Hamburg.[3]

This article focuses on Eastern European Jews' views of Germans before, during, and after immigration to America. Images of Germans should be understood in the context of the Jewish encounter with modernity. Modernizing Jews initially idealized the non-Jews whom they perceived as more developed and carriers of a higher culture; however, this pattern of initial admiration was often followed by disenchantment. Idealization required geographical distance; when Jews came into close contact with Germans, their attitudes often changed. Utilizing a vast array of sources, such as the Yiddish and Hebrew press both in Eastern Europe and in New York, unpublished and published oral history accounts, memoirs, autobiographies, and letters, this study uses a transnational framework to advance our knowledge not only of Jewish attitudes and intergroup relations, but also of the complex and often-contradictory effects of modernization on immigration.

The examination of Eastern European Jewish perceptions of Germans improves our understanding of the knotty ways in which various immigrant groups both replicated *and* modified their previous interrelations after arriving in America. In addition, this case study runs counter to the intuitive narrative of linear acculturation, in which prospective immigrants knew very little about their new country and after arrival gradually became more and more Americanized. Already in the Old Country, would-be immigrants imagined their future country, often idealized it, but grew disenchanted with their new country after arrival. Distant cultures became less alluring upon direct interaction.[4]

The imagery of Germans is particularly interesting, as it denoted progress and modernity within Jewish society, when nineteenth-century modernizers (and many others) held in high esteem all things German. The German origin of the *Haskalah* (Jewish Enlightenment) movement, and the situation where German literature and science represented a more advanced *Kultur* than anything the Gentile world in Eastern Europe seemed to offer, explain that esteem. In Austrian-ruled Galicia and Bukovina, German was the language of the state and cultural elites. Bohemian-born Abraham Kohn, a proponent of the *Haskalah*, who became (1843) Lemberg's (Lviv) Rabbi, asserted, "The German mother tongue alone is . . . that on whose ground we can acquire true culture," and concluded that no "Slavic dialect" was able to compete with German. Yoysef Margoshes, who would become a communal activist and an important Yiddish journalist in New York, grew up in an orthodox family in Lemberg during the 1870s and 1880s and recalled that none of his friends "displayed even the least interest" in learning Polish (not to mention Ukrainian), but only German. Yiddish journalist and humorist Khone Gotesfeld, who also grew up in Galicia around 1900, described how his father and other parents in his native shtetl of Skale insisted that "A Jew must know German," and therefore he was sent to a private tutor. In his shtetl, even when people were sharply divided over a host of issues, "everyone had deep respect for German." In Russia, government policy in the 1840s fortified that disposition by encouraging an extensive use of German at the government-sponsored schools for Jewish children and viewing Germany as a cultural model. The proximity of the Yiddish language to German facilitated the making of the German language the gateway to European culture. When the Yiddish poet Yoysef Rolnik was on his way to America (1899), he arrived in the port city of Libau (today Latvia's Liepāja). Upon arrival, Rolnik stopped and stared at the window of a local bookstore, which displayed German books. Years later he recalled, "I felt that I am almost in Germany, in Europe."[5]

Already before the mid-nineteenth century the term "daytsh" or "daytshish" (German) was common when referring to almost any new custom or social phenomenon, and also designated the new type who personified the *Haskalah* in his language, ideas, and looks: without a hat, without a beard, without sidelocks and wearing a short jacket ("German" style) rather than a caftan. In one of his short stories, the famed Yiddish writer Sholem Aleichem (Sholem Rabinovitsh) mocked a character who was "a Jewish German or a German Jew," and whose clean-shaven face was "smooth like a plate." German culture and manners, channeled through German and Eastern European proponents of the *Haskalah*—as well as Jewish bankers and merchants in Galicia and cities across the Pale of Settlement like Warsaw, Odessa, Berdichev, and

Zamoshtsh—were the symbols of modernity and a shibboleth between the enlightened and their orthodox opponents. Even the fiercest detractors of the new ideas, like Hasidim, reluctantly admitted the weight of the new Gentile knowledge. They objected, of course, to the government's Germanization effort in Austrian-ruled Galicia and attacked the "berlintshikes" (as advocates of the *Haskalah* were often called) as unable to understand the real meaning of life. But also in Hasidic tales, the *daytshn* were full of knowledge and shrewd. The German was seen as a bearer of higher culture and science with a universal appeal, a world of difference from what Yiddish-speaking Jews knew from their encounters with surrounding Slavic peasantry and Russian officials. Though there were German colonists in Russia, the contact with them remained infrequent, something that made the idealization of German culture easier.[6]

By the late nineteenth century, the respect for Germans and their culture was still noticeable among Yiddish-speaking Jews. In 1870, an unnamed reader wrote to the Yiddish newspaper *Kol mevaser* (Heralding Voice) about a simple, uneducated Jew in his shtetl who wanted "to pass for a *daytsh*," because he thought "only in that lies real education!" The recollections of people who grew up across Tsarist Russia's Pale of Settlement in the mid-to-late nineteenth century conveyed such reverence: future revolutionary and Yiddishist Chaim Zhitlovsky noticed that his father and neighbors had a clearly distinct attitude toward Germans. Zhitlovsky's father felt deep respect toward Germans: "The German nature had made a tremendous impression on him." His father was particularly impressed by the German's "absolute honesty," where "a word is a word!" and even a simple German like a local locksmith was clean and well-dressed. The Hebrew critic, poet, and educator, Avraham Ya'akov Paperna, who lived in many places across the Pale of Settlement, recalled how the Jewish bourgeoisie aped German culture so that even a vulgar parvenu had "the statues of Schiller and Goethe on marble columns" in his house. The Yiddish poet Abraham Reyzin recalled how his father admired German poetry, and when a certain verse impressed him, he used to call him, and ask, "Do you really understand it? You should have known German better." The Zionist leader Shmaryahu Levin wrote in his memoir, "I admired the strict order of German life in general; I admired the German drive for education and knowledge . . . I admired even more the German language and literature, with which I became more familiarized than the Russian."[7]

With the growing connections between Germany and Eastern Europe in the later part of the century, the image of Germans became increasingly more realistic. The rise of pseudo-scientific, racial antisemitism in Germany from the late 1870s on legitimized its espousal by the Russian intelligentsia. Although it did not dethrone Germany from its position as a bastion of high culture, the anti-Jewish tirades showed Jews that the land of Goethe and Schiller was also that of antisemites like Wilhelm Marr, Adolf Stoecker, and Heinrich von Treitschke. The disappointment was evident in the exclamation of the moderate-orthodox Hebrew periodical, *Ha-magid* (The Herald) in 1881, "hatred is the result of the German character and soul." *Ha-magid*'s rival, the Warsaw Hebrew weekly *Ha-tsefirah* (The Dawn or The Morning), equated (1881) anti-Jewish violence in Germany (in the city of Neustettin) with Russian pogroms, stating, "the Germans, who boast of their enlightenment, are not more elevated in virtue and human spirit than their likeminded brethren, the ignorant Russian masses." During the eruption (1883) of anti-Jewish riots across Hungary in the wake of the Tiszaeszlár blood libel, the same paper determined "most instigators are Germans," and described how "small groups of Germans" traveled around, agitating the masses against the Jews.[8]

Furthermore, most of the approximately 2.5 million East European Jews who immigrated to America between 1881 and 1924 had made their way through Germany, heading to one of the major European ports. While transients stayed in Germany for various periods, most of them had brushed against German border officials, policemen, train conductors, innkeepers and ordinary Germans. Germany's administrative structure had granted local and state bureaucrats almost unlimited power over foreigners, which made Eastern Europeans vulnerable to arbitrary treatment by unsympathetic bureaucrats. Paul Nathan, head of German Jewry's chief relief agency, commented that the medical control of transients was "the most stringent imaginable."[9]

Under such circumstances, even simple actions like delousing could turn traumatic. Russian-born author Mary Antin, whose 1912 autobiography, *The Promised Land*, brought her nationwide recognition, passed through Germany in 1894; she remembered how she and other immigrants were taken off the train and hurried by "white-clad Germans shouting commands, always accompanied with 'Quick! Quick!'—the confused passengers obeying all orders like meek children . . . strange looking people driving us about like dumb animals." While Antin penned her recollection before World War I, the long shadow of the Holocaust is clearly seen in the autobiography of future Zionist leader Meyer Weisgal, who traveled through Germany a decade after Antin. Mentioning "the grim efficiency of the Germans, their treatment of us as cattle," Weisgal saw it as "a rehearsal" for the Holocaust. Other immigrants recalled harsh German officials. Passing through Germany in 1894,

Warsaw-born Minnie Goldstein remembered a railroad employee in Berlin, a tall German, who looked "as angry as a mad dog," and threatened the twelve-year-old Goldstein and her mother with a whip.[10]

Such experiences were far from exceptional. To be sure, some immigrants savored what Abraham Cahan, the influential editor of the *Jewish Daily Forward* and a towering figure in the Jewish labor movement in America, depicted as "the difference between a highly civilized country, and a country like Russia. I admired the tidiness and cleanliness of everyone and everything. I was stunned." Many memoirs and autobiographies, nonetheless, detail running into disagreeable Germans, whether in Germany proper or on board America-bound German ships. The emergence of political and pseudo-biological antisemitism in Germany after its unification (in 1871) also contributed to the travails of transient Jewish immigrants in Imperial Germany. Pushed aside on crowded streets, called "damn Jews," and handled as the scum of the earth, Jewish immigrants found there was more to Germany than high culture, running water and cleanliness. Three decades after Yisroel Kopelov passed through Germany, an immigrant by the name of Isaac Donen traveled (1913) by a similar route through Germany and described the Germans: "proud people, cultured antisemites, who look down on every non-German."[11]

Unpleasant and frequent brushes with hostile German crewmembers and passengers aboard German ships to America are also ubiquitous in many accounts. A pioneer of the Jewish labor movement in America, Bernard Vaynshteyn, sailed (1882) to America aboard a German ship and recalled the hostility of the German crew, who called them "Russian pigs." Minnie Goldstein described how one of the young German stewards cursed them, "Damn Jews! All they eat are onions!" A letter signed by ten Jewish immigrants from Minneapolis that appeared (1891) in *Ha-tsefirah* warned potential Jewish immigrants not to choose German ships because of "the ignorant Germans" and mentioned how the German crewmembers "did not spare spitting" at them and occasionally beat them up.[12]

After the passage through Germany and the arrival in America, Jewish observers saw the long shadow of German antisemitism cast west of the Atlantic as well. In 1865, the leading German-Jewish periodical *Allgemeine Zeitung des Judenthums* (General Newspaper of Judaism), which Eastern European proponents of the *Haskalah* often quoted in their publications, complained about the hostility of German immigrants in America, including radical ones, toward Jews. "We owe all *rishes* [antisemitism] in America to those freedom heroes [a sarcastic reference to German revolutionaries]—originally the American knows nothing about *rishes."* Similarly, Rabbi Henry Vidaver, who served congregations in New York, Philadelphia and San Francisco, termed in 1865 Germans in America as "Sons of Haman" (the biblical sworn enemy of the Israelites). Writing from St. Louis in *Ha-magid*, Vidaver warned that, "most Christian Germans are like bottles filled with antisemitism; with antisemitism they were created in the womb . . . [Germans] arrive by the thousands and tens of thousands in America, the land of freedom, and bring the seed of antisemitism to implant in the hearts of the Americans who are not accustomed to it." In 1898, the Hebrew satirist Abraham Kotlyor published a parody that used a Talmudic formula of measurement to distinguish between the Yankees, whose worst offense was chewing tobacco, and others: "ten measures of drunkenness were given to the world, the Irish took nine . . . and the rest of the world took one. . . . Ten measures of antisemitism were given to the world, the Germans took them all."[13]

Nearly twenty years later (1884), *Ha-tsefirah* published a report by a man from Chicago who identified as Ben Ha-shilony. The writer pictured in bright colors the "exalted" Republican presidential candidate James G. Blaine who was "beloved" by the American people. Blaine, who was actually infamous for his corruption even by Gilded Age standards, received commendations in the Jewish press for intervening on behalf of Russian and Romanian Jews. Yet the Germans in America opposed him, Ha-shilony argued, because Blaine backed the temperance movement and objected to the usage of the German language in Ohio and Pennsylvania. Ha-shilony cautioned that the German-Americans were trying to assert their nationalism, "and if, God forbid, they should succeed, then woe unto us Jews, because the Germans hate us here more than in their country," and the German customer often said to the Jewish peddler, "I don't buy from a damn Jew." Such writings did not only differentiate between Americans and Germans, attributing the country's negative features to the latter, but also saw Americans as a bulwark against anti-Jewish enmity that German immigrants brought over from Europe.[14]

Once in America, the attitude of Eastern European Jewish immigrants toward Germans in the closing years of the nineteenth century remained quite ambivalent. Many Yiddish-speaking Jews shared the affection for German culture shown by German Jews, holding German language and culture as an indicator of refinement and modernity. One Yiddish historian commented that among Yiddish-speaking Jews there was a "deeply seated, exaggerated respect for German culture." Certain immigrants tried to pass as German Jews, although when they tried to speak "datsh," noted Yiddish journalist Yankev Magidov, you "could split your sides laughing." Galician-born Louis Borgenicht, who came to New York in 1889 and became a successful clothing manufacturer, wrote that he was raised to look upon anything "'German' as the stamp of excellence in trade, science, thought." One of the important Hebraists in America, Wolf (Zeʹev) Schur, whom a rival Jewish journalist called "dirty," responded (1892) in an angry letter to a friend: "I'm not a Russian Jew who just left the ghetto . . . and in my house reigns cleanliness like that of the Germans."[15]

Yiddish-speaking immigrants were drawn to Manhattan's Southeast sections, in the area known as "Little Germany" (mainly south of Fourteenth Street and east of the Bowery). In time, the influx of Eastern European Jews, Italians, Greeks and other groups would de-Germanize Little Germany, pushing out Germans of the Mosaic persuasion, too. Before and during that process, however, Yiddish-speaking Jews lived in close proximity to a large German population, whose language they could understand, and whose culture was often more accessible to them than American culture. Thus, to a certain degree, the nearby German community life provided a paradigm for the recently arrived immigrants.[16]

Jewish immigrants viewed German organizational forms as role models for themselves in the late nineteenth century. The *landsmanshaftn* (hometown associations) were the most popular organizational form among Jewish immigrants in America in the late nineteenth and early twentieth centuries. *Landsmanshaftn* included various types of associations (orthodox, socialist, or Zionist), most of which were heavily influenced by German organizational culture and the German *Vereine* (associations). While the immigrants had a high opinion of American fraternal orders and lodges, the German model was easier to emulate in terms of physical proximity, language and the sway of existing German-Jewish fraternal orders. Besides the Germanized Yiddish that seemed to introduce an aura of grandeur, Jewish societies readily adopted the regalia, rituals and rules common in German orders and lodges. Looking back in 1911, the Workmen's Circle monthly, *Der Fraynd* (The Friend), praised the socialist German workers' mutual benefit society as the "spiritual father" of the Jewish order, and mentioned it as the first socialist benefit order in America.[17]

Jewish radicals' high regard for their German comrades was not for all things German per se, but rather intertwined with class and ideological affiliation. Since Jewish socialists and anarchists came in close contact with likeminded Germans, their frame of reference was that particular segment of the German population, which then became "the Germans." German immigrants in New York established a strong labor movement, which impressed a young

Jewish cigar-maker called Samuel Gompers as "aggressive and rational."
Already before the Workmen's Circle fashioned itself (1892) after a German socialist mutual benefit society, Russian Jewish intellectuals modeled the United
Hebrew Trades (UHT, founded in 1888 in a meeting at the German labor ly-
ceum on Fourth Street) after the United German Trades. German unions also
contributed money in 1890 to establish the UHT's weekly.[18]

The self-confidence, class-consciousness and theoretical accomplish-
ment that emanated from the German left-of-center environment in New York
profoundly impressed Jewish radicals. Russian Jewish youths, with their pot-
pourri of socialism, anarchism, positivism and collectivism, brought over from
Russian revolutionary circles, flocked to lecture halls and taverns, thirstily listening to talks by Sergius Schewitsch (a scion of the Latvian nobility who was
educated in Germany and bridged Russian and German cultures), German
socialists like Friedrich Sorge and Alexander Jonas, or anarchists like the fiery
Johann Most. Jewish socialists regularly read the socialist *Volkszeitung* (People's
Newspaper) while Jewish anarchists preferred Most's *Freiheit* (Freedom).
German radicals often spoke to gatherings of Jewish *Genossen* (comrades)
and the latter attempted to use their less-than-perfect German when talking
in meetings of German socialists. The longtime secretary of UHT, Bernard
Vaynshteyn, sympathized with German workers—who were largely socialists, according to him—as opposed to Irish workers, who were conservative.
At times the conditions of German workers were considered the standard by
which to pass judgment. In the early 1890s, when Vaynshteyn visited a Jewish
bakery in a basement on Orchard Street, he was shocked by the filth and the
sight of the half-naked bakers who slaved away next to the ovens. One of the
bakers justified ("in half-German") their situation by crying out: "Things are
not much better at the German bakeries."[19]

Nonetheless, the images of Germans were more ambivalent, often marred
after direct contact between Jewish immigrants and German Americans. Many
immigrants recounted unpleasant encounters with Germans, whether at the
workplace or on the street. Some negative feelings remained from the trans-
continental journey; those were coupled with the pains of dislocation and uncertainty (and in some memoirs also a subsequent antipathy toward Germany,
especially after 1933), which frequently put Germans in a bad light. In spite of
the aforesaid respect for German culture, the German people Jews met seemed
less alluring. In New York, signs that barred Jews from stores and apartments
were common in turn-of-the-century German neighborhoods. Orthodox
and Zionist journalist, Joseph Isaac Bluestone, recalled a German landlord on

Delancey Street who had flatly refused (1882) to rent apartments to Jews. Years later, another German landlord on First Avenue called Jews "untidy and dirty." Jewish immigrants who worked at predominantly German shops did not escape the antagonism of their coworkers. When Yisroel Kopelov moved to New Jersey (mid-1880s) and began working at a garment shop, most of his coworkers were Germans, who "did not hide their hatred toward Jews." Later, when he began peddling in New York City, he recalled that, "The Germans were much cleaner [than the Irish]", but "in their hatred to Jews, the Germans surpassed the Irish many times over."[20]

In the 1890s, the mostly German waiters and bartenders union in New York refused to accept Jews, admitting only a few who could speak German well, thus forcing the Jewish waiters to form their own union. In the early years of the twentieth century, sixteen-year-old Sam Carasik came from Bobroysk to Baltimore, where he worked at a shop that made wooden fixtures. On his first day, he thought he was back at the port of Bremen: most workers were the same big Germans with "potbellies that looked like kegs." Carasik felt that the workers hated the few Jews who worked there and "straight away on my first day I heard the phrase goddamn Jew."[21]

The reverberations of German political antisemitism were felt across the Atlantic and augmented the anti-Jewish streak among Germans. In December 1895, a sample of that political brand arrived in New York City in the person of Hermann Ahlwardt, a German antisemitic agitator. Leading uptown Jews refused to speak of him, or expressed confidence that Americans would reject the demagogue's message, while eminent figures among New York's German-Americans strongly denounced Ahlwardt. For the Jewish immigrants who were alert to his visit, nevertheless, the fulminations of a German politician embodied a wider German tendency. A conservative Yiddish weekly, *Yidishe gazetn* (Jewish Gazette) termed the German Americans who welcomed Ahlwardt as "the Milwaukee donkeys," since it was a Milwaukee antisemite, Waldemar Wernich, who was one of those who invited Ahlwardt to America. The latter newspaper (most likely the editor, John Paley) mocked Ahlwardt's pose as having a PhD, "although he didn't even learn how to spell 'sauerkraut' without making ten mistakes." Jews did not stand idle. When Ahlwardt was scheduled to make a speech at Manhattan's Cooper Union, Harlem stockbroker Arthur Goldsmith put an ad asking for volunteers to pelt the German with rotten eggs. A few Jews took up his offer throwing eggs, booing or hissing when Ahlwardt spoke at Cooper Union, in Brooklyn, and in New Jersey. Although local Germans dissociated themselves from Ahlwardt, visits of antisemitic politicians like him or Adolf Stoecker (1893) did not help to dispel the perception of Germans as almost-inherently anti-Jewish.[22]

The problem of rowdyism proved even more troublesome than Ahlwardt. German youths were more than a match for Irish gangs, with whom they sometimes operated in tandem. Yehuda David Eisenstein, a Polish-born prolific scholar and writer who came to New York in 1872 at the age of eighteen and was active in orthodox circles, complained equally about youths of Irish and German parents who beat up and injured Jewish peddlers. In reference to the establishment of the American Hebrew League of Brooklyn (1899), Eisenstein was filled with anger at the hooliganism of children of German and Irish immigrants, whom he called the "garbage of Europe" and "scum of the earth." Those immigrants who binged on alcohol while listening to *Wacht am Rhein* ("Guard on the Rhine" was a popular nationalist song in Germany after 1840), could not control their offspring who roam the streets, pelt Jews with stones or "pull the beards and sidelocks" of old men. Other Jews complained about being terrorized by mixed gangs of Germans and Irish. In February 1900, a Brooklyn Jew was arrested after he shot a young man described as the head of an Irish-German gang that used to throw stones at his house.[23]

Since immigrant Jews viewed Germans as originating from a higher culture than the Irish, many immigrants (as well as American-born) were reluctant to make negative generalizations about them. Morris Hillquit (still called Hillkowitz in the 1880s), who would become a key figure in the Socialist Party, asserted that German workers outranked American workers by far in "political intelligence." Yisroel Beneqvit, who emigrated from the Pale to New York in 1888 and became an active anarchist, noted that Americans "had no progressive ideas" in comparison to the German intelligentsia of New York. The appreciation was not limited to radical circles; when Jewish observers mentioned German instinctive disposition toward antisemitism and alcoholic beverages, such negative qualities usually related to certain redeeming features. Thus a conservative and Zionist writer and activist, Abraham H. Fromenson, who worked against Christian missionaries, coedited the conservative *Yidishes Tageblat* (Jewish Daily News), and was diametrically opposed to Hillquit and Beneqvit, shared their differentiation between the Irish and Germans. Fromenson wrote in 1899 that any Jew "who has strayed into the Irish or *low* German quarters" would be "the victim of cowardly brutality." The star of the Yiddish theater, Boris Tomashevsky, alongside his father, were amazed to see how much a German could drink, yet Tomashevsky also came to appreciate German "calmness." Popular Yiddish humorist and translator

Tashrak (penname of Yisroel-Yoysef Zevin) often referred to Germans as more civilized than the Irish, but also more antisemitic. In a 1904 feuilleton, titled, "In Crotona Park," Tashrak mentioned the Jewish influx into that section of the Bronx. Rather than try to resist that influx, "the Germans behave respectfully"—they simply pack their belongings and move out to Brooklyn or Jersey City: "The Germans are wiser than the Irish, and know that a fight against the Jews is a lost one."[24]

The outbreak of World War I in Europe in 1914, and the enormous suffering of the Jewish population living in what had become the war's eastern front, exemplify the pattern of early enthusiasm of Eastern European Jewish immigrants toward Germany and Germans, followed by disenchantment and bitterness. With the onset of war, the Yiddish press in America provided harrowing reports about the atrocities committed by Tsar Nicholas's soldiers: scorched-earth withdrawals, kidnappings, looting, torture, rape, and sadistic savagery. Furthermore, the Russians also initiated a series of massive expulsions of hundreds of thousands of Jews from their homes in the western regions of the Pale of Settlement, ordering them to leave their homes, often at no more than twelve hours' notice. The ominous news reports from Europe were filled with the names of *shtetlekh* and cities from which many immigrants had come, and the misery was the fate of Jewish immigrants' parents, siblings, and offspring.[25] In a fever-pitch outburst of relief work activity, numerous *landsmanshaftn*, synagogues, and charitable societies organized benefits and bazaars, and provided monetary assistance as well as hundreds of volunteers to help solicitations and collections.[26]

Apart from most immigrant Jews' deep loathing for the hated Tsarist regime, there were Jews who hailed from the Habsburg Empire (Hungary, Galicia, and Bukovina): they were typically ardent Austrian patriots, and especially admired Emperor Franz Joseph, whom they considered protector of the Jews.[27] Perhaps more important, amid the atrocities of Russian troops, the German or Austrian military seemed as the last hope, and the image of the cultured Germans became ubiquitous, especially in 1914–15. In the summer of 1914, Abraham Cahan enlightened his readers about the warring sides: "In truth, the Germanic peoples are more advanced, stronger and more energetic than the Slavs." A week later, Cahan argued, "all civilized people sympathize with Germany, every victorious battle against Russia is a source of joy." Cahan's colleague, the Yiddish journalist and historian Herts Burgin, concluded, "the interests of the European masses and civilization in general can gain more from Germany's victory than from a victory by Russia, France, England, etc."[28]

Representations of Germans and Austrians as civilized defenders against Russian barbarism would continue through 1916, if not later. In the summer of 1915, when the German army retook Austrian Galicia, and also conquered the large Jewish centers in Warsaw, Bialystok, and Kovno, Yiddish newspapers struggled to exceed one another in celebrating the German and Austrian victories: when Lemberg was recaptured, the Yiddish Orthodox daily, *Morgen zhurnal* (Morning Journal), congratulated Galician Jews, who were liberated "from the rule of the Asiatic barbarian." Abraham Cahan, who returned from a May 1915 visit in Eastern Europe, declared at a socialist mass meeting in Carnegie Hall, "The German of today is a better man than he ever was." The *Forverts* extolled the German rule in Warsaw and showed a picture of a Hasidic rabbi in Lodz under a humorous caption: "Now he is a *daytsh*": Hasidim were the bitter opponents of the *maskilim* (proponents of the *Haskalah*), who were often called *daytshn*. By cleverly fusing a familiar Jewish type (*daytsh*) to the new occupiers, the *Forverts* relayed to its readers a homey, soothing image of the German, which was diametrically opposed to that of the bloodthirsty Russian/ Cossack. In 1916 a Jewish dentist on Suffolk Street, Dr. B. Schwartz, published his practice in an ad titled "Germany strikes all the enemies of the Jews," which claimed, "God sent Germany to punish Russia and Romania" for their cruelty toward Jews.[29]

In such an atmosphere it was little wonder that the Yiddish humorist weekly, *Der Groyser Kundes* (Big Stick) remarked in 1914, "The German soldiers are positively the best in the world: they are 'made in Germany.'" *Varhayt* (Truth) published in 1915 a feuilleton by an unnamed author, which mentioned, "If there's really a little antisemitism here in New York, you can be sure that most of it was on account of the Germans." In the past, "who if not the Brooklyn *daytshukes*" [a pejorative for Germans] used to pull the beards of Jews on the East New York (Brooklyn) cars and "mimic, curse, and insult Jewish women and girls." Since the war began, however, "the old hatred is taken back," and one could not find "two other races that would live so peacefully, truly sleep under one blanket, as the Jews and Germans."[30]

The conditions of war and the sheer ruthlessness of the Tsarist army reestablished the image of Germans as carriers of a higher and more benevolent culture, especially as opposed to Russian, or "Slavic," brutality. The feuilleton's reference to German antisemitism, however, implies that acute awareness of German antisemitism still remained. Once the United States joined the war in April 1917, the non-radical Yiddish press drastically changed its stance from a pro-German to a pro-Allied position. The wartime vilification of the brutal "Huns" and all things German further damaged the image of Germans in Jewish eyes. After the Tsar was toppled (March 1917), Russian Jews had no reason to support the authoritarian Germany against their former home country, which emancipated its Jewish population. Jews received additional reports from Eastern Europe about deteriorating economic conditions under German occupation, leading to hunger and smuggling, and subsequent German punitive measures against local Jewish communities. Well before America entered the war, the *Tog* (The Day) critically scrutinized the German character, noting that Germans "are too much in love with themselves." Yiddish writer Tashrak penned a humoristic sketch in March 1917 that relayed how all things German fell from grace for New York Jews: lodge members refused to talk Germanized Yiddish anymore at their meetings. Everyone hoped America would beat the Germans, and German Jews pretended to be Litvakes (Lithuanian Jews).[31]

After the March 1917 Revolution in Russia, Jewish socialists had little sympathy for Germany, and the far-reaching change in the image of Germans also permeated the circles that objected to America's entry into the war. A friend of the influential socialist activist and journalist Tsivyen (penname of Ben-Tsiyen Hoffman), described him as "in love with German culture." By August 1917, nonetheless, Tsivyen wrote about the "barbaric, bloodthirsty Germans that have to be wiped from the face of the earth so humanity may live in peace." Moreover, after the Soviets signed (March 1918) a humiliating separate peace treaty with Germany at Brest-Litovsk, where they ceded vast territories to the Central Powers, most Jewish radicals saw it as German belligerence that emphasized the vulnerability of the young Soviet regime. Even the most pro-German Jewish radical of yesteryear no longer saw the Germans as a bulwark of civilization against the Slavs, but rather as those culpable for the outbursts of anti-Jewish violence and dire food shortage in Eastern Europe. A Jewish organizer of the Structural Iron workers in New York, Sol Broad, said, "There was a friction between the Jews and the German-Austrian element because the Jews favored the war after the Brest-Litovsk Treaty. The German-Austrian element has been somewhat antisemitic." By February 1918, leading Yiddish journalist, William Edlin, claimed privately that "everybody" among New York's Jewish immigrants was becoming anti-German, and that transformation was especially noticeable among Jewish socialists. A week later, Adolph Germer, the German-American secretary of the Socialist Party, wrote to Morris Hillquit that "95% of their [Jewish] membership have changed front" and support the war against Germany.[32]

*****

A perceptive observer of Yiddish-speaking immigrants in New York City, the journalist Hutchins Hapgood, concluded (1902) that Jews were "susceptible to their Gentile environment, when that environment is of a high order of civilization."[33] The attractiveness of German culture, as well as the representations of Germans before, during, and after migration should be understood within the intriguing dynamics of immigration and modernization. Whereas modernizing Jews often put Germans on a pedestal, and viewed them as bearers of a higher, more advanced culture, that process of initial veneration eventually turned to disappointment. The idealization of German culture was largely dependent on a certain geographical distance between Germany and the large Jewish population centers of Eastern Europe. As more concrete contacts were established, various expressions of rejection and anti-Jewish enmity turned high regard into disillusionment.

This pattern of Jews' initial idealization of a culture that seemed more advanced followed by disappointment when brushing up against the prejudices of everyday life held true for Russia as well as Germany. Jewish modernizers who once hailed Russian culture and sought Jewish integration, later witnessed antisemitism and rejection. Jewish enlighteners were drawn to high culture—the cultures of empires, whether in Berlin, Vienna, or St. Petersburg. As historian Yuri Slezkine has rightly observed, Jews who wanted to speak the language of universalism chose those languages (such as German and Russian) which "were a claim to a prestigious high-cultural tradition." To be sure, the appeal of such cultures had practical reasons as well. More often than not, Jews aligned themselves with the central authorities who protected them from violent mob attacks; many communities also relied on Gentile rulers for their livelihood. Acquaintance with the languages of the central government and those spoken across vaster swathes of land assured better chances to conduct business or just eke out a livelihood. Yet the Jewish attraction to modern, advanced cultures was genuine and not only due to economic reasons. As historian Ezra Mendelsohn has justly noted, late-nineteenth-century Jews wanted to transform themselves into Russians, Poles and Germans, not Belorussians, Latvians, Lithuanians, or Ukrainians.[34] A similar pattern of initial idealization and later disenchantment would also occur with respect to old-stock, white Americans, which Yiddish sources often termed "Yankees" or "real" Americans. The image of "Yankees" shared some of the optimistic assumptions that modernizing Jews had about the upper echelons of non-Jewish society in Europe. However, the rise of American nativism and recurring attempts to close America's gates, and the xenophobic panic that spread during World War I and ensuing Red Scare would lead to more sober assessments of "Yankee benevolence."[35]

While replicating some aspects of their interrelations with Germans in the Old World, other aspects were quite different for Eastern European Jews after their arrival in America. In the United States, Germans were one group among many, and Jewish immigrants associated them with the pains of urban displacement, social dislocation, and hooliganism. The Great War reinforced the dynamics of initial admiration followed by embitterment, but added a new component, as by April 1917 Germany became an enemy of the United States. Thus Jewish resentment over German antisemitism and mistreatment of Jewish population on the eastern front fitted within the larger framework of American democracy's fight against German tyranny.

Studying the images of Germans among immigrant Jews links American Jewish history to the larger field of American immigration and ethnic history. Scholars in those fields have revealed that the process of Americanization/assimilation/acculturation, however defined, was far less voluntary than usually assumed and entailed forced conformism and exclusion as well as integration. More specifically, some scholars have explored immigrants' idealization of America prior to immigration and their growing disenchantment with their new country after arrival.[36] Such framework would advance our knowledge not only of Jewish attitudes and of intergroup relations, but also of the intricate effects of modernization, which would continue to shape such relations west of the Atlantic as well.

Notes

1. Y. Kopelov, *Amol in amerike* (Warsaw: Brzoza, 1928), 15–18. The letter was published in *Yudisher emigrant* (St. Petersburg), Nov. 27, 1908, 12–13. Unless otherwise
   noted, all the translations to English are mine.

2. A succinct discussion of the historiography is in Tobias Brinkmann, "'German
   Jews?': Reassessing the History of Nineteenth-Century Jewish Immigrants in
   the United States," in *Transnational Traditions; New Perspectives on American
   Jewish History*, ed. Ava F. Kahn and Adam D. Mendelsohn (Detroit: Wayne State
   University Press, 2014), 145–9. Hasia R. Diner, *The Jews of the United States, 1654
   to 2000* (Berkeley: University of California Press, 2004), 80–95. Avraham Barkai,
   Branching Out: German-Jewish Immigration to the United States, 1820–1914 (New
   York: Holmes & Meier, 1994). Stanley Nadel, "Jewish Race and German Soul in
   Nineteenth Century America," *American Jewish History* 77 (1987): 6–26. See also,
   Adi Gordon and Gil Ribak, "German-Jewish Migration to the United States," in
   Germany and the Americas: Culture, Politics and History, ed. Thomas Adam (Santa
   Barbara: ABC-Clio, 2005), 13–22.

3. Immigration statistics are in "A Reader in the Demography of American Jews,"
   American Jewish Year Book 77 (1977): 319. Ira Glazier, ed., *Migration from the Russian
   Empire: Lists of Passengers Arriving at U.S. Ports* (Baltimore: Genealogical Publishing
   Co., 1997), 3:viii–ix, xv–xvi. Naomi W. Cohen, *Encounter with Emancipation: The
   German Jews in the United States, 1830–1914* (Philadelphia: Jewish Publication
   Society, 1984), 12. See also, Pamela Nadell, "The Journey to America by Steam:
   The Jews of Eastern Europe in Transition," *American Jewish History* 71 (1981):
   269–84. Zosa Szajkowski, "Sufferings of Jewish Emigrants to America in Transit
   to America through Germany," *Jewish Social Studies* 39 (1977): 105–16. Lloyd P.
   Gartner, "Jewish Migrants en Route from Europe to North America: Traditions
   and Realities," *Jewish History* 1 (1986): 49–67. John D. Klier, "Emigration Mania
   in Late Imperial Russia: Legend and Reality," in *Patterns of Migration, 1850–1914*,
   ed. Aubrey Newman and Stephen W. Massil (London: Jewish Historical Society of
   England, 1996), 21–29.

4. Ewa Morawska, "A Replica of the 'Old-Country' Relationship in the Ethnic Niche:
   East European Jews and Gentiles in Small-Town Western Pennsylvania, 1880s–
   1930s," *American Jewish History* 77 (1987): 27–86. Ewa Morawska, "From Myth
   to Reality: America in the Eyes of East European Peasant Migrant Laborers," in
   *Distant Magnets: Expectations and Realities in the Immigrant Experience, 1840–
   1930*, ed. Dirk Hoerder and Horst Roessler (New York: Holmes & Meier, 1993),
   241–63. Gianfausto Rosoli, "From 'Promised Land' to 'Bitter Land': Italian Migrants
   and the Transformation of a Myth," in *Distant Magnets*, 222–40.

5. Yoysef Margoshes, *Erinerungen fun mayn lebn* (New York: Max Mayzel Farlag,
   1936), 81. Khone Gotesfeld, *Vos ikh gedenk fun mayn lebn* (New York: Fareynikte

galitsyaner yidn in amerike, 1960), 41, 44–45, 103, 114. Yoysef Rolnik, *Zikhroynes* (New York: With the help of the David Ignatoff Fund, 1954), 109. See also, "Prussia," *Ha-tsefirah,* May 8, 1862, 101–2. Kohn is quoted in Israel Zinberg, *A History of Jewish Literature* (Cincinnati and New York: Hebrew Union College Press and Ktav Publishing, 1977–78), 10:106. Shmuel Werses, *Hakitsa 'ami: sifrut ha-haskalah be-'eedan ha-modernizatsya* (Jerusalem: Magnes, 2001), 269–70. Michael Stanislawski, *Tsar Nicholas I and the Jews: The Transformation of Jewish Society in Russia, 1825–1855* (Philadelphia: Jewish Publication Society, 1983), 45, 60, 115. Yehuda Slutsky, *Ha-'itonut ha-yehudit-rusit ba-me'ah ha-tsha-'esre* (Jerusalem: Bialik, 1970), 15–18. On Rabbi Kohn, see Michael Stanislawski, *A Murder in Lemberg: Politics, Religion, and Violence in Modern Jewish History* (Princeton: Princeton University Press, 2007), 52–64.

6. All dates are given according the Gregorian calendar. See the report of the Hebrew critic A. Y. Paperna from Warsaw, "Letters from Warsaw" [in Hebrew], *Ha-karmel,* March 9, 1868, 35. See also, the story "Dos meserl" (The Pocketknife) by Sholem Aleichem, *Ale verk fun Sholem Aleichem* (New York: Sholem Aleichem folksfond oysgabe, 1925), 7:14, 30. Marie Schumacher-Brunhes, "The Figure of the Daytsh in Yiddish Literature," in *Jews and Germans in Eastern Europe: Shared and Comparative Histories,* ed. Tobias Grill (Oldenbourg, Germany: De Gruyter, 2018), 72–87. Israel Bartal, "The Image of Germany and German Jewry in East European Jewish Society During the 19th Century," in *Danzig, Between East and West: Aspects of Modern Jewish History,* ed. Isadore Twersky (Cambridge, MA: Harvard University Press, 1985), 3–17. Shlomo Yosef Zevin, *Sipurei Chasidim* (Tel Aviv: Avraham Tsiyoni, 1955), 427. The Ger Rebbe defended German Jews before his disciples despite their infidelity (Louis I. Newman, ed. and trans., in collaboration with Samuel Spitz, *The Hasidic Anthology: Tales and Teachings of the Hasidim* [New York: Bloch, 1944], 290). On the German culture's influence in Russia, see John D. Klier, *Imperial Russia's Jewish Question, 1855–1881* (Cambridge, UK: Cambridge University Press, 1995), 106, 154–6.

7. Untitled article by Not a Daytsh, *Kol mevaser* [in Yiddish], Dec. 1, 1870, 343. Chaim Zhitlovsky, *Zikhroynes fun mayn lebn* (New York: Zhitlovsky's Jubilee Committee, 1935), 1:160–1. Avaraham Ya'akov Paperna, *Kol ha-ktavim,* ed. Israel Zmora (Tel Aviv: Machbarot le-sifrut, 1952), 318–9. Abraham Reyzin, *Epizodn fun mayn lebn* (Vilna: Kletzkin, 1929), 1:7–8. Shmaryahu Levin, *Me-zichronot chayai,* trans. Z. Vislevsky (Tel Aviv: Dvir, 1935), 3:15–16. There are many other examples—see the memoir of Galician-born Louis Borgenicht, *The Happiest Man: The Life of Louis Borgenicht as Told to Harold Friedman* (New York: Putnam's Sons, 1942), 305. Abraham Cahan, *Bleter fun mayn lebn* (New York: Forverts, 1926), 1:156. Mordkhe Spektor, *Mayn lebn* (Warsaw: Achisefer, 1927), 2:5.

8. Many of the news items in those newspapers were unsigned. "The Jewish Question," *Ha-magid,* March 2, 1881, 69 (this Hebrew weekly came out in Germany, but its

readership was made mostly of Jews in Russia). "Chronicles," *Ha-tsefirah*, July 26, 1881, 217. "Woe Is Me," *Ha-tsefirah*, Sept. 4, 1883, 260. See also, "The Fanatics' Recklessness in Germany," *Ha-tsefirah*, Jan. 11, 1881, 3. "Riots against the Jews in Germany," *Ha-tsefirah*, March 18, 1884, 75–76. Future Zionist leader Nachum Sokolov made an interesting comparison between the sophistication of German antisemitism and "Slavic" brutality: "Observer of the Jewish People," *Ha-tsefirah*, Jan. 3, 1882, 397. On the context of the Tiszaeszlár affair see Hillel J. Kieval, "Neighbors, Strangers, Readers: The Village and the City in Jewish-Gentile Conflict at the Turn of the Nineteenth Century," *Jewish Studies Quarterly* 12 (2005): 61–79. Peter Pulzer, *The Rise of Political Anti-Semitism in Germany & Austria* (1964; rev. ed. Cambridge, MA: Harvard University Press, 1988), 47–57, 72–119.

9. Nadell, "The Journey to America by Steam," 269–84. Szajkowski, "Sufferings of Jewish Emigrants," 105–16 (Nathan is quoted ibid., 107). Gartner, "Jewish Migrants," 49–67. Gur Alroey, *Ha-ma'hapecha ha-shketah: ha-hagirah ha-yehudit me-ha'imperiya ha-rusit, 1875–1924* (Jerusalem: Zalman Shazar, 2008), 150–91. Jack Wertheimer, *Unwelcome Strangers: East European Jews in Imperial Germany* (New York: Oxford University Press, 1987), 50–51, 176–81. Steven Aschheim, *Brothers and Strangers: The East European Jew in German and German Jewish Consciousness, 1800–1923* (Madison: University of Wisconsin Press, 1982), 3–62.

10. Mary Antin, *The Promised Land* (1912; new ed. New York: Penguin, 1997), 138–39. Meyer Weisgal, *So Far: An Autobiography* (New York: Random House, 1971), 19. See also the memoir of Pauline Notkoff, in *Voices from Ellis Island [microform] : An Oral History of American Immigration: A Project of the Statue of Liberty-Ellis Island Foundation* (Frederick, MD: University Publications of America, c. 1987), #27:6, https://lccn.loc.gov/91955600. Minnie Goldstein's account is in Jocelyn Cohen and Daniel Soyer, eds. and trans., *My Future Is in America: Autobiographies of Eastern European Jewish Immigrants* (New York: New York University Press, in conjunction with the YIVO Institute for Jewish Research, 2006), 25–26. Goldstein's experience is very similar to that of an anonymous Jew almost twenty years later: *Yudisher emigrant*, May 28, 1912, 6.

11. Cahan, *Bleter fun mayn lebn*, 2:51–52. Kopelov, *Amol in amerike*, 15–18. "Isaac Donen," #100:23, *American Jewish Autobiographies Collection* (YIVO). Numerous memoirs conveyed similar experiences: see the memoir of Yiddish linguist Alexander Harkavy, *Prakim me-khayay* (New York: Hebrew Publishing, 1935), 37–38. Gregory Weinstein, *The Ardent Eighties: Reminiscences of an Interesting Decade* (New York: International Press, 1928), 14. I. A. Beneqvit, *Durkhgelebt un durkhgetrakht* (New York: Kultur federatsye, 1934), 2:15–17. Boris D. Bogen, *Born a Jew* (New York: Macmillan, 1930), 32–34. Joseph Isaac Bluestone, "Memoirs of J. I. Bluestone," in *Joseph Isaac Bluestone Papers*, box #1 (not in a folder), 31–36, American Jewish Historical Society.

12. B. Vaynshteyn, *Fertsik yor in der yidisher arbeter bavegung* (New York: Veker, 1924),

15–16. Goldstein's account is in *My Future Is in America*, 27–28. "Minneapolis," *Ha-tsefirah*, Nov. 5, 1891, 942. See also, A. Berlow (Vorleb), #70:36–38, *American Jewish Autobiographies Collection* (YIVO). Bluestone, "Memoirs of J. I. Bluestone," 36.

13. "North America," *Allgemeine Zeitung des Judenthums*, March 28, 1865, 202. On that publication, see Hans Otto Horch, "Le-toldotav shel *ha-'Allgemeine Zeitung des Judenthums*," *Kesher* 5 (1989): 12–20. "America," *Ha-magid*, Feb. 1, 1865, 36 ("sons of Haman" appears in that piece). On Vidaver see Morris B. Margolies, "The American Career of Rabbi Henry Vidaver," *Western States Jewish Historical Quarterly* 16 (1983): 30–43. Abraham Kotlyor, *Derekh 'erets ha-khadasha* (Warsaw: Shapiro, 1898), 10. On the imagery of the Irish among Jewish immigrants, see Gil Ribak, "'Beaten to Death by Irish Murderers': The Death of Sadie Dellon (1918) and Jewish Images of the Irish," *Journal of American Ethnic History* 32 (2013): 41–74.

14. "Chicago," *Ha-tsefirah*, July 15, 1884, 210. See also, *Ha-tsefirah*, July 29, 1884, 224. One of the prominent leaders of American Jewry in the twentieth century, Rabbi Stephen S. Wise, recalled how Blaine's speech stirred him as a ten-year-old child— *Challenging Years: The Autobiography of Stephen Wise* (New York: G. P. Putnam's Sons, 1949), 4–5.

15. The historian is Y. Khaykin, *Yidishe bleter in amerike* (New York: self-pub., 1946), 243. "Split your sides" is in Yankev Magidov, *Der shpigl fun der ist sayd* (New York: self-pub., 1923), 21–22. On Polish Jews who tried to pass as German Jews (in California) see Norton B. Stern and William M. Kramer, "What's the Matter with Warsaw?" *American Jewish Archives Journal* 37 (1985): 301–4. Borgenicht, *Happiest Man*, 305 (quotes in the original). Schur's letter to Yosef Yehuda Leib Sosnitz (March 31, 1892) is printed in E. R. Malachi, ed., *'Igrot sofrim* (New York: Dr. Shmuel Miller's Publication, 1931), 120–21 (Yechezkel Sarasohn was the offender). On Schur see Jacob Kabakoff, "The Role of Wolf Schur as Hebraist and Zionist," in *Essays in American Jewish History* (no ed., Cincinnati: American Jewish Archives, 1958), 425–56. See also, Hasia R. Diner, "Before the Promised City: Eastern European Jews in America Before 1880," in *An Inventory of Promises: Essays on American Jewish History in Honor of Moses Rischin*, ed. Jeffrey S. Gurock and Marc Lee Raphael (New York: Carlson, 1995), 43–62.

16. B. Hoffman (Tsivyen), *Fuftzik yor kloakmakher yunyon, 1886–1936* (New York: Cloak Operators Union Local 117, 1936), 24–25. Yoysef Kahan, *Di Yidish-anarkhistishe bavegung in amerike* (Philadelphia: Radical Library, Workmen's Circle, 1945), 34–40. Hyman B. Grinstein, *The Rise of the Jewish Community of New York, 1654–1860* (Philadelphia: Jewish Publication Society, 1945), 31–33. Ronald Sanders, *The Lower East Side Jews: An Immigrant Generation* (formerly titled *The Downtown Jews* in 1969; corrected edition published in 1987; repr. Mineola, NY: Dover, 1999), 46–47, 75–79. Stanley Nadel, *Little Germany: Ethnicity, Religion and Class in New York City, 1845–1880* (Urbana: University of Illinois Press, 1990), 68–69, 99–103, 161. Rudolf Glanz, *Studies in Judaica Americana* (New York: Ktav, 1970), 122–51.

17. *Der fraynd*, March 1911, 117–18. *Parlamentarishe ruls vi tsu firen mitingen fun yunyons, lodzhen, un andere faraynen* (New York: Arbeter tsaytung, 1891), 3–5. See the Yiddish WPA study, *Di yidishe landsmanshaftn fun nu york* (New York: Yiddish Writers' Union, 1938), 68–108. Daniel Soyer, *Jewish Immigrant Associations and American Identity in New York, 1880–1939* (1997; repr., Detroit: Wayne State University, 2001), 30, 38, 48–81, 204–5. Nathan M. Kaganoff, "The Jewish Landsmanshaftn in New York City in the Period Preceding World War I," *American Jewish History* 76 (1986): 56–66. Cf. Michael R. Weisser, *A Brotherhood of Memory: Jewish Landsmanshaftn in the New World* (New York: Basic, 1985). Klaus Hoedl, *Vom Shtetl an die Lower East Side* (Vienna: Boehlau, 1991), 175–82. On similar societies among non-Jewish immigrants, see John Bodnar, *The Transplanted: A History of Immigration in Urban America* (Bloomington: Indiana University Press, 1985), 120–30.

18. Samuel Gompers, *Seventy Years of Life and Labor* (New York: Dutton & Co., 1925), 47, 69–71. Vaynshteyn, *Fertsik yor*, 78–80. Hartmut Keil, "German Working-Class Radicalism after the Civil War," in *The German-American Encounter: Conflict and Cooperation between Two Cultures, 1800–2000*, ed. Frank Trommler and Elliot Shore (New York: Berghahn, 2001), 37–48. Stanley Nadel, "From the Barricades of Paris to the Streets of New York: German Artisans and the European Roots of American Labor Radicalism," *Labor History* 30 (1989): 47–75. Morris U. Schappes, "The Political Origins of the United Hebrew Trades," *Journal of Ethnic Studies* 5 (1977): 13–41. Tony Michels, *A Fire in Their Hearts: Yiddish Socialists in New York* (Cambridge, MA: Harvard University Press, 2005), 41–49.

19. Emma Goldman, *Living My Life* (New York: Alfred Knopf, 1931), 1:34–40. Beneqvit, *Durkhgelebt un durkhgetrakht*, 2:74. Vaynshteyn, *Fertsik yor*, 56, 78–79, 90. Idem, *Di yidishe yunyons in amerike* (New York: Fareynigte yidishe geverkshaftn, 1929), 427–28. Magidov, *Shpigl*, 21–22. Cahan, *Bleter fun mayn lebn*, 2:87–90. Shoel Yanovsky, *Ershte yorn fun yidishn frayhaytlekhen sotzialism* (New York: Fraye arbeter shtime, 1948), 83–85, 92–95. Chaim Leyb Vaynberg, *Fertzik yor in kamf far sotzialer bafrayung* (Los Angeles: Vaynberg bukh komitet, 1952), 24–26. Paul Avrich, *Anarchist Portraits* (Princeton: Princeton University Press, 1988), 178–82. Carl Wittke, *The German-Language Press in America* (Frankfort: University of Kentucky Press, 1957), 112, 173–74.

20. Bluestone, "Memoirs," 54. The other German landlord's story is in Avrom Pinkhes Unger, *Mayn heymshtetl strykov* (New York: Arbeter Ring, 1957), 240–41. Kopelov, *Amol in amerike*, 133–5, 157, 163–4. See the report of Yehuda Buchalter about German immigrants' beer drinking—*Ha-tsefirah*, Oct. 21, 1884, 317. On the displacement of German workers in the garment industry, see US Census Bureau, *Populations* (1880), 754, 759; US Census Bureau, *Populations* (1890), 2:table 109. US Industrial Commission, *Report of the Industrial Commission*, 14:83. Judith

Greenfeld, "The Role of the Jews in the Development of the Clothing Industry," *YIVO Annual* 2–3 (1947–48): 180–204.

21. Vaynshteyn, *Fertsik yor*, 505–7. Sam Carasik, #173:60, 64–65, *American Jewish Autobiograohies Collection* (YIVO). See also the Yiddish play by Yankev Ter, "Der amerikaner arbeter," *Natur un lebn* (New York: Baron, 1898), 25–28.

22. *Ha-'Ivry*, Nov. 22, 1895 (not paginated). *Yidishe gazetn*, Nov. 29, 1895, 1. Dec. 6, 1895, 17. Dec. 13, 1895, 4, 17. Dec. 20, 1895, 5. See also *Abend-blat*, Dec. 6, 1895, 1. Dec. 16, 1895, 1. See also the reports in *Ha-tsefirah*, Dec. 26, 1895, 1100–1. Jan. 2, 1896, 1131. Jan. 3, 1896, 1134. Jan. 7, 1896, 1145. *New York Times*, Nov. 22, 1895, 9. Dec. 4, 1895, 5. Dec. 9, 1895, 3. Dec. 13, 1895, 2. Dec. 15, 1895, 9. On Wernich, see the *Milwaukee Sentinel*, Dec. 16, 1895, 2. Years later, the New York's Police Commissioner at the time, Theodore Roosevelt, wrote that he assigned Jewish policemen to guard Ahlwardt: Theodore Roosevelt, *An Autobiography* (1913, repr. Charleston, SC: BiblioBazaar, 2007), 174. Naomi W. Cohen, "American Jewish Reactions to Anti-Semitism in Western Europe, 1875–1900," *Proceedings of the American Academy for Jewish Research* 45 (1978): 34–35. On Ahlwardt's career, see Pulzer, *Rise of Political Anti-Semitism*, 106–10.

23. Yehuda David Eisenstein, *Otsar zikhronotay* (New York: self-pub., 1929), 79, 98. *Ha-tekhiya*, Feb. 23, 1900, 7. Herbert Asbury, *The Gangs of New York: An Informal History of the Underworld* (New York: Alfred Knopf, 1928), 233.

24. Morris Hillquit, *Loose Leaves from a Busy Life* (New York: Rand School, 1934), 41. Beneqvit, *Durkhgelebt un durkhgetrakht*, 2:74. *Yidishes tageblat*, June 12, 1899, 8 (Fromenson, italics added). Boris Tomashevsky, *Mayn lebns-geshikhte* (New York: Trio, 1937), 99, 239. Y. Y. Zevin, "In krotona park," *Tashrak's beste ertselungen* (1910, 5th ed.; New York: Hebrew Publishing Company, 1929), 1:19–21. See also "Yoshke the Dog," *Tashrak's beste ertselungen*, 1:39–43; and "The Jews of the 'White Eagle,'" *Tashrak's beste ertselungen*, 1:57–61. See also the recollection of garment union leader, Joseph Schlossberg, *Columbia University Oral History Research Office Collection*, 9–13. Cf. a letter by Wilhelmina Wiebusch (1884) to her family in Germany about her work as a housemaid for a Jewish family in Brooklyn, in Walter D. Kamphoefner et al., eds., *News from the Land of Freedom: German Immigrants Write Home* (trans. from the German by Susan Carter Vogel; Ithaca, NY: Cornell University Press, 1991), 595–96.

25. For a full analysis of Jewish immigrants' allegiances during World War I, see Gil Ribak, "'A Victory of the Slavs Means a Deathblow to Democracy': The Onset of World War I and the Images of the Warring Sides among Jewish Immigrants in New York, 1914–1916," in *War and Peace in Jewish Tradition: From the Ancient World to the Present*, ed. Yigal Levin and Amnon Shapira (Oxford, UK: Routledge, 2012), 203–17. *Forverts*, Aug. 6, 1915, 4. *American Jewish Year Book* 5676 (1915–16): 225–27, 244–46, 269. On the dissemination of information in New York about the suffering of Russian Jews, see the letter from Ber Borokhov to S. Niger, Oct.

25, 1914, in Matityahu Mintz, ed., *'Igrot ber borokhov, 1897–1914* (Tel Aviv: Am Oved, 1989), 613. Yiddish folklorist and playwright S. An-ski (Shloyme Zaynvl Rapoport) described the Russian soldiers' cruelty in "Khurbm galitsye," *Gezamlte shriftn* (Warsaw: Farlag An-ski, 1925), 4:10–14. Eric Lohr, *Nationalizing the Russian Empire: The Campaign Against Enemy Aliens During World War I* (Cambridge, MA: Harvard University Press, 2003), 137–50.

26. *Yidishes tageblat*, Sept. 8, 1915, 4. *Forverts*, April 24, 1915, 12. Morris Engelman, *Four Years of Relief and War Work by the Jews of America, 1914–1918* (New York: Shoen, 1918). Soyer, *Jewish Immigrant Associations*, 161–89. Mary McCune, *"The Whole Wide World without Limits": International Relief, Gender Politics, and American Jewish Women, 1890–1913* (Detroit: Wayne State University Press, 2005), 43–77.

27. On Polish and Hungarian Jews' high regard for Franz Joseph, see the interview with Helen Weinstein, tape I-65, *NYC Immigrant Labor History Project*, Tamiment Institute, New York University. Gotesfeld, *Vos ikh gedenk*, 41–42. M. Tsipin, "Di es-traykh-serbishe milkhome in dem higen galitsyaner-ungarishen kvartal," *Varhayt*, July 29, 1914, 4. "Galitsyaner vinshen tsu nikolay'en un litvakes zogen 'amen,'" *Forverts*, July 31, 1914, 4. Y. Magidov, "A getsvungener krig," *Morgen zhurnal*, Aug. 3, 1914, 4. Borgenicht, *Happiest Man*, 33.

28. The first quote by Cahan is in, "Estraykh un ire slavishe felker," *Forverts*, July 31, 1914, 4; his second quote is in "England maynt oykh nit di hagode," *Forverts*, Aug. 7, 1914, 4. H. Burgin, "Vemen zolen mir vinshen zig?" Aug. 20, 1914, 4. On the German army and Eastern European Jews, see Tobias Grill, "'Pioneers of Germanness in the East'? Jewish-German, German, and Slavic Perceptions of East European Jewry during the First World War," in *Jews and Germans in Eastern Europe*, 125–59.

29. "Di simkhe bay estraykhishe yidn," *Morgen zhurnal*, June 24, 1915, 4. Cahan is quoted in the *New York Times*, May 2, 1915, 5. "Yetst iz er a 'daytsh,'" *Forverts*, Aug. 11, 1915, 4. Schwartz's ad was published under the title, "Daytshland shlogt ale yidishe sonim," *Yidishes Tageblat*, Dec. 15, 1916, 8. See a similar ad in the humor-ist *Der Groyser Kundes* (Big Stick), Oct. 13, 1914, 10. Linguist Hirsh Abramovitch recounted how "almost" all the Jews in Vilna were elated by the German conquest of the city (September 1915) in his memoir, *Farshvundene geshtaltn: zikhroynes un siluetn* (Buenos Aires: Tsentral farband fun poylishe yidn in argentine, 1958), 262–64, 297–98. Vejas Gabriel Liulevicius, *War Land on the Eastern Front: Culture, National Identity, and the German Occupation in World War I* (Cambridge, UK: Cambridge University Press, 2000), 17–21.

30. *Der Groyser Kundes*, Aug. 7, 1914, 8. *Varhayt*, Jan. 14, 1915, 8. See also, A. Zeldin, "Di legend vegen daytshe gvures," *Tog*, April 14, 1916, 4. On cooperation between Jews and Germans prior to the US entry into the war, see Zosa Szajkowski, *Jews, Wars, and Communism: The Attitude of American Jews in World War I, the Russian Revolutions of 1917, and Communism (1914–1945)* (New York: Ktav, 1972), 1:66–

67; and Joseph Rappaport, *Hands Across the Sea: Jewish Immigrants and World War I* (Lanham, MD: Hamilton Books, 2005), 48–49.

31. "Dytshe blindkayt," *Tog*, March 31, 1917, 8. Tashrak, "Nishto mer keyn daytshen in blotetown," *Yidishe gazetn*, March 30, 1917, 11. On the anti-German mood, see David M. Kennedy, *Over Here: The First World War and American Society* (New York: Oxford University Press, 1980), 59–69; and John Higham, *Strangers in the Land: Patterns of American Nativism, 1860–1925* (1955, new ed. New York: Atheneum, 1978), 204–19, 278–79. On the worsening conditions under German occupation in Eastern Europe in 1917, see the recollections in the interview of Pauline Notkoff, Sept. 11, 1985, #27:2, *Voices from Ellis Island*; and fellow Bialystoker Gertrude Yellin, Feb. 10, 1986, #144:4, *Voices from Ellis Island*. See also, Liulevicius, *War Land on the Eastern Front*, 182.

32. Tsivyen's friend is Dovid Shub, *Fun di amolike yorn* (New York: Cyco, 1970), 450. Tsivyen wrote in the *Fraynd*, Aug. 1917, 9. See also the depiction of Germans as "savages" with a superiority complex in *Der Groyser Kundes*, July 20, 1917, 6. Interview with Sol Broad, March 6, 1919, in *David J. Saposs Papers*, box #22, folder #2, Wisconsin State Historical Society. William Edlin, to George Creel, Feb. 28, 1918, folder #76, *William Edlin Papers* (YIVO). Adolph Germer, to Morris Hillquit, March 4, 1918, reel #2, *Morris Hillquit papers*, Wisconsin State Historical Society.

33. Hutchins Hapgood, *The Spirit of the Ghetto* (1902, repr. New York: Schocken, 1965), 3.

34. Yuri Slezkine, *The Jewish Century* (Princeton, NJ: Princeton University Press, 2004), 64. Ezra Mendelsohn, *On Modern Jewish Politics* (New York: Oxford University Press, 1993), 38–39. That pattern was true also for Jews who wrote in Yiddish and/or Hebrew. See also, David Biale, *Power and Powerlessness in Jewish History* (New York: Schocken, 1986), 64–67. Jacob Katz, *Tradition and Crisis: Jewish Society at the End of the Middle Ages* (1958, repr. Syracuse, NY: Syracuse University Press, 2000), 44–51.

35. Gil Ribak, *Gentile New York: The Images of Non-Jews among Jewish Immigrants* (New Brunswick, NJ: Rutgers University Press, 2012).

36. An excellent overview of the topic is in Gary Gerstle, "Liberty, Coercion, and the Making of Americans," *Journal of American History* 84 (1997): 524–58. See also, Higham, *Strangers in the Land*, 97–105, 136–44, 186–93, 234–63. Todd J. Pfannestiel, *Rethinking the Red Scare: The Lusk Committee and New York's Crusade Against Radicalism, 1919–1923* (New York: Routledge, 2003), 123–33. Noah Pickus, *True Faith and Allegiance: Immigration and American Civic Nationalism* (Princeton, NJ: Princeton University Press, 2005), 3–4, 107–23. Cecilia Elizabeth O'Leary, *To Die For: The Paradox of American Nationalism* (Princeton, NJ: Princeton University Press, 1999), 220–45. See also, Morawska, "A Replica of the 'Old-Country'"; idem, "From Myth to Reality"; Rosoli, "From 'Promised Land' to 'Bitter Land.'"

Bibliography

Abend-blat, Dec. 6, 1895.

———, Dec. 16, 1895.

Abramovitch, Hirsh. *Farshvundene geshtaltn: zikhroynes un siluetn.* Buenos Aires: Tsentral farband fun poylishe yidn in argentine, 1958.

Aleichem, Sholem. "Dos meserl" (The Pocketknife) in *Ale verk fun Sholem Aleichem,* Vol. 7. New York: Sholem Aleichem folksfond oysgabe, 1925.

Alroey, Gur. *Ha-ma'hapecha ha-shketah: ha-hagirah ha-yehudit me-ha'imperiya ha-rusit, 1875–1924.* Jerusalem: Zalman Shazar, 2008.

"America," *Ha-magid*, Feb. 1, 1865.

American Jewish Year Book 5676 (1915–16).

An-ski S. (Shloyme Zaynvl Rapoport). "Khurbm galitsye." In *Gezamlte shrift*, 4:10–14. Warsaw: Farlag An-ski, 1925.

Antin, Mary. *The Promised Land.* New York: Penguin, 1997. First published 1912.

Asbury, Herbert. *The Gangs of New York: An Informal History of the Underworld.* New York: Alfred Knopf, 1928.

Aschheim, Steven. *Brothers and Strangers: The East European Jew in German and German Jewish Consciousness, 1800–1923.* Madison: University of Wisconsin Press, 1982.

Avrich, Paul. *Anarchist Portraits.* Princeton: Princeton University Press, 1988.

Barkai, Avraham. *Branching Out: German-Jewish Immigration to the United States, 1820–1914.* New York: Holmes & Meier, 1994.

Bartal, Israel. "The Image of Germany and German Jewry in East European Jewish Society during the 19th Century." In *Danzig, Between East and West: Aspects of Modern Jewish History*, edited by Isadore Twersky, 3–17. Cambridge, MA: Harvard University Press, 1985.

Beneqvit, I. A. *Durkhgelebt un durkhgetrakht.* New York: Kultur federatsye, 1934.

Biale, David. *Power and Powerlessness in Jewish History.* New York: Schocken, 1986.

Bodnar, John. *The Transplanted: A History of Immigration in Urban America.* Bloomington: Indiana University Press, 1985.

Bogen, Boris D. *Born a Jew.* New York: Macmillan, 1930.

Borgenicht, Louis. *The Happiest Man: The Life of Louis Borgenicht as Told to Harold Friedman.* New York: Putnam's Sons, 1942.

Brinkmann, Tobias. "'German Jews?': Reassessing the History of Nineteenth-Century Jewish Immigrants in the United States." In *Transnational Traditions: New Perspectives on American Jewish History*, edited by Ava F. Kahn and Adam D. Mendelsohn, 144–64. Detroit: Wayne State University Press, 2014.

Burgin, H. "Vemen zolen mir vinshen zig?" Aug. 20, 1914.

Cahan, Abraham. *Bleter fun mayn lebn.* New York: Forverts, 1926.

"Chicago." *Ha-tsefirah*, July 15, 1884.

"Chronicles." *Ha-tsefirah*, July 26, 1881.

Cohen, Jocelyn, and Daniel Soyer, eds. and trans. *My Future Is in America: Autobiographies of Eastern European Jewish Immigrants*. New York: New York University Press, in conjunction with the YIVO Institute for Jewish Research, 2006.

Cohen, Naomi W. "American Jewish Reactions to Anti-Semitism in Western Europe, 1875–1900." *Proceedings of the American Academy for Jewish Research* 45 (1978): 29–65.

———. *Encounter with Emancipation: The German Jews in the United States, 1830–1914*. Philadelphia: Jewish Publication Society, 1984.

"Daytshland shlogt ale yidishe sonim." *Yidishes Tageblat*, Dec. 15, 1916.

"Di simkhe bay estraykhishe yidn." *Morgen zhurnal*, June 24, 1915.

Di yidishe landsmanshaftn fun nu york. New York: Yiddish Writers' Union, 1938.

Diamond, Jack J. "A Reader in the Demography of American Jews." *American Jewish Year Book* 77 (1977): 251–319.

Diner, Hasia R. "Before the Promised City: Eastern European Jews in America Before 1880." In *An Inventory of Promises: Essays on American Jewish History in Honor of Moses Rischin*, edited by Jeffrey S. Gurock and Marc Lee Raphael, 43–62. New York: Carlson, 1995.

———. *The Jews of the United States, 1654 to 2000*. Berkeley: University of California Press, 2004.

"Dytshe blindkayt." *Tog*, March 31, 1917.

Eisenstein, Yehuda David. *Otsar zikhronotay*. New York: Self-published, 1929.

Engelman, Morris. *Four Years of Relief and War Work by the Jews of America, 1914–1918*. New York: Shoen, 1918.

"England maynt oykh nit di hagode." *Forverts*, Aug. 7, 1914.

"Estraykh un ire slavishe Felker." *Forverts*, July 31, 1914.

"The Fanatics' Recklessness in Germany." *Ha-tsefirah*, Jan. 11, 1881.

Forverts, April 24, 1915.

———, Aug. 6, 1915.

Der fraynd, March, 1911.

———, Aug. 1917.

"Galitsyaner vinshen tsu nikolay'en un litvakes zogen 'amen.'" *Forverts*, July 31, 1914.

Gartner, Lloyd P. "Jewish Migrants en Route from Europe to North America: Traditions and Realities." *Jewish History* 1 (1986): 49–67.

Gerstle, Gary. "Liberty, Coercion, and the Making of Americans." *Journal of American History* 84 (1997): 524–58.

Glanz, Rudolf. *Studies in Judaica Americana*. New York: Ktav, 1970.

Glazier, Ira, ed. *Migration from the Russian Empire: Lists of Passengers Arriving at U.S. Ports*. Baltimore: Genealogical Publishing Co., 1997.

Goldman, Emma. *Living My Life*. New York: Alfred Knopf, 1931.

Gompers, Samuel. *Seventy Years of Life and Labor*. New York: Dutton & Co., 1925.

Gordon, Adi, and Gil Ribak. "German-Jewish Migration to the United States." In

Germany and the Americas: Culture, Politics and History, edited by Thomas Adam, 13–22. Santa Barbara: ABC-Clio, 2005.

Gotesfeld, Khone. *Vos ikh gedenk fun mayn lebn*. New York: Fareynikte galitsyaner yidn in amerike, 1960.

Greenfeld, Judith. "The Role of the Jews in the Development of the Clothing Industry." *YIVO Annual* 2–3 (1947–48): 180–204.

Grill, Tobias. "'Pioneers of Germanness in the East'? Jewish-German, German, and Slavic Perceptions of East European Jewry during the First World War." In *Jews and Germans in Eastern Europe: Shared and Comparative Histories*, edited by Tobias Grill, 125–59. Oldenbourg, Germany: De Gruyter, 2018.

Grinstein, Hyman B. *The Rise of the Jewish Community of New York, 1654–1860*. Philadelphia: Jewish Publication Society, 1945.

Der Groyser kundes (Big Stick), Aug. 7, 1914.

———, Oct. 13, 1914.

———, July 20, 1917.

Ha-'Ivry, Nov. 22, 1895.

Hapgood, Hutchins. *The Spirit of the Ghetto*. New York: Schocken, 1965. First published 1902.

Harkavy, Alexander. *Prakim me-khayay*. New York: Hebrew Publishing, 1935.

Ha-tekhiya, Feb. 23, 1900.

Ha-tsefirah, July 29, 1884.

———, Oct. 21, 1884.

———, Dec. 26, 1895.

———, Jan. 2, 1896.

———, Jan. 3, 1896.

———, Jan. 7, 1896.

Higham, John. *Strangers in the Land: Patterns of American Nativism, 1860–1925*. New York: Atheneum, 1978. First published 1955.

Hillquit, Morris. *Loose Leaves from a Busy Life*. New York: Rand School, 1934.

Hoedl, Klaus. *Vom Shtetl an die Lower East Side*. Vienna: Boehlau, 1991.

Hoffman (Tsivyen), B. *Fuftzik yor kloakmakher yunyon, 1886–1936*. New York: Cloak Operators Union Local 117, 1936.

Horch, Hans Otto. "Le-toldotav shel ha-'Allgemeine Zeitung des Judenthums." *Kesher* 5 (1989): 12–20.

"The Jewish Question." *Ha-magid*, March 2, 1881.

Kabakoff, Jacob. "The Role of Wolf Schur as Hebraist and Zionist." In *Essays in American Jewish History*, 425–56. No editor; Cincinnati: American Jewish Archives, 1958.

Kaganoff, Nathan M. "The Jewish Landsmanshaftn in New York City in the Period Preceding World War I." *American Jewish History* 76 (1986): 56–66.

Kahan, Yoysef. *Di Yidish-anarkhistishe bavegung in amerike*. Philadelphia: Radical Library, Workmen's Circle, 1945.

Kamphoefner, Walter D. et al., eds. *News from the Land of Freedom: German Immigrants Write Home*. Translated from the German by Susan Carter Vogel. Ithaca, NY: Cornell University Press, 1991.

Katz, Jacob. *Tradition and Crisis: Jewish Society at the End of the Middle Ages*. Syracuse, NY: Syracuse University Press, 2000. Originally printed 1958.

Keil, Hartmut. "German Working-Class Radicalism after the Civil War." In *The German-American Encounter: Conflict and Cooperation between Two Cultures, 1800–2000*, edited by Frank Trommler and Elliot Shore, 37–48. New York: Berghahn, 2001.

Kennedy, David M. *Over Here: The First World War and American Society*. New York: Oxford University Press, 1980.

Khaykin, Y. *Yidishe bleter in amerike*. New York: Self-published, 1946.

Kieval, Hillel J. "Neighbors, Strangers, Readers: The Village and the City in Jewish-Gentile Conflict at the Turn of the Nineteenth Century." *Jewish Studies Quarterly* 12 (2005): 61–79.

Klier, John D. "Emigration Mania in Late Imperial Russia: Legend and Reality." In *Patterns of Migration, 1850–1914*, edited by Aubrey Newman and Stephen W. Massil, 21–29. London: Jewish Historical Society of England, 1996.

———. *Imperial Russia's Jewish Question, 1855–1881*. Cambridge, UK: Cambridge University Press, 1995.

Kopelov, Y. *Amol in amerike*. Warsaw: Brzoza, 1928.

Kotlyor, Abraham. *Derekh 'erets ha-khadasha*. Warsaw: Shapiro, 1898.

Levin, Shmaryahu. *Me-zichronot chayai*. Translated by Z. Vislevsky. Tel Aviv: Dvir, 1935.

Liulevicius, Vejas Gabriel. *War Land on the Eastern Front: Culture, National Identity, and the German Occupation in World War I*. Cambridge, UK: Cambridge University Press, 2000.

Lohr, Eric. *Nationalizing the Russian Empire: The Campaign Against Enemy Aliens During World War I*. Cambridge, MA: Harvard University Press, 2003.

Magidov, Yankev. "A getsvungener krig." *Morgen zhurnal*, Aug. 3, 1914.

———. *Der shpigl fun der ist sayd*. New York: Self-published, 1923).

Malachi, E. R., ed. *'Igrot sofrim*. New York: Dr. Shmuel Miller's Publication, 1931.

Margolies, Morris B. "The American Career of Rabbi Henry Vidaver." *Western States Jewish Historical Quarterly* 16 (1983): 30–43.

Margoshes, Yoysef. *Erinerungen fun mayn lebn*. New York: Max Mayzel Farlag, 1936.

McCune, Mary. "*The Whole Wide World without Limits*": *International Relief, Gender Politics, and American Jewish Women, 1890–1913*. Detroit: Wayne State University Press, 2005.

Mendelsohn, Ezra. *On Modern Jewish Politics*. New York: Oxford University Press, 1993.

Michels, Tony. *A Fire in Their Hearts: Yiddish Socialists in New York*. Cambridge, MA: Harvard University Press, 2005.

Milwaukee Sentinel, Dec. 16, 1895.

"Minneapolis." *Ha-tsefirah*, Nov. 5, 1891.

Mintz, Matityahu, ed. *'Igrot ber borokhov, 1897–1914*. Tel Aviv: Am Oved, 1989.

Morawska, Ewa. "A Replica of the 'Old-Country' Relationship in the Ethnic Niche: East European Jews and Gentiles in Small-Town Western Pennsylvania, 1880s–1930s." *American Jewish History* 77 (1987): 27–86.

———. "From Myth to Reality: America in the Eyes of East European Peasant Migrant Laborers." In *Distant Magnets: Expectations and Realities in the Immigrant Experience, 1840–1930*, edited by Dirk Hoerder and Horst Roessler, 241–63. New York: Holmes & Meier, 1993.

Nadel, Stanley. "From the Barricades of Paris to the Streets of New York: German Artisans and the European Roots of American Labor Radicalism." *Labor History* 30 (1989): 47–75.

———. "Jewish Race and German Soul in Nineteenth Century America." *American Jewish History* 77 (1987): 6–26.

———. *Little Germany: Ethnicity, Religion and Class in New York City, 1845–1880.* Urbana: University of Illinois Press, 1990.

Nadell, Pamela. "The Journey to America by Steam: The Jews of Eastern Europe in Transition." *American Jewish History* 71 (1981): 269–84.

Newman, Louis I., ed. and trans., in collaboration with Samuel Spitz. *The Hasidic Anthology: Tales and Teachings of the Hasidim.* New York: Bloch, 1944.

New York Times, Nov. 22, 1895.

———, Dec. 4, 1895.

———, Dec. 9, 1895.

———, Dec. 13, 1895.

———, Dec. 15, 1895.

———, May 2, 1915.

"North America." *Allgemeine Zeitung des Judenthums*, March 28, 1865.

Not a Daytsh. *Kol mevaser* [in Yiddish], Dec. 1, 1870.

O'Leary, Cecilia Elizabeth. *To Die For: The Paradox of American Nationalism.* Princeton, NJ: Princeton University Press, 1999.

"Observer of the Jewish People." *Ha-tsefirah*, Jan. 3, 1882.

Paperna, Avaraham Ya'akov. *Kol ha-ktavim.* Edited by Israel Zmora. Tel Aviv: Machbarot le-sifrut, 1952.

———. "Letters from Warsaw" [in Hebrew]. *Ha-karmel*, March 9, 1868.

Parlamentarishe ruls vi tsu firen mitingen fun yunyons, lodzhen, un andere faraynen. New York: Arbeter tsaytung, 1891.

Pfannestiel, Todd J. *Rethinking the Red Scare: The Lusk Committee and New York's Crusade Against Radicalism, 1919–1923.* New York: Routledge, 2003.

Pickus, Noah. *True Faith and Allegiance: Immigration and American Civic Nationalism.* Princeton, NJ: Princeton University Press, 2005.

"Prussia." *Ha-tsefirah*, May 8, 1862.

Pulzer, Peter. *The Rise of Political Anti-Semitism in Germany & Austria.* Rev. ed. Cambridge, MA: Harvard University Press, 1988. Originally published 1964.

Rappaport, Joseph. *Hands Across the Sea: Jewish Immigrants and World War I.* Lanham, MD: Hamilton Books, 2005.

Reyzin, Abraham. *Epizodn fun mayn lebn.* Vilna: Kletzkin, 1929.

Ribak, Gil. "'A Victory of the Slavs Means a Deathblow to Democracy': The Onset of World War I and the Images of the Warring Sides among Jewish Immigrants in New York, 1914–1916." In *War and Peace in Jewish Tradition: From the Ancient World to the Present,* edited by Yigal Levin and Amnon Shapira, 203–17. Oxford, UK: Routledge, 2012.

———. "'Beaten to Death by Irish Murderers': The Death of Sadie Dellon (1918) and Jewish Images of the Irish." *Journal of American Ethnic History* 32 (2013): 41–74.

———. *Gentile New York: The Images of Non-Jews among Jewish Immigrants.* New Brunswick, NJ: Rutgers University Press, 2012.

"Riots against the Jews in Germany." *Ha-tsefirah,* March 18, 1884.

Rolnik, Yoysef. *Zikhroynes.* New York: With the help of the David Ignatoff Fund, 1954.

Roosevelt, Theodore. *An Autobiography.* Charleston, SC: BiblioBazaar, 2007. Originally published 1913.

Rosoli, Gianfausto. "From 'Promised Land' to 'Bitter Land': Italian Migrants and the Transformation of a Myth." In *Distant Magnets: Expectations and Realities in the Immigrant Experience, 1840–1930,* edited by Dirk Hoerder and Horst Roessler, 222–40. New York: Holmes & Meier, 1993.

Sanders, Ronald. *The Lower East Side Jews: An Immigrant Generation.* Formerly titled *The Downtown Jews.* 1969. Corrected edition 1987; repr. Mineola, NY: Dover, 1999.

Schappes, Morris U. "The Political Origins of the United Hebrew Trades." *Journal of Ethnic Studies* 5 (1977): 13–41.

Schumacher-Brunhes, Marie. "The Figure of the Daytsh in Yiddish Literature." In *Jews and Germans in Eastern Europe: Shared and Comparative Histories,* edited by Tobias Grill, 72–87. Oldenbourg, Germany: De Gruyter, 2018.

Shub, Dovid. *Fun di amolike yorn.* New York: Cyco, 1970.

Slezkine, Yuri. *The Jewish Century.* Princeton, NJ: Princeton University Press, 2004.

Slutsky, Yehuda. *Ha-'itonut ha-yehudit-rusit ba-me'ah ha-tsha-'esre.* Jerusalem: Bialik, 1970.

Soyer, Daniel. *Jewish Immigrant Associations and American Identity in New York, 1880–1939.* 1997. Reprint, Detroit: Wayne State University, 2001.

Spektor, Mordkhe. *Mayn lebn.* Warsaw: Achisefer, 1927.

Stanislawski, Michael. *A Murder in Lemberg: Politics, Religion, and Violence in Modern Jewish History.* Princeton: Princeton University Press, 2007.

———. *Tsar Nicholas I and the Jews: The Transformation of Jewish Society in Russia, 1825–1855.* Philadelphia: Jewish Publication Society, 1983.

Stern, Norton B., and William M. Kramer, "What's the Matter with Warsaw?" *American Jewish Archives Journal* 37 (1985): 301–4.

Szajkowski, Zosa. *Jews, Wars, and Communism: The Attitude of American Jews in World War I, the Russian Revolutions of 1917, and Communism (1914–1945)*. New York: Ktav, 1972.

———. "Sufferings of Jewish Emigrants to America in Transit to America through Germany." *Jewish Social Studies* 39 (1977): 105–16.

Tashrak. "Nishto mer keyn daytshen in blotetown." *Yidishe gazetn*, March 30, 1917.

Ter, Yankev. "Der amerikaner arbiter." In *Natur un lebn*, 25–28. New York: Baron, 1898.

Tomashevsky, Boris. *Mayn lebns-geshikhte*. New York: Trio, 1937.

Tsipin, M. "Di estraykh-serbishe milkhome in dem higen galitsyaner-ungarishen kvartal." *Varhayt*, July 29, 1914.

Unger, Avrom Pinkhes. *Mayn heymshtetl strykov*. New York: Arbeter Ring, 1957.

Varhayt, Jan. 14, 1915.

Vaynberg, Chaim Leyb. *Fertzik yor in kamf far sotzialer bafrayung*. Los Angeles: Vaynberg bukh komitet, 1952.

Vaynshteyn, B. *Di yidishe yunyons in amerike*. New York: Fareynigte yidishe geverkshaftn, 1929.

———. *Fertsik yor in der yidisher arbeter bavegung*. New York: Veker, 1924.

Voices from Ellis Island [microform]: An Oral History of American Immigration: A Project of the Statue of Liberty-Ellis Island Foundation. Frederick, MD: University Publications of America, c. 1987. https://lccn.loc.gov/91955600.

Weinstein, Gregory. *The Ardent Eighties: Reminiscences of an Interesting Decade*. New York: International Press, 1928.

Weinstein, Helen. Interview, tape I-65. *NYC Immigrant Labor History Project*. New York: Tamiment Institute, New York University.

Weisgal, Meyer. *So Far: An Autobiography*. New York: Random House, 1971.

Weisser, Michael R. *A Brotherhood of Memory: Jewish Landsmanshaftn in the New World*. New York: Basic, 1985.

Werses, Shmuel. *Hakitsa 'ami: sifrut ha-haskalah be-'eedan ha-modernizatsya*. Jerusalem: Magnes, 2001.

Wertheimer, Jack. *Unwelcome Strangers: East European Jews in Imperial Germany*. New York: Oxford University Press, 1987.

Wise, Stephen S. *Challenging Years: The Autobiography of Stephen Wise*. New York: G. P. Putnam's Sons, 1949.

Wittke, Carl. *The German-Language Press in America*. Frankfort: University of Kentucky Press, 1957.

"Woe Is Me." *Ha-tsefirah*, Sept. 4, 1883.

Yanovsky, Shoel. *Ershte yorn fun yidishn frayhaytlekhen sotzialism*. New York: Fraye arbeter shtime, 1948.

"Yetst iz er a 'daytsh.'" *Forverts*, Aug. 11, 1915.

Yidishe gazetn, Nov. 29, 1895.

———, Dec. 6, 1895.

————, Dec. 13, 1895.

————, Dec. 20, 1895.

Yidishes tageblat, June 12, 1899.

————, Sept. 8, 1915.

Yudisher emigrant (St. Petersburg), Nov. 27, 1908.

————, May 28, 1912.

Zeldin, A. "Di legend vegen daytshe gvures." *Tog*, April 14, 1916.

Zevin, Shlomo Yosef. *Sipurei Chasidim*. Tel Aviv: Avraham Tsiyoni, 1955.

Zevin, Y. Y. *Tashrak's beste ertselungen*. 5th ed. New York: Hebrew Publishing Company, 1929. Originally published 1910.

Zhitlovsky, Chaim. *Zikhroynes fun mayn lebn*. New York: Zhitlovsky's Jubilee Committee, 1935.

Zinberg, Israel. *A History of Jewish Literature*. Cincinnati and New York: Hebrew Union College Press and Ktav Publishing, 1977–78.

Other Maps: Reflections on European Jewish Refugees' Migration to the United States in the Early Postwar Era[1]

by Libby Garland

HE REFUGEE AND THE SOCIAL WORKER

In June 1954, Ann Petluck of the United Service of New Americans (USNA) spoke in Toronto at a conference of non-governmental organizations. Her talk, "Activities of Non-Governmental Organizations on Behalf of Migrants in Their Capacities as Aliens," took listeners through the complex logistical and legal work that aid organizations like hers had been doing during the postwar era. Petluck, the Assistant Executive Director of the USNA, spoke from her long experience as a lawyer, social worker and immigrant advocate. The USNA was part of a network of US-based Jewish organizations, including the Hebrew Immigrant Aid Society (HIAS) and the American Joint Distribution Committee (JDC), that provided critical assistance to Jewish migrants in the postwar world, from locating relatives to navigating documentary requirements to providing advocacy vis-à-vis government authorities.[2]

Petluck, perhaps to make up for her talk's unwieldy title (it was "rather formidable," she conceded to her audience) opened with an anecdote that she called "a classic story" about a refugee talking with a social worker about the matter of where he might go:

> They have before them a map of the world and they are discussing the requirements for the various countries of immigration. As they go over the requirements for each country, it becomes apparent that

> this poor man would not be eligible. At last in despair he turns to the
> worker and says: "Haven't you any more maps?"[3]

This brief Borgesian parable of cartographic wishfulness was clearly meant to illustrate something. Petluck did not, however, explain what. Instead, she left the story hanging, briskly moving on to her lawyerly summary of the work conducted by agencies like her own. I, however, want to pause and consider this cryptic, apocryphal opener because its ambiguities capture some important dynamics in the larger story about postwar migration that Petluck was discussing that day. The tale seems meant to speak wryly, at the expense of a naïve refugee who refuses to grasp geopolitical realities, to the intense challenges faced by the staff of organizations like Petluck's, which were trying to assist their clients in a postwar world of nation-states that tightly controlled passage across their borders.

Whether Petluck intended it or not, though, the tale suggests other interpretations. The exchange between refugee and social worker, and, in particular, the refugee's question—*Haven't you any more maps?*—contains complicated layers of desperation and possibility. To be sure, the question points the social worker, and us, toward the constraints presented by the global order of sovereign states that sought to control the movements of people. The question also, however, simultaneously points beyond these constraints, toward the resourcefulness, stubbornness, imagination, and labor that were as essential to making migration happen as trains or ships. Fictional or no, the refugee's question is neither idle nor naïve. Even in the highly bounded mid-twentieth-century world, migration and the rules that governed it were profoundly contested terrain. The meanings of those maps the refugee and social worker were poring over were not static, nor were they solely determined by the decrees of states. Jewish refugees and US Jewish aid organizations understood, like the refugee in Petluck's story understood, that other maps were possible, that the meaning of borders and legal requirements could be contested. They understood that the parameters of the international migratory regime—documents and bureaucracies meant to assert territorial sovereignty—were fundamentally unstable when seen from up close. Aid groups leveraged that instability as best they could to push and pull at that migration regime on behalf of their Jewish refugee clients. And the aid groups in turn were pushed from below by those clients, who never stopped insisting on the need for alternative maps.

This chapter explores stories found among the vast records of American Jewish aid groups working after World War II with European Jewish refugees who hoped to make their home in the United States. It considers the sorts of granular moments that Petluck's story presents. The ways that refugees and the staff of aid agencies confronted massive legal and logistical barriers to migration, and scrambled to construct paths of mobility around or through them, matter greatly. At war's end and for many years afterwards, it was unclear where European Jews who survived the war would make their homes. Hundreds of thousands ultimately made their way to Palestine and then, after 1948, the state of Israel; others went to places such as Canada, South Africa, or Latin American countries. A large number of Jewish refugees, however, hoped to reach the United States, where many had family.[4] That many succeeded in doing so is a testament to the efforts of refugee advocates, and to these refugees and their families themselves. It is these stories of those Jews hoping to get from Europe to the United States, and of their advocates, that I focus on here. The offices of Jewish aid organizations in the United States and abroad, where people came for help in navigating the legal and documentary parameters of migration; the correspondence surrounding the cases of refugees threatened with exclusion or deportation; the meetings advocacy organizations' staff held with officials to hash out the specific meanings of government policies—all of these were spaces in which postwar Jewish migration to the United States was effected or blocked, one person, family, document, decision, or policy at a time.

The period after World War II marked an important turning point for US immigration policy toward refugees, a moment in which the state began to make new large-scale commitments—however qualified and grudging—to accepting foreign victims of persecution, and to defining "refugees" as different from other immigrants.[5] In the immediate postwar era, US law and policy created new possibilities for refugees to migrate to the United States, and many of the 137,000 Jews who arrived in the United States between 1945 and 1952 came because of these measures.[6] But these partial openings in an intensely restrictive immigration system did not, by themselves, make Jewish migration to the United States happen. The intense labor of refugees and aid groups, in the face of chaotic places, policies, and bureaucracies, made migration happen. This dynamic is not unique to the history of Jewish refugees or to postwar Europe. Rather, it is important to see how Jewish refugees and the organizations that advocated for them participated in a larger history of people on the move pushing hard at the closed system of national borders. Many scholars have explored the way the postwar European refugee crisis—the vexing "problem" of displaced people who fit nowhere into the world order—became central to the production of the modern refugee regime, a system rife with contradictions, limitations, and possibilities.[7] But whatever set of possibilities for migration this regime presented, migration was not merely something that happened to refugees and their advocates. The cumulative force of these people's individual and collective labor, too, was critical in forcing open those possibilities—in making the maps meet their needs.

The behind-the-scenes moments of such labor spill out everywhere in the archival record. If such moments make it clear that state polices, by themselves, did not (and do not) produce migration, they nevertheless resist being easily shaped into or conveyed by larger-scale narratives of historical change.[8] But the masses of paper left behind by Ann Petluck and her colleagues—piles upon piles of paper—can also invite us to sit with the smaller moments contained within them. The frameworks of refugee studies and border studies are useful here in pointing us to the meanings such moments might hold. Like the refugee in Petluck's story, scholars in these fields remind us not to take the concepts of nation-states, territorial sovereignty, borders and the rules governing migration across them, simply as givens, or as the natural backdrop to history. Indeed, refugees' histories by definition "cut across the cartographic logic of the territorial state," disrupting the tidy "imagination of the world as a world of the modern state-system," in which the relationships between states, citizens and territories are assumed to be clearly defined, and the default mode of organizing people's connection to place.[9] Jewish aid organizations and the refugees they worked with *had* to understand that the orderliness of the world as rendered in maps was misleading, and that they were operating on contested and unstable terrain. Indeed, they used that contested realm as the space within which they could press their cases for mobility.

A NOTE ON THE TERM "REFUGEE"

In keeping with the project of unpacking Ann Petluck's story, I often refer to the Jewish migrants I discuss here as "refugees," meaning, broadly, that they were people who had been "forced outside the political community indefinitely." Many had been deported to Nazi concentration and death camps, or were fleeing postwar persecution, and were in need of safe passage and safe haven.[10] "Refugee" is, however, always a problematic term. Even as it points to the instability of the political and legal status of those it describes, the word "refugee" obscures the instability of its own meanings. It homogenizes and erases identities and experiences, as the generic naming (and namelessness) of "the refugee" in Petluck's story suggests.[11] And like "borders" and "nation," it is a term that has not tended to be the object of analysis for historians of American Jewish immigration.[12] But "refugee" is always a term marked by conceptual struggle. Indeed, after World War II, an often-bewildering number of terms flew around in reference to those violently uprooted during the war and by postwar upheavals: *refugees, deportees, stateless persons, expellees, persecutees.* "Displaced persons," or DPs, another term I use here in keeping with the language of the time, was a multipronged category. The Allies initially deployed the term in the context of their plans to repatriate the millions of deported and expelled civilians in the zones of Europe their militaries occupied. Later, "displaced persons" came to refer to those for whom the Allies took some responsibility for maintaining and resettling. It was used more loosely, as well, in more general discussions about the human dislocation caused by the war.[13]

The related term, "refugee," sometimes used interchangeably with "displaced person" or other terms, was also a concept in flux. If "refugee" often signified abjection, helplessness and need, it was also becoming more firmly linked in this era to the idea that at least certain violently displaced and persecuted people could make claims on sovereign nations—an idea enshrined in the 1951 Geneva Convention Relating to the Status of Refugees.[14] Being deemed a refugee was a position of desperation, but it also conferred a status that could serve as a potential key to otherwise locked doors of nation-states' borders. This was so even as refugees' need for asylum was never recognized as taking precedence over nations' right to control migration.[15]

Other scholars have ably explored the tense debates over who in postwar Europe, as well as in the many other places where millions of people were dislocated by the war, would count as "legitimate" refugees or displaced persons and who—particularly outside of Europe—would not, and what implications the outcome of such debates held for governments, occupying forces, aid organizations, and migrants themselves.[16] What I want to highlight here is the way that staking a claim to mobility as a "refugee" or "displaced person" came with no guarantee of recognition, and was rarely clear-cut. It was generally a labor-intensive, drawn-out process. In the postwar era, Jewish migrants and American Jewish aid organizations were central to the project of making such claims. These claims had to be forged not just once but, as those piles and piles of archived paper show, at many points, in a multitude of documents, applications, and hearings.

AMERICAN JEWISH AID ORGANIZATIONS
IN ALLIED OCCUPATION ZONES

In early 1945, as hostilities stuttered to an end in Europe, social worker and migration expert Cecilia Razovsky Davidson arrived in France. On the strength of her decades of experience heading up immigration and refugee work with groups including the National Council for Jewish Women and the National Refugee Service, Razovsky Davidson was hired as a Displaced Persons Specialist with the United Nations Relief and Rehabilitation Agency (UNRRA). This was the US-led international organization established in 1943 to address the humanitarian needs of war refugees and war-battered nations. The UNRRA, in turn, loaned Razovsky Davidson to the JDC, which was operating an office in Paris. No one could be more prepared for the job than Razovsky Davidson. "I must admit that the work is just the right kind for me in view of my past training," she wrote in a letter after her first month in Paris. "I get a great deal of satisfaction from it."[17] Still, setting up a refugee aid operation in war-ravaged France was a seemingly Sisyphean task. Office supplies like typewriters and erasers were scarce; severe food shortages meant that office staff sometimes fainted from hunger. Razovsky Davidson herself constantly battled severe gastrointestinal troubles brought on by the meager diet.[18] And the task—the scale of the human displacement that aid workers like Razovsky Davidson were there to address—was daunting. The entire region was a migratory zone. "Every place we went we would see groups of people marching along," Razovsky Davidson said, describing displaced persons who "have left some camp and are on their way somewhere."[19]

Razovsky Davidson was witnessing but a small proportion of the staggering numbers of people World War II and its aftermath had violently displaced across multiple continents. In Europe alone, in early 1945, tens of millions of people were in motion—ethnic German "expellees" from eastern Europe, eastern Europeans brought as forced laborers to Germany by the Nazi regime, concentration camp survivors, prisoners of war, and others. It was and remains unclear exactly how to count the populations of the displaced. The Allied forces reckoned that they would take responsibility for repatriating something on the order of eight million displaced people in the European territories they now occupied; those millions of people who were displaced but defined as belonging to the nationality of former enemies did not fall into this category. Millions were repatriated to eastern Europe, sometimes forcibly, many unwillingly.[20] By late 1945, however, about a million people deemed "unrepatriable," including Jewish death camp survivors along with others who were understood to be threatened with persecution should they return home, remained marooned in the occupied zones. Among them were about 100,000 Jews. Over the next few years many more Jews fled violence in Poland and elsewhere in the region for the Allied occupied zone, eventually bringing the number of Jewish refugees in that zone to somewhere around 300,000, largely concentrated in Germany.[21]

The organizations seeking to render aid and facilitate migration worked, in many ways, in close partnership with state actors, both military and civilian, which understood that the funds and machinery of these groups would be critical to their larger objectives of bringing order and stability to the region. Cecilia Razovsky Davidson and the JDC, along with HIAS and other American Jewish organizations, were an integral part of what historian Stephen Porter calls the "benevolent empire," the expanding network of non-governmental organizations that helped realize a new US project of humanitarian interventionism. This project melded the ideas and practices of the New Deal welfare state with the enlarged role the United States assumed in foreign affairs.[22] The state relied on voluntary agencies to perform a critical portion of this humanitarian labor. They brought their professional expertise in social work, relief, and migration to the work they did in conjunction with the UNRRA and Allied military forces to manage the flow of people and humanitarian aid.[23] Jewish agencies, with their decades of experience in such international work, provided a model for what large-scale non-governmental humanitarian engagement might look like.[24]

In particular, American Jewish groups' expertise on migration issues proved crucial in their work with the region's Jewish refugees.[25] Razovsky Davidson and her colleagues were on intimate terms with the endlessly complicated terrain of US immigration policy and procedures, and had experience working in trying conditions and coordinating with each other across international divides. As Petluck's tale reminds us, the interactions of these organizations and refugees could be fraught with tension. Refugees did not always trust the social workers and other staff they encountered. They faced condescending or pathologizing attitudes. They often became frustrated with organizations' limitations to help them. Still, the JDC, HIAS, and other American Jewish organizations played a key role mediating the bureaucratic and legal structures of migration, as they did in providing other forms of aid. Thus, many refugees found themselves turning to these groups, even if they had to push for what they wanted and needed, as the refugee in Petluck's story was doing when he was unwilling to accept the limitations of the social worker's maps.

FINDING RELATIVES AND ESTABLISHING
CONTACT ACROSS BORDERS

The most urgent imperative at war's end for most of the displaced was getting back in touch with loved ones.[26] Conveying information across vast and fragmented geographic terrain was a desperately complicated task. In the wake of the war, communications in much of Europe were in shambles. There was no reliable postal service. Survivors used whatever means they could devise to find those from whom they had been separated. In the Allied occupied zones, refugees trekked on foot from camp to camp, posting announcements in public spaces and newspapers, and making inquiries by word of mouth.[27] And as Petluck's anecdotal refugee would have known well, borders and immigration laws were not the only hurdles for those Jewish refugees in Europe who wished to emigrate to the United States or elsewhere. There was, first, the need to find family members abroad—those to whom refugees might go, and who could help with money, transportation, and the thicket of legal documents. The re-establishing of personal communication networks was a critical first step in migration. Information, messages, and documents often had to cross borders before people could. But communication, like people, did not just flow. Transnational communication pathways had to be painstakingly assembled— created where there were none. Aid organizations, and refugees themselves, were integral to this process.

Just as they used whatever means they could to locate loved ones who might still be in Europe, so refugees used whatever avenues they could devise in order to find relatives farther abroad. In November 1945, for example, a Jewish refugee in Italy wrote the New York-based *Forverts* with a plea for the newspaper to help him find family members in the United States.[28] American soldiers were another possible conduit of information across the Atlantic. Rita Benmayor, a Greek Jew, told the psychologist David Boder, who interviewed her in Paris in 1946, that she had asked a Greek-American GI she met to try to contact her uncle. All Benmayor knew was her uncle's name, and that he lived in Hartford, Connecticut. But somehow the soldier located him, and put the two in touch. The uncle organized the affidavit and other documents Benmayor needed.[29]

Many Jewish refugees, however, turned first to Jewish aid organizations, with their considerable logistical capacities, for assistance in finding relatives, whether in Europe or abroad, even as those relatives abroad often sought organizations' help in getting in touch with family they hoped had survived the war in Europe.[30] In April 1945, for example, a hundred and eighteen Jewish

concentration camp survivors, upon being liberated, wrote a collective letter to French military officials asking to be put in touch with the JDC. They
explained that they had relatives in "America, Russia, Palestine," and beyond,
and that "to bring us in contact with those [relatives] would be of inestimable
value." Razovsky Davidson described how Jewish survivors in Heidelberg put
messages for relatives around the world on small scraps of paper. Someone
enclosed the scraps in a wooden shoebox, and in that way the notes reached
JDC's Paris office.[31]

Putting families in touch across national divides, in the absence of
functioning communications systems, was obviously extremely complicated.
Razovsky Davidson described the improvisational channels the JDC was using
in 1945 to put Jewish refugees in displaced persons camps in touch with their
families elsewhere in the world: "Quakers going in with ambulances could usually take messages in and soldiers and chaplains could take messages out."[32]
Setting up systems to put people in contact required expertise in language,
geography, and information management.[33] Razovsky Davidson reported that
one of her very first projects on arriving in Paris was "setting up a Central File
and Card Index of special categories of Displaced Persons in France," a massive
undertaking that entailed creating "a Cardex for all inquiries from relatives
emanating from England and the Western Hemisphere concerning refugees
in France, Holland, Belgium, Roumania and Hungary."[34] Even after she left,
information remained in a chaotic state. "Lists with incomplete data seem to
circulate all over Europe without much rhyme or reason," lamented one JDC
worker in the late spring of 1945.[35] That summer, Razovsky Davidson reported
that the JDC's effort to set up a "national registry location for Germany," where
the great majority of Jewish refugees were congregating, was ongoing.[36]

As the years went on, families both within the United States and abroad
continued to seek help from the JDC and other organizations to find each
other, often as the first step in a migration process. "Hundreds of letters in all
languages reach the offices of United Service each week from survivors of Nazi
persecution who hopefully request help in locating relatives in this country,"
the USNA reported in 1948, and the organization needed "imagination and in-
genuity" to pursue the tenuous leads it had. Abram Gold, for example, looking
for his cousins Bernard and Louis Gold, could only tell the USNA that Bernard
was a barber and Louis a tailor. A USNA worker pursued the lead by getting
in touch with several local trade unions. Six were stumped, but a seventh,
in fact, was able to point the location worker toward Bernard, who in turn
was in touch with Louis. The two "were overjoyed to hear that [their cousin

Abram]" was still alive.[37] In their location work, American Jewish aid organizations coordinated with each other and their local partners, as well as with other US aid organizations.[38] They also worked with national and international initiatives to centralize data about displaced people such as the International Tracing Service, established after much wrangling and confusion in 1947 by the International Refugee Organization, the UNRRA's successor.[39]

To be sure, aid organizations' efforts at putting refugees in touch with relatives were sometimes a mess. Early on after the war, a large number of groups tried to provide tracing services, but without figuring out how to coordinate their data-gathering or location efforts with each other.[40] Refugees were frustrated by organizations' strict adherence to bureaucratic processes. And, not surprisingly given the challenges, location work often resulted in failure.[41] From January to November 1947, for example, the USNA got fifteen thousand queries; in the same period it successfully resolved six thousand, some of them from 1946.[42] Nevertheless, each contact demanded by refugees and their relatives, each contact established via the index cards and forms that aid agencies deployed to build their databases, was a critical step in creating the possibility for migration. This was not the doing of policy. It was not the work of states.[43] It was the persistence of refugees and their families, and the know-how and legwork of aid groups, that made this transnational flow of information possible.

A DOCUMENTARY MAZE

Establishing contact with loved ones abroad was, of course, just one step in creating the possibility for international migration. The fictional conversation between refugee and social worker with which this chapter began revolved around the barriers to migration posed by potential receiving nations' "requirements," which in practice meant—as it still means—a deeply frustrating bureaucratic bedlam of applications and documentation, one that took up enormous amounts of energy on the part of refugees and aid workers.[44] Aid agencies and refugees daily grappled with the fact that, as Ann Petluck noted in her 1954 speech in Toronto, the "right to move" was predicated on a brutally complicated process of acquiring documents and permissions. "We are living in a world," she observed, "where usually the mere crossing of a border entails the production of a travel document, the obtention of a visa to enter, plus a possible physical examination, plus fees, etc., etc. Often documents are required to leave, to pass through another country, and to enter."[45] This international system of controlling migration via passports and visas, and, as Aristide Zolberg puts it, "remote control" over would-be immigrants, had fully emerged in the interwar period, and the postwar world held to this regime of documentedness.[46] But what Jewish refugees and aid workers alike by necessity understood were the contradictions and chaos underlying the demands for documentedness, which in turn rested on a vision of a world with relationships between citizens and states that were as clear as lines on a map. Refugees, after all, were often stateless people without access to the sorts of official papers that states demanded for migration purposes. Those refugees and aid workers engaged in the daily labor of effecting migration not only understood that systems of migration control were rife with contradictions but also that leveraging this instability in the workings of government bureaucracy was often key to pressing people's cases for mobility.

In his remarks at the USNA's annual meeting in 1949, the organization's Executive Director Joseph Beck reflected on the substantial bureaucratic hurdles posed by the 1948 Displaced Persons Act. This law was a deep disappointment to the American Jewish activists who had played a key role in the coalition pushing for expanding refugee admissions postwar. It contained provisions that made it clearly stacked against Jewish refugees, such as giving preference to agricultural workers and requiring that applicants had to have been residing in Allied occupied territory by December 1945.[47] And while the law was nominally designed to admit more refugees to the United States, Beck explained, its documentary requirements "literally created a maze, a maze through which few newcomers have, up until this time, found their way."[48]

The United States already expected "regular" immigrants to pass through a massive obstacle course to obtain the documents the law had demanded of all immigrants since the 1920s, including individual affidavits of support and related financial documents from relatives in the United States. As Beck reminded his audience, thousands of Jewish refugees in Europe and elsewhere were applying for visas under this existing law. For those who might only be eligible through the Displaced Persons Act, the process of becoming documented was now even harder. The law required that a daunting array of documents had to be assembled and processed and shuttled among the appropriate authorities for refugees to be approved by all the relevant authorities. Affidavits from aid agencies pledging sponsorship of individuals, including guarantees of employment and housing, went to the newly established Displaced Persons Commission (DPC) first in Washington, then abroad. The DPC generated paperwork for each case. Photos, birth certificates, marriage certificates, police reports, and proof of residence in the occupied zones also had to go to the DPC, which in turn sent them to the military's Counter Intelligence Corps (CIC) for a security check. The next obstacle for refugees was a medical exam. After that, they could apply for a US visa under the Displaced Persons Act. More medical checks at the point of embarkation followed.[49]

The Displaced Persons Act was part of a multistage postwar response to the refugee crisis in which the United States conflictedly opened some new pathways to immigration for Jewish and other refugees.[50] In August 1945, Earl Harrison, former Commissioner of Immigration and Naturalization, issued a sharply critical report on the situation of DPs (particularly Jews) in the Allied occupied zones, urging that both Palestine and the United States provide more opportunities for refugee resettlement.[51] In December 1945, in the wake of that report, President Truman directed that DPs should get preference for visas under existing US immigration laws.[52] Approximately 28,000 Jewish refugees were able to enter on the basis of this directive.[53] An amended version of the Displaced Persons Act that passed in 1950 removed some of the provisions that made it hard for many Jewish refugees to qualify, including moving the cutoff date for presence in the Allied zone to January 1949.[54] It did not, however, make the documentary requirements any lighter, and, indeed, the National Security Act passed that same year now required that visa applicants be screened for any history with Communist organizations, which would disqualify them.[55]

Amidst all these changes, one thing remained constant: none of the processes connected with US migration control ran in smooth or consistent ways. Government bureaucracies were chaotic. Thus, one thing that achieving documentedness meant in actual practice was a perpetual quest for information and clarification. Sometimes nobody had answers, not even the government officials in charge. In June 1945, for example, Murray LeVine, Executive Director of HIAS's Philadelphia's office, reported on his meeting with an official at the State Department's Visa Division in Washington to try to pin down how refugees might obtain visas. LeVine and the officials discussed at length the nitty-gritty of which forms needed filing and with whom. The process of granting visas in Europe was "confused and experimental," LeVine wrote, with consulates still short-staffed. "Changes will come frequently," he warned his colleagues, as indeed they would.[56] HIAS workers were particularly baffled by the Visa Division's insistence that would-be immigrants obtain an exit visa from the country in which they found themselves before US officials would even begin the visa process. How this could work in practice was unclear. "We would like very much for you to send us at once a complete detailed description of how exit visas can be obtained before a destination visa is granted or promised," Ilja Dijour of the New York HIAS office wrote his Paris colleague. "We want to know all the formalities involved."[57]

Jewish aid organizations put an enormous amount of work into figuring out the documentary "formalities involved" and conveying them to their staff, who in turn helped refugee clients with these formalities as best they could. Hashing out such minutiae was time-consuming for aid organizations and maddening for refugees, but each point of negotiation mattered if the work was going to get done. If HIAS staff were frustrated after their meeting with the Visa Division about the demand for exit permits from refugees, they were at least able to get officials to confirm that applicants could continue to use the familiar affidavit forms that they had used before the war, and that they did not need to submit a certified copy of a sponsor's income tax to show that the prospective immigrant would not become a public charge.[58] New rules under Truman's 1945 order and the Displaced Persons Act allowed voluntary agencies to provide written guarantees of housing and employment for refugees themselves. These "corporate affidavits" were a major new effort to be coordinated, of course, and revealed just how much policies that seemed humanitarian on their face relied on the labor of aid agencies for their implementation. But they also helped make many refugees' migration more possible.[59] Form by filled-out form, then, aid organizations and their refugee clients constructed ways through the documentary maze.

Refugees themselves often had extensive experience in navigating the disconnects between their reality and officialdom's insistence on documentation and control. Leonard Dinnerstein writes about the lively industry of black market "document factories" in postwar Europe that provided an alternate mode of creating the papers that displaced persons needed for both everyday existence and migration purposes.[60] Such strategies were risky. The JDC reported that in the year after the war, some Jewish refugees in German DP camps and surrounding communities were arrested for unauthorized entry into the US occupied zone and for "possession of improper identification papers."[61] That refugees frequently took such risks suggests how necessary these were. Unauthorized movement and unsanctioned means of becoming documented were basic survival strategies.

The Displaced Persons Act of 1948 provided new impetus for refugees to obtain documents outside official channels, and to invent relationships to geography that those documents supposedly testified to. To be eligible for a visa under the law, refugees were supposed to prove that they had resided in the Allied zones since December 22, 1945.[62] But tens of thousands of Jews had come later, including a great many fleeing ongoing antisemitic violence in Poland and elsewhere.[63] Forged or irregularly procured documents attesting to residence in those western European zones since the cutoff date thus became one tool that refugees might use to obtain a visa to the United States. This was what Solomon Wiesel did. Wiesel was a Romanian Jew. He had been a prisoner of both the Nazis and the Russians. His wife and baby girl were murdered in the gas chambers of Auschwitz. After the war, Wiesel fled, "without passport and papers," to Hungary, then Czechoslovakia, and finally got himself to Germany, arriving in the American zone in 1948. Through friends, he obtained a document from the police chief in the town of Mühldorf certifying that he had resided there since 1945, with which he qualified for a visa under the Displaced Persons Act.[64]

Jewish aid organizations, for their part, found themselves on the defensive at home and abroad about the irregular modes through which refugees became documented.[65] Accusations that American Jewish organizations were facilitating unsanctioned immigration had a long history, and rhymed with a prominent strain of antisemitic, anti-immigrant opinion in the United States that held the Displaced Persons Act to be an alarming departure from restrictionist immigration policy. Jewish groups argued that reports of widespread document fraud were exaggerated. They also contended that US authorities— in particular, the Immigration and Naturalization Service (INS)—were quick to assume fraud when none existed, as in the case of Leisa Lowinger. Lowinger's application was approved by the Displaced Persons Commission, the CIC and the US Consulate. The INS, however, wanted more proof of Lowinger's residence in the US zone in Germany "although more than fifteen pieces of documents were issued to them."[66]

The refugee Erzia Suss encountered similar difficulties. In 1945, at the age of fifteen, Suss was "liberated in Germany," after which she returned to Hungary to search for family. She returned to Germany in early 1946, but did not disclose this chronology on a form she filled out for the IRO "for fear that she may not be eligible for emigration to the United States." She later admitted to her 1946 return to Germany, and the US consulate saw no problem with her case. The INS, though, "charged the applicant with willful misrepresentation" and ruled to exclude her. The JDC helped Suss appeal her case.[67]

Even as Jewish aid groups argued in legal and public forums that refugees' relationships to documentedness were proper—perhaps just marred by technicalities—organizational staff working on the ground understood the disconnect between bureaucratic processes and migrant realities. Razovsky Davidson, for example, described ways that refugees enacted their own versions of documentedness. "People will claim nationalities of their own for various reasons," she explained, and aid organizations and government authorities would be hard-pressed to track people through the papers they carried. She reported that the French underground had "prepared forged documents wholesale" for many refugees during the war, thereby saving "thousands upon thousands" of lives. She mused that some refugees "will never give up these papers, so no one will ever know their real identity." She also noted that many refugees were prepared to "change their nationalities and names" when they needed to, for example by switching papers with someone else.[68] Razovsky Davidson was noting, in other words, the arbitrariness of the very concepts undergirding the system of international migration controls and the emerging international refugee regime. National identities were not stable, and documents were not bearers of truth. Refugees, of necessity, understood and acted on this. They understood that undertaking international migration was less like going through a door and more like making it through a maze. Bending the bureaucratic processes to their own realities was a critical tool for doing so.

NAVIGATING THE MAZE IN THE UNITED STATES

Petluck observed in her Toronto speech that the work organizations like hers did with Jewish refugees didn't end when those refugees embarked for or arrived at US shores. The bureaucratic maze extended into the interior of the nation itself. Refugees' relationship to territorial belonging could remain precarious. Many faced potential exclusion at the ports of entry. And even those admitted to the territory of the United States had to confront the system of legal border-guarding that divided them from native-born citizens. "The migrant is now an alien in his new country. Many legal problems immediately confront him," Petluck explained, speaking of refugees' experiences in both the United States and elsewhere. "He may have to carry an alien registration card; he may have to make an annual address report; he may be subject to deportation," and even those who were naturalized could face the threat of having their citizenship revoked.[69] For Jewish refugees who arrived in the United States, as for other immigrants, borders were not only geographic, but also present in the regime of exclusion and deportation.[70] Even after securing a visa, many had encounters in which they had to argue for their right to be within the nation, and aid organizations were often enlisted to help them do this.

Because the workings of immigration policy were rarely straightforward, Petluck and her colleagues found themselves in constant discussions with US government officials. These were not simply fact-finding missions. They were also a form of negotiation. The lengthy meetings in which staff members of Jewish aid organizations queried those officials on the contradictions and confusion inherent in immigration policies, as when HIAS met with the Visa Division in 1945 to figure out new procedures and forms, were often frustrating for those trying to aid refugees. But these meetings were also occasions when organizations' staff pushed officials to clarify and resolve issues—to negotiate and hash out the details. Petluck served as part of an umbrella group of immigrant advocacy organizations that formalized this process, meeting on a monthly basis with government officials. She observed just how many procedures remained unclear after new policies came into effect, and how the government officials charged with implementing the law were clearly somewhat at sea. "The members of the Board [of Immigration Appeals] indicated," she reported, "that these new regulations were new to them too and that they were feeling their way." Government officials did not share refugee advocates' goals, but were, in these cases, willing to discuss procedures together. What could "aliens" and aid agencies do, for example, if the deadline to appeal a decision excluding an immigrant had passed? Which government officials could they go to in cases of denials?[71] Even if Petluck and her counterparts at other agencies were not coming into such meetings with the power to *make* policy, they were, through this persistent form of labor, leveraging officials' uncertainty to help shape what the workings of existing policies would actually be.

Aid organizations deployed their intimate understanding of state processes to help refugees to navigate them. The National Council of Jewish Women (NCJW), USNA and HIAS regularly advocated for refugees who were detained on arrival in the United States because immigration officials found fault with their papers or their statements about their political affiliations, or suspected them of having health issues that would render them excludable. The organizations also advocated for those facing deportation, particularly refugees who had been able to enter the country on some sort of temporary status, such as visitor or student visas, and now faced expulsion.

Aid organizations acting as advocates for refugees often found themselves having to follow refugees' lead. Refugees did not always accept official rules about which places they could migrate to or remain in, and took the initiative to define the relationship between themselves and national territories when they needed to do so. But challenging the legal boundaries of migration could get refugees in trouble. The story of Solomon Wiesel, mentioned above, provides one example of how. In 1949, he was admitted to the United States as a displaced person; this admission rested on his proof of having lived in Germany since before December 22, 1945. Wiesel made his home in Allentown, Pennsylvania, where he worked as a butcher. But a later investigation found that his visa was "procured by fraud" because he had lied about the timing of his sojourn in Germany. The US government ordered him deported. The USNA submitted a brief on his behalf to the Board of Immigration Appeals. Despite the USNA's advocacy, the appeal was denied; Wiesel might have faced deportation. But Wiesel, with the support of Allentown ministers, perhaps also coordinated by the USNA, was able to get the deportation order reversed by means of a private bill passed by Congress.[72]

Polish-Jewish refugees Irene-Wanda and Victor Goldstein, similarly, made a case, in conjunction with aid agencies, for their right to be present in the United States. Both had lost their families, who were killed in concentration camps. They were able to obtain visas to the Dominican Republic. After a few months there, they got temporary visas to visit the United States for medical care for Irene-Wanda. They stayed. They later applied to regularize their status under a provision of the Displaced Persons Act that allowed for temporary visitors to do so, but were denied on the basis of not facing persecution in the Dominican Republic. Their permission to enter that country, however, had lapsed, and they were "actually displaced," the NCJW argued, with no country to accept them. Like Wiesel, they ran out of avenues for appeal with the INS, which had ordered them deported. Congress granted the Goldsteins permanent residence in May 1955.[73]

CONCLUSION

Ann Petluck ended her talk that day in 1954 on a wistful note, one that evoked the conundrum faced by the refugee in her opening story. "The interplay of the needs of the individual and the sovereign rights of a country is ever-fascinating, and often frustrating," she told her audience. "They need not be inconsistent. One of the great responsibilities of the NGOs is to see that these two equities get closer together."[74] Like the refugee in her story, though, Petluck clearly understood just how much the rules of migration were inconsistent with individual needs. Aid agencies like hers did not argue for or show the way to a borderless world, one in which the right to move was never overshadowed by nations' insistence on migration control as a sovereign right. Petluck and her colleagues, following the needs and cues of refugees themselves, stretched, but did not dismantle, the rules and systems that determined the meanings of the world's maps. The archival record of these groups' labor, and the labor of refugees themselves, does not necessarily reveal a history of resistance to the bordering of the world. Nevertheless, it speaks to the remarkable space of negotiation their labor identified. It also speaks to a history of an ongoing insistence on the right to move, on the possibility, that is, of crafting other maps.

Notes

1. I am grateful to Steve Gold and Steve Ross for including my contribution in this volume, and for their comments. Infinite thanks go to Rachel Buff, Beth Dill, and Deborah Wilk, whose virtual writing support sustained me throughout the devastating pandemic spring, and whose insightful editing accounts for whatever clarity this piece might offer. Any errors are of course my own.

2. The USNA was established in 1946 when the National Refugee Service merged with the National Council for Jewish Women's Service for Foreign Born. Beth B. Cohen, *Case Closed: Holocaust Survivors in Postwar America* (New Brunswick: Rutgers University Press, 2006), 18. By 1947, the USNA had grown so rapidly that it became the "second largest social service voluntary agency in the country, topped only by the Red Cross" (B. B. Cohen, *Case Closed,* 21).

3. Ann S. Petluck, Speech before Non-Governmental Organizations, June 30, 1954, Hebrew Immigrant Aid Society (HIAS) Records, I-363 (hereafter HIAS), Box 132, Folder "Migration Department—Speeches by Ann S. Petluck, Director," American Jewish Historical Society, New York, NY (hereafter AJHS).

4. See, for example, Atina Grossmann, *Jews, Germans, and Allies: Close Encounters in Occupied Germany* (Princeton: Princeton University Press, 2007), 181. Grossmann observes here that "the United States was still a kind of *goldene Medina,* a dream destination if they could only get there. . . . It was no accident that the dusty streets in Föhrenwald Displaced Persons camp were named New York, Michigan, or Wisconsin Avenue." Refugees were thus creating, in a sense, "other maps"—placing, through language, the imagined destinations under their feet before anyone gave them permission to be there.

5. Although the United States had no extensive refugee admission policy before World War II, there was precedent for regarding refugees differently within immigration law before the war. On US policies meant to provide haven for refugees in earlier eras, see Julian Lim, "Immigration, Asylum, and Citizenship: A More Holistic Approach," *California Law Review* 101, no. 4 (2013): 1013–78, http://scholarship. law.berkeley.edu/californialawreview/vol101/iss4/3; Yael Schacher, "Exceptions to Exclusion: A Prehistory of Asylum in the United States, 1880–1980" (PhD diss., Harvard University, 2015).

6. Leonard Dinnerstein, *America and the Survivors of the Holocaust* (New York: Columbia University Press, 1982), 288.

7. See, for example, Gerard Daniel Cohen, *In War's Wake: Europe's Displaced Persons in the Postwar Order* (New York: Oxford University Press, 2011); Peter Gatrell, *The Making of the Modern Refugee* (Oxford: Oxford University Press, 2013); Emma Haddad, *The Refugee in International Society: Between Sovereigns* (Cambridge: Cambridge University Press, 2008); Nevzat Soguk, *States and Strangers: Refugees and Displacements of Statecraft* (Minneapolis: University of Minnesota Press, 1999).

8. For a related argument about how Jewish immigration lawyers played a crucial role in supporting migration in an earlier era, see Britt Tevis, "'The Hebrews Are Appearing in Court in Great Numbers': Toward a Reassessment of Early Twentieth-Century American Jewish Immigration History," *American Jewish History* 100, no. 3 (2016): 319–47.

9. Soguk, *States and Strangers*, 54, 34. One of the most important contemporary theorists of the vexed relationship between refugees—particularly stateless people—and nation-states was Hannah Arendt, herself a German Jewish refugee to the United States, who elaborated many of her ideas in *The Origins of Totalitarianism,* rev. ed. (New York: Harcourt Brace Jovanovich, 1976), chap. 9.

10. Haddad, *The Refugee in International Society*, 42.

11. Haddad, *The Refugee in International Society*, 34–37; Soguk, *States and Strangers*, 53–54; Liisa H. Malkki, "Refugees and Exile: From 'Refugee Studies' to the Natural Order of Things," *Annual Review of Anthopology* 24 (1995): 510–12.

12. Historians writing about postwar refugees in the European context, however, have been more attentive to exploring the complexities of the term "refugee," along with terms like "displaced person." See, for example, G. D. Cohen, *In War's Wake*, esp. chap. 2; Anna Holian, *Between National Socialism and Soviet Communism: Displaced Persons in Postwar Germany* (Ann Arbor: University of Michigan Press, 2011), chap. 1. For a rich exploration of how and when postwar Asian migrants were defined as "refugees," see Laura Madokoro, *Elusive Refuge: Chinese Migrants in the Cold War* (Cambridge, MA: Harvard University Press, 2016), esp. chaps. 1 and 2.

13. In the early postwar period, Allied authorities used "refugee" to refer to those displaced people who were in their nation of origin, and "displaced persons" to those who had crossed international borders, in contrast to current parlance. G. D. Cohen, *In War's Wake,* 38; Jenny Edkins, *Missing: Persons and Politics* (Ithaca: Cornell University Press, 2011), 61–62; Gatrell, *The Making of the Modern Refugee*, 94–96; Haddad, *The Refugee in International Society*, 129–31; Holian, *Between National Socialism and Soviet Communism*, 42–45.

14. Recent explorations of postwar developments in ideas about the claims refugees had a right to make on sovereign nations include Gatrell, *The Making of the Modern Refugee*, and Haddad, *The Refugee in International Society*.

15. On debates pre-and postwar about what the right to asylum would actually look like for refugees, especially vis-à-vis national sovereignty, see G. D. Cohen, *In War's Wake,* 91–98.

16. See, for example, G. D. Cohen, *In War's Wake*; Haddad, *The Refugee in International Society*; Madokoro, *Elusive Refuge*; Malkki, "Refugees and Exile," 497–503; Ilana Feldman, "Difficult Distinctions: Refugee Law, Humanitarian Practice, and Political Identification in Gaza," *Cultural Anthropology* 22, no. 1 (2007): 129–69. On the issue of what has been at stake in the refugee label more generally, see Andrew E. Shaknove, "Who Is a Refugee?" *Ethics* 95, no. 2 (January 1985): 274–84; Roger

Zetter, "Labelling Refugees: Forming and Transforming a Bureaucratic Identity," *Journal of Refugee Studies* 4, no. 1 (1991): 39–62 and idem, "More Labels, Fewer Refugees: Remaking the Refugee Label in an Era of Globalization," *Journal of Refugee Studies* 20, no. 2 (2007): 172–92.

17. Cecelia Razovsky Davidson to C. H. Cramer, March 20, 1945, Papers of Cecilia Razovsky, P-290 (hereafter CR), Box 6, Folder 1, AJHS.

18. Sylvia Milrod, "Collected Notes on Lecture #3, Cecelia Razovsky Davidson," July 26, 1945, CR, Box 6, Folder 1, AJHS; Cecilia R. Davidson to [Morris Davidson], May 13, 1945, CR, Box 1, Folder 4, AJHS. On Razovsky Davidson's sojourn in France, see also Laura Hobson Faure, "American Jewish Mobilization in France After World War II: Crossing the Narratives," *Transatlantica* 1 (2014): 5–7, http://journals.openedition.org/transatlantica/6961.

19. Sylvia Milrod, "Collected Notes on Lecture #2, Cecelia Razovsky Davidson," July 26, 1945, CR, Box 6, Folder 1, Box 6, AJHS.

20. Grossmann, *Jews, Germans, and Allies*, 131–32; Haddad, *The Refugee in International Society*, 130–32; Holian, *Between National Socialism and Soviet Communism*, 37–42; Mark Wyman, *DP's: Europe's Displaced Persons, 1945–1951* (Ithaca: Cornell University Press, 1998), chap. 3.

21. G. D. Cohen, *In War's Wake*, 126–27; Grossmann, *Jews, Germans, and Allies*, 132; Holian, *Between National Socialism and Soviet Communism*, 37. On the complexities of tabulating displaced persons, see Dinnerstein, *America and the Survivors of the Holocaust*, 273–82; Grossmann, *Jews, Germans, and Allies*, 315–16 n. 8 and 316–17 n. 11.

22. Stephen Porter, *Benevolent Empire: U. S. Power, Humanitarianism, and the World's Dispossessed* (Philadelphia: University of Pennsylvania Press, 2017), esp. chap. 3.

23. On the work that aid agencies did, in conjunction with government and military officials, toward "care and maintenance," see G. D. Cohen, *In War's Wake*, chap. 3. Regarding the tense relationships among the military, UNRRA, and aid groups, see Grossmann, *Jews, Germans, and Allies*, 154–56. On the related notion of the postwar refugee regime's work of "care and control," see Holian, *Between National Socialism and Soviet Communism*, 29 and 282–83, n. 2; Malkki, "Refugees and Exile," 497–503.

24. Porter, *Benevolent Empire*, 87.

25. Jacques Vernant, *The Refugee in the Post-War World* (London: George Allen & Unwin Ltd., 1953), 520.

26. Edkins, *Missing*, 49, 67; Grossmann, *Jews, Germans, and Allies*, 134; Wyman, *DP's*, 55.

27. Edkins, *Missing*, 48–53; Wyman, *DP's*, 55. Indeed, many of the people Cecilia Razovsky Davidson described seeing on the move may well have been searching for loved ones.

28. B. B. Cohen, *Case Closed*, 8, 179 n. 3.

29. Rita Benmayor, interview by David P. Boder, August 5, 1946, Paris, France, "Voices

of Technology," Illinois Institute of Technology, accessed July 10, 2020, http://iit. aviaryplatform.com/r/mc8rb6wd5b.

30. Jenny Edkins recounts the history of postwar tracing efforts in extensive detail in *Missing*, chap. 3.

31. Sylvia Milrod, "Collected Notes on Lecture, Cecelia Razovsky Davidson," July 25, 1945, CR, Box 6, Folder 1, AJHS.

32. Ibid.

33. Wyman, *DP's*, 55–57.

34. Cecelia Razovsky Davidson, memo to T. T. Scott, February 23, 1945, CR, Box 6, Folder 1, AJHS.

35. Linda G. Levi, "Family Searching and Tracing Services of JDC in the Second World War Era," in *Tracing and Documenting Nazi Victims Past and Present,* ed. Henning Borggräfe, Christian Höschler, and Isabel Panek (Berlin and Boston: Walter de Gruyter, 2020), 75.

36. Sylvia Milrod, "Collected Notes on Lecture, Cecelia Razovsky Davidson," July 25, 1945, CR, Box 6, Folder 1, AJHS.

37. Annual Meeting, January 1948, Box 23, Folder 1, United Service for New Americans Records, I-93, AJHS, accessed July 17, 2020, https://archives.cjh.org/repositories/3/ archival_objects/895107.

38. In 1944, the JDC, HIAS, the National Council of Jewish Women, the National Refugee Service and others established the Central Location Index to coordinate inquiries and data about refugees and their families. Levi, "Family Searching and Tracing Services," 70–71.

39. Edkins, *Missing*, chap. 3.

40. Ibid., 59.

41. Grossmann, *Jews, Germans, and Allies*, 154.

42. Annual Meeting, January 1948, Box 23, Folder 1, United Service for New Americans Records, I-93, AJHS, accessed July 17, 2020, https://archives.cjh.org/repositories/3/ archival_objects/895107. The Central Location Index, more broadly, received inquiries concerning finding some 750,000 people, of which it was able to locate 50,000 (40,000 of whom had survived the war). Levi, "Family Searching and Tracing Services," 73.

43. Jenny Edkins makes the point that, indeed, the work of reconnecting displaced people and their families was initially of little interest to military and government officials, who were more interested in controlling and relocating populations than in helping displaced people rebuild their lives. Edkins, *Missing*, 59, 64, 73.

44. Mark Wyman recounts a joke that circulated in the world of DP camps about the US migration bureaucracy: "One DP was asked whether he would be willing to join the U.S. Army. He said he would. Then the Immigration officer asked, 'If, while in the Army, you had a chance to capture Stalin, what would be the worst punishment you could give him?' The DP shot back: 'I'd bring him here to Funk Kaserne

and make him go through processing for emigration to the States!'" (Wyman, *DP's*, 198).

45. Ann S. Petluck, Speech before Non-Governmental Organizations, June 30, 1954, HIAS, Box 132, Folder "Migration Department—Speeches by Ann S. Petluck, Director," AJHS.

46. Aristide R. Zolberg, *A Nation by Design: Immigration Policy in the Fashioning of America* (New York: Russell Sage Foundation, 2006), 264–67.

47. Dinnerstein, *America and Survivors of the Holocaust*, 171; Libby Garland, *After They Closed the Gates: Jewish Illegal Immigration to the United States, 1921–1965* (Chicago: University of Chicago Press, 2014), 191; Maddalena Marinari, *Unwanted: Italian and Jewish Mobilization against Restrictive Immigration Laws, 1882–1965* (Chapel Hill: University of North Carolina Press, 2020), 105.

48. Proceedings of Annual Meeting, USNA, January 8–9, 1949, HIAS, Box 56, Folder "Annual Meetings of Members and Directors, 1949," AJHS.

49. Dinnerstein, *America and the Survivors of the Holocaust*, 189–91.

50. On the political battles waged by American Jews and other groups for legislation to admit postwar refugees, see, for example, Danielle Battisti, *Whom We Shall Welcome: Italian Americans and Immigration Reform, 1945-1965* (New York: Fordham University Press, 2019); Carl J. Bon Tempo, *Americans at the Gate: The United States and Refugees During the Cold War* (Princeton: Princeton University Press, 2008); Dinnerstein, *America and the Survivors of the Holocaust*; Marinari, *Unwanted*, chaps. 4–6; Daniel J. Tichenor, *Dividing Lines: The Politics of Immigration Control in America* (Princeton: Princeton University Press, 2002), 181–203.

51. Dinnerstein, *America and the Survivors of the Holocaust*, 298–300.

52. Dinnerstein, *America and the Survivors of the Holocaust*, 113; Garland, *After They Closed the Gates*, 188; Grossmann, *Germans. Jews, and Allies*, 141; Marinari, *Unwanted*, 102–3.

53. Dinnerstein, *America and the Survivors of the Holocaust*, 252.

54. Dinnerstein, *America and the Survivors of the Holocaust*, 249–50; Garland, *After They Closed the Gates*, 191; Marinari, *Unwanted*, 108–9.

55. Dinnerstein, *America and the Survivors of the Holocaust*, 251–52; Garland, *After They Closed the Gates*, 193; Marinari, *Unwanted*, 109–10.

56. Murray LeVine, memo to Isaac Asofsky, June 15, 1945, Records of the HIAS-HICEM Offices in Europe; RG 245.5 (hereafter HIAS-HICEM), MKM 19.42, Folder 394, YIVO Institute for Jewish Research, New York (hereafter YIVO).

57. Ilja Dijour to Wladimir Schah, June 22, 1945, HIAS-HICEM, MKM 19.42, Folder 394, YIVO.

58. "Questions and Answers on New Immigration Procedures," June 14, 1945, HIAS-HICEM, MKM 19.42, File 394, YIVO.

59. B. B. Cohen, *Case Closed*, 32–33; Dinnerstein, *America and Survivors of the Holocaust*, 113–4; 185.

60. Dinnerstein, *America and Survivors of the Holocaust*, 196.
61. Leo W. Schwarz to Dr. Joseph Schwartz, "Summary Analysis of AJDC Program in the U. S. Zone of Occupation, Germany, January 13 1947," 1945–1954 Geneva Collection, American Jewish Joint Distribution Committee Archives, accessed July 1, 2020, http://search.archives.jdc.org/notebook_ext.asp?item=2057018. Other charges mentioned in the report included those for similarly irregular forms of survival, namely engaging in the black market and "possession of foreign currencies." The report explained that modifications to the law in April 1946 helped decriminalize self-documentedness and unauthorized entry.
62. Dinnerstein, *America and the Survivors of the Holocaust*, 174; Garland, *After They Closed the Gates*, 191; Marinari, *Unwanted*, 105.
63. G. D. Cohen, *In War's Wake*, 138–9; Dinnerstein, *America and the Survivors of the Holocaust*, 166; Holian, *Between National Socialism and Soviet Communism*, 37.
64. H.R. Rep. No 356, 84th Cong., 1st sess. (March 3, 1955).
65. Dinnerstein, *America and the Survivors of the Holocaust*, 235–36, Garland, *After They Closed the Gates*, 189.
66. Gladys Roth, memo to A[rthur] Greenleigh, January 2, 195[1], HIAS, Box 58, Folder "Subversive Activities, 1950–1951," AJHS.
67. Ibid.
68. Sylvia Milrod, "Collected Notes on Lecture #3, Cecelia Razovsky Davidson," July 26, 1945, CR, Box 6, Folder 1, AJHS.
69. Ann S. Petluck, Speech before Non-Governmental Organizations, June 30, 1954, HIAS, Box 132, Folder "Migration Department—Speeches by Ann S. Petluck, Director," AJHS.
70. As border studies scholar Thomas Nail succinctly puts it, "Borders are not only at the territorial periphery, but all over the place and include all the social mechanisms that materially deprive any person of territorial, political and economic status" ("Sanctuary, Solidarity, Status!" in *Open Borders: In Defense of Free Movement*, ed. Reece Jones [Athens, GA: University of Georgia Press, 2019], 31). John Torpey makes a similar point about what he calls the "two dimensions of 'state control of borders,' one of which is about controlling movement, and the other about controlling membership ("States and the Regulation of Migration in the Twentieth-Century North Atlantic World," in *The Wall Around the West: State Borders and Immigration Controls in North America and Europe,* ed. Peter Andreas and Timothy Snyder [New York: Rowman and Littlefield, 2000], 33).
71. Ann S. Petluck, memo to I&R Staff, June 13, 1952, HIAS, Box 58, Folder "Immigration & Naturalization Regulations, 1952," AJHS.
72. H. R. Rep. No. 356, 84th Cong., 1st sess. (March 3, 1955); Private Law 252, August 1, 1955 (66 Stat. I63).
73. H. R. Rep. No. 282, 84th Cong., 1st sess. (March 22, 1955); Private Law 84-30, May 23, 1955 (69 Stat. A11).

74. Ann S. Petluck, Speech before Non-Governmental Organizations, June 30, 1954, HIAS, Box 132, Folder "Migration Department—Speeches by Ann S. Petluck, Director," AJHS.

Bibliography

1945–1954 Geneva Collection. American Jewish Joint Distribution Committee Archives.

Arendt, Hannah. *The Origins of Totalitarianism.* Rev. ed. New York: Harcourt Brace Jovanovich, 1976.

Battisti, Danielle. *Whom We Shall Welcome: Italian Americans and Immigration Reform, 1945-1965.* New York: Fordham University Press, 2019.

Bon Tempo, Carl J. *Americans at the Gate: The United States and Refugees During the Cold War.* Princeton: Princeton University Press, 2008.

Cohen, Beth B. *Case Closed: Holocaust Survivors in Postwar America.* New Brunswick: Rutgers University Press, 2006.

Cohen, Gerard Daniel. *In War's Wake: Europe's Displaced Persons in the Postwar Order.* New York: Oxford University Press, 2011.

Dinnerstein, Leonard. *America and the Survivors of the Holocaust.* New York: Columbia University Press, 1982.

Edkins, Jenny. *Missing: Persons and Politics.* Ithaca: Cornell University Press, 2011.

Faure, Laura Hobson. "American Jewish Mobilization in France After World War II: Crossing the Narratives." *Transatlantica* 1 (2014): 1–13. http://journals.openedition.org/transatlantica/6961.

Feldman, Ilana. "Difficult Distinctions: Refugee Law, Humanitarian Practice, and Political Identification in Gaza." *Cultural Anthropology* 22, no. 1 (2007): 129–69.

Garland, Libby. *After They Closed the Gates: Jewish Illegal Immigration to the United States, 1921-1965.* Chicago: University of Chicago Press, 2014.

Gatrell, Peter. *The Making of the Modern Refugee.* Oxford: Oxford University Press, 2013.

Grossmann, Atina. *Jews, Germans, and Allies: Close Encounters in Occupied Germany.* Princeton: Princeton University Press, 2007.

Haddad, Emma. *The Refugee in International Society: Between Sovereigns.* Cambridge: Cambridge University Press, 2008.

Hebrew Immigrant Aid Society Records. American Jewish Historical Society, New York, NY.

Holian, Anna. *Between National Socialism and Soviet Communism: Displaced Persons in Postwar Germany.* Ann Arbor: University of Michigan Press, 2011.

Levi, Linda G. "Family Searching and Tracing Services of JDC in the Second World War Era." In *Tracing and Documenting Nazi Victims Past and Present,* edited by Henning Borggräfe, Christian Höschler, and Isabel Panek, 59–94. Berlin and Boston: Walter de Gruyter, 2020.

Lim, Julian. "Immigration, Asylum, and Citizenship: A More Holistic Approach." *California Law Review* 101, no. 4 (2013): 1013–78.

Madokoro, Laura. *Elusive Refuge: Chinese Migrants in the Cold War.* Cambridge, MA: Harvard University Press, 2016.

Malkki, Liisa H. "Refugees and Exile: From 'Refugee Studies' to the Natural Order of Things." *Annual Review of Anthopology* 24 (1995): 495–523.

Marinari, Maddalena. *Unwanted: Italian and Jewish Mobilization against Restrictive Immigration Laws, 1882–1965.* Chapel Hill: University of North Carolina Press, 2020.

Nail, Thomas. "Sanctuary, Solidarity, Status!" In *Open Borders: In Defense of Free Movement,* edited by Reece Jones, 23–33. Athens, GA: University of Georgia Press, 2019.

Papers of Cecilia Razovsky. American Jewish Historical Society, New York, NY.

Porter, Stephen. *Benevolent Empire: U.S. Power, Humanitarianism, and the World's Dispossessed.* Philadelphia: University of Pennsylvania Press, 2017.

Records of the HIAS-HICEM Offices in Europe. YIVO Institute for Jewish Research, New York.

Schacher, Yael. "Exceptions to Exclusion: A Prehistory of Asylum in the United States, 1880–1980." PhD diss., Harvard University, 2015.

Shaknove, Andrew E. "Who Is a Refugee?" *Ethics* 95, no. 2 (January 1985): 274–84.

Soguk, Nevzat. *States and Strangers: Refugees and Displacements of Statecraft.* Minneapolis: University of Minnesota Press, 1999.

Tevis, Britt. "'The Hebrews Are Appearing in Court in Great Numbers': Toward a Reassessment of Early Twentieth-Century American Jewish Immigration History." *American Jewish History* 100, no. 3 (2016): 319–47.

Tichenor, Daniel J. *Dividing Lines: The Politics of Immigration Control in America.* Princeton: Princeton University Press, 2002.

Torpey, John. "States and the Regulation of Migration in the Twentieth-Century North Atlantic World." In *The Wall Around the West: State Borders and Immigration Controls in North America and Europe,* edited by Peter Andreas and Timothy Snyder, 31–54. New York: Rowman and Littlefield, 2000.

United Service for New Americans Records. American Jewish Historical Society, New York, NY.

Vernant, Jacques. *The Refugee in the Post-War World.* London: George Allen & Unwin Ltd., 1953.

Wyman, Mark. *DP's: Europe's Displaced Persons, 1945–1951.* Ithaca: Cornell University Press, 1998.

Zetter, Roger. "Labelling Refugees: Forming and Transforming a Bureaucratic Identity." *Journal of Refugee Studies* 4, no. 1 (1991): 39–62.

———. "More Labels, Fewer Refugees: Remaking the Refugee Label in an Era of Globalization." *Journal of Refugee Studies* 20, no. 2 (2007): 172–92.

Zolberg, Aristide R. *A Nation by Design: Immigration Policy in the Fashioning of America.* New York: Russell Sage Foundation, 2006.

"It's the Community That We've Made": Jewish Migration to East Lansing, Michigan, in the Postwar Era

by Kirsten Fermaglich

I n 1967, David and Beverly Wiener and their two daughters left their supportive graduate student housing community in Syracuse, New York and arrived in East Lansing, Michigan, ready for David to start his new job as an assistant professor in the American Thought and Language program at Michigan State University. David was born in Philadelphia, grew up in a Jewish neighborhood there, and his entire tight-knit family had gone to school in the Philadelphia area. His mother was deeply upset with David's decision to take a job halfway across the country. But at least one fellow graduate of Syracuse assured him that he wouldn't stay long at MSU; he could stay for a few years and then move elsewhere.[1]

David and Bev, however, have remained in East Lansing for over fifty years. David enjoyed his work at the university at first, and they found themselves making friends easily, joining two communities that would become central to their lives in Michigan, in some ways substituting for their close families and communities on the East Coast. The first community was political: they made friends with liberals of many different religious backgrounds, forming a young liberal group that called for the desegregation of East Lansing, and took other steps towards racial and class equality in the Lansing area. That community became formative in David's professional identity, and ultimately gave him an alternative career path: he left academia for politics in the late 1970s, and worked for his friend, Lansing mayor David Hollister, for twenty years.[2]

The second community was a group of young Jewish families who had almost all come to East Lansing to work at MSU or Lansing Community College. They celebrated Jewish holidays together, created new rituals, and established a Hebrew school for their children, called Rishon. They developed different pathways for their children to become *b'nai mitzvot*; David and Bev's older daughter Rebecca presented research on Jewish immigration from Eastern Europe, while their younger daughter Susan wanted a more traditional bat mitzvah, requiring the group to find a Torah. And they became a part of the larger religious landscape of the capital area of Michigan. The members of Rishon—including David and Bev—ultimately joined some disaffected, mostly academic, members of the only synagogue in town at the time, Shaarey Zedek, to form a new congregation, Kehillat Israel (KI). Without a rabbi for years, KI functioned as a small, tight-knit community, with roughly two-thirds of its initial congregation made up of academic families.[3] Members taught one another how to lead services and created innovative programs to teach their children Jewish ritual and liturgy. With a tiny Jewish population and only one extant Jewish institution in mid-Michigan before 1970, young Jewish academic families like the Wieners forged their own Jewish community.

David and Bev found themselves embracing Michigan, learning to love camping and the scenery of the Midwest and uncovering both the Jewish and the non-Jewish beauties of the state. While some East Coast friends complained about Michigan's flat, boring landscape and homogeneous food culture, David found himself appreciating its beauty and diversity. Travelling back home from Detroit one night, after eating corned beef sandwiches at the Stage Deli, David remembered thinking, "you know, this is a gorgeous place, with these beautiful skies. And I said, it's so big that these hills are just kind of flattened out. So, you could think of them as mountains, only they got flattened out. So, it's just a matter of perspective."[4]

The Wieners' story in East Lansing is part of a larger pattern of the post-World War II era that has rarely been studied or even acknowledged by historians. As higher education boomed and restrictions on Jews in academia lifted, the years after World War II saw thousands of young Jews from Jewish neighborhoods in big cities, mostly on the coasts, going to graduate school and then finding jobs in higher education in college towns and small cities throughout the country.[5] Few scholars have identified this movement as a significant wave of internal migration within the United States. American Jewish historians have been preoccupied with other larger, more visible migration patterns, particularly the mass migration of Jews from Central and Eastern Europe in the nineteenth and early twentieth centuries. While many scholars today argue that the study of immigration should be reconsidered as a study of migration, and that there is an important relationship between migration within a state and migration between states, American Jewish historians have typically focused on immigration and paid less attention to internal migration.[6]

There have been several important studies of Jewish internal migration within the United States, but they have primarily highlighted the expansion of Jewish peddlers and traders across the United States during the nineteenth century. Both Hasia Diner's recent work on peddlers and Shari Rabin's exploration of Jews on the frontier offer crucial insights about the significance of mobility and transience in the formation of Jewish identity and community in America. Much like David and Bev Wieners' experience in twentieth century East Lansing, peddlers like M.S. Polack on the nineteenth century frontier found themselves in locations with few Jews, using creativity and flexibility to devise new rituals and build community.[7]

Historians like Lila Corwin Berman and Deborah Dash Moore have looked at internal migration in the twentieth century through two major migration movements after World War II—Jewish suburbanization and Sunbelt migration—and they too have offered significant insight into the experiences of academic Jews during this era. Berman has noted the significance of place in American Jewish life, as Jews migrated to suburbs but continued to identify themselves with the city. Meanwhile, Moore has described the frontier-like spirit of Jews moving to the cities of Miami and Los Angeles, building institutions that promoted experiential and egalitarian education.[8] As we will see in this article, the Jews of East Lansing similarly prized experiential learning and egalitarianism. Unlike in Miami and Los Angeles, however, no mass migration of Jews arrived in the capital area of Michigan in the years after World War II. There were few attractions to mid-Michigan—either in its climate or its economy—that encouraged the chain migrations of Sunbelt communities like Miami or Los Angeles. Without that critical mass, Lansing Jews attracted no handsome, dynamic, entrepreneurial leaders, like those who travelled to Miami and Los Angeles seeking new pulpits to shape in their own image. Academic Jews also no longer lived near their families, as did suburban Jews, who might have lived only a fifteen-minute drive away from their parents and grandparents and still found themselves politically and culturally tied to the city of their childhood. By contrast, in their new college towns hundreds of miles from their former communities and far from their parents and grandparents, academic Jews found themselves identifying less with the cities and communities of their origins and instead seeking a new Jewish family and community and constructing a new Jewish identity.

Several historians have documented the impact of this influx of Jewish academics within the intellectual life of their various disciplines.[9] And indeed, for many academics, that impact was crucial: in East Lansing, numerous Jewish scholars found themselves making a mark in their disciplines, like sociology, education, and history. But few scholars have analyzed the social impact of this migration for Jews themselves or their communities. Community leaders in the 1960s and 1970s were indeed quite worried that the move into academia would separate young ambitious, intellectual Jews from the Jewish community, but no historians have identified or addressed this anxiety, or the actual experiences of these academic Jews after they moved.[10]

Although my research is only in its beginning stages, oral histories of academics (and family members) born between 1931 and 1956 who moved to East Lansing in the 1960s, 1970s and 1980s, and synagogue documents from Congregation Kehillat Israel suggest that the experience of migration to a small college town with few Jews, like East Lansing, during an era of religious experimentation and educational boom actually intensified and made more meaningful the Jewish identities of many Jewish academic migrants.[11] Jewish academic families who moved to East Lansing in the 1960s and 1970 participated in the religious experimentation of the era's Jewish counterculture, as did many other Jewish men and women in New York, Los Angeles, and other large cities, but that religious experimentation took on very different meaning for Jewish men and women who had moved across the country from their families to a profoundly non-Jewish environment, one very different from the one they had experienced as children.

BACKGROUNDS

Most of the Jews who moved to East Lansing in the 1960s, 1970s, and 1980s to work in education grew up in heavily Jewish neighborhoods in cities and suburbs on the coasts (both New York and California) or in the Midwest (Chicago, Cleveland or Detroit). Ken Glickman remembered his Cleveland Heights neighborhood being "very rich" in Jewish culture.[12] Marcia Horan estimated that her Lincolnwood suburban neighborhood just outside of Chicago was about eighty to eighty-five percent Jewish.[13] Paul Menchik remembered of growing up in Crown Heights, Brooklyn: "I didn't really know a white Christian until I went to college. It was very much cloistered."[14] Emily Tabuteau remembered only two families that she believed were non-Jewish from her entire Prospect Heights, Brooklyn neighborhood.[15] And in the Fairfax neighborhood of Los Angeles, where Don Kaufman spent his early childhood, he joked that on Jewish holidays, the local high school held classes in the phone booth.[16]

A number of migrants remembered streets studded with synagogues and shuls, shopping districts laden with Jewish delis and kosher markets, and neighborhood kids who "roamed the streets," sometimes stopping traffic for play.[17] As children, their neighborhood friends tended to be Jewish, as were their elementary school friends. Some Jewish migrants made close friendships through their synagogues or youth groups, which were deeply embedded in the fabric of their neighborhoods and family lives.[18] For others, it was extended family that dominated social life. Most grew up with grandparents, aunts, uncles, and cousins living in the same neighborhood or nearby; several spent their weekends, holidays, and hours after school playing with cousins, and participating in large family get-togethers regularly.[19]

As they travelled through middle school and high school, they sometimes remembered branching out and making non-Jewish friends. Rich Block lived in a predominantly Jewish neighborhood in Chicago growing up, but he remembered that his position on the high school football team helped him make non-Jewish friends for the first time, an experience of being a minority that had a lasting impact on him. His wife, Marcia Horan, purposely applied for a year-long program in urban studies at a predominantly African American high school in Chicago to reach out to non-Jews and non-whites as a high school student. Karen Glickman's best friend in high school in Cleveland Heights was the daughter of a Methodist minister; Steve Yelon remembered one of his best friends, Jimmy Thompson, inviting him over to decorate his Christmas tree and play with his Christmas presents.[20]

But to a large extent, it was Jewish family, neighbors, and friends that governed the early social lives of most of these young Jewish men and women. And it was Jewish institutions—from Orthodox shuls around the block to B'nai Brith youth organizations to Boy Scout troops to kosher butchers—that formed the backdrop for these friendships and relationships. Beverly Wiener remembered that although she was not at all observant religiously, she regularly attended Saturday morning services at her Conservative synagogue in Rochester because they fit seamlessly into her extracurricular and social schedule: "I was in inter-high band at 8:00 and inter-high orchestra at 9:00 and at 10:00 I could walk over to the Conservative synagogue and join the junior congregation for the last part and then we would move to the regular congregation for the last part of the [services] and then we had tea and coffee and cookies and then I would go with a friend to a movie."[21] Art Seagull's mother desperately wanted him to become a rabbi at one of the synagogues in their Weequahic neighborhood in Newark, NJ—though not the local Orthodox shul they attended, where he was the leader of the Zionist youth group.[22] Marcia Horan's parents worked at a large Reform synagogue in Chicago—her mother was the religious school principal and her father was the director of the children's choir—and so she lived her life at the synagogue: "I thought I ran the place." She also became deeply involved in her synagogue's branch of the Chicago Federation of Temple Youth (CFTY).[23] David Wiener remembered participating actively in his synagogue's Jewish youth group all through high school, with Friday night services and Saturday night dances: "it was the center of our community."[24]

Yet, for many other Jews, those institutions were just part of the backdrop: many took being Jewish for granted, never went to Shabbat services as children, and avoided youth groups. In Paul Menchik's neighborhood, "It was the exception, not the rule, to be a regular synagogue-goer."[25] Marcia Horan remembered that very few of her neighborhood friends went to services the way that her family did: "You didn't really have to be [observant]. Everybody did Passover, everybody did Rosh Hashanah, Yom Kippur. Everything closed down in my neighborhood. . . . If you grow up in a Jewish neighborhood, you know, Christmas didn't even creep in. It's kind of irrelevant."[26] Lisa Fine noted: "In my view, Jewishness was background noise because it was so ubiquitous, you didn't pay attention to it."[27] Out of her eight closest girlfriends in Brooklyn, Emily Tabuteau remembered, seven were Jewish, but none of their families went to synagogue.[28] Indeed, Jewish institutions, friends, and family in Jewish neighborhoods enabled many Jews who would eventually migrate to East Lansing to develop Jewish identities as children that had nothing to do with the practice of the religion itself, a pattern that Jonathan Sarna and others have noted was typical for American Jewish neighborhoods in the first half of the twentieth century.[29]

And it is worth noting that Jewish institutions frequently shaped young Jews' lives, even when their families were not actually members of those institutions, or even residents of the neighborhood anymore. Several Jewish men, like Stan Kaplowitz and Paul Menchik, went to Orthodox shuls in the neighborhood for their religious education or bar mitzvah ceremonies, even though their immediate families did not attend services or belong to those shuls.[30]

Steve Yelon's family lived in a neighborhood with multiple synagogues with famous cantors and although the family were not frequent synagogue-goers, they would sometimes stand outside the synagogues, "just to listen [to the cantors], especially in the warm weather. They would crank the windows open and we would listen in. . . . They were amazing."[31] Lisa Fine remembered that even when her family left the Jewish neighborhood of Borough Park, they kept returning to go shopping at Jewish stores, especially to buy the deli specialties they couldn't find in the new neighborhood.[32] And Paul Menchik remembered adults walking to shul in his neighborhood on Friday nights, and Lubavitcher kids from a nearby Hasidic enclave playing punchball in his schoolyard, even though he did not grow up with this level of Orthodoxy.[33]

Indeed, these men and women were raised with a wide range of denominational backgrounds. Stan Kaplowitz and Emily Tabuteau grew up in secular leftist homes; Kaplowitz attended a secular Yiddish shul for religious education.[34] David Wiener's family were early supporters of Mordecai Kaplan and the Reconstructionist ideal.[35] Marcia Horan's family was deeply enmeshed in the Reform movement.[36] Karen and Ken Glickman both attended large Conservative synagogues.[37] And others described homes that might be called traditional, somewhere between Conservative and Orthodox: their parents might keep kosher at home, but not in restaurants; their grandparents might take them to Orthodox shuls on Saturday morning but their parents never went to services and joined the Conservative synagogue because it had more child-friendly Sunday school. For most, denomination was loose and less meaningful than the fact of Jewishness itself.[38]

Camp was another Jewish institution that shaped many of these Jewish men and women's childhoods. Some of the camps were denominational, though others were not: Marcia Horan attended the Olin Sang Ruby Institute, a Reform-affiliated camp, while Steve Yelon went to an unaffiliated camp that was nonetheless predominantly Jewish, with Friday night services.[39] Several, including Arthur Elstein, Josef Konvitz, and David Wiener, attended Camp Ramah, affiliated with the Conservative movement.[40] Still others, like Bev Wiener and Ruth and Arthur Seagull, worked as counselors at Jewish camps.[41] These camp experiences were important in many of these men and women's childhoods. They made close friendships, learned ritual and songs, and developed confidence in their athletic and leadership abilities. As intended by their founders, this immersion in a Jewish space with Jewish songs, rituals and friends made a deep impression on many migrants: "That was a very important part of my upbringing," Steve Yelon remembered, "I had a lot of friends from that. They had nothing to do with Yeshiva. They had nothing to do with high school. But it was a completely different group, all Jewish."[42]

Lest this portrait seem overly nostalgic, it is worth noting that quite a few migrants—particularly women—did not have particularly fond or rosy memories of their Jewish neighborhoods or communities at all. A number of people, like Marcia Horan, Toba Kaplowitz, and Lisa Fine, saw their overwhelmingly Jewish high schools as overly materialistic, shallow, intolerant, and homogeneous.[43] Indeed, Lisa Fine found herself out of step with high school social circles because she looked "too white bread": not Jewish enough.[44] While most male migrants interviewed seem to have had an easier time finding friends in their neighborhoods and schools through shared experiences, women may have faced a higher bar for behavior and looks in their overwhelmingly Jewish worlds. And to be sure, by the 1960s, many young Jews, both men and women, were becoming critical of their Jewish communities, synagogues, and families, seeing them dominated by wealth and hypocrisy.[45] The Jews who eventually moved to East Lansing did not all share this critique, but some certainly did.

It is important to note that the Jewish migrants interviewed were not all grounded exclusively in Jewish neighborhoods or in Jewish communities as children. In addition to their experiences in Jewish neighborhoods, some migrants had experiences in more mixed neighborhoods, like Boyle Heights in Los Angeles or Midwood Park in Brooklyn, where Jews lived together with Italian Catholics, Latinos, African Americans, and Arab Americans.[46] Perhaps even more importantly, other Jewish migrants had very different, less urban and less Jewish experiences growing up. Fran Yelon grew up in Alton, Illinois, a small city with few Jews and one synagogue with a travelling rabbi.[47] A few faculty children, like Josef Konvitz and Judy Bisno Shulman, grew up themselves in academic communities with few Jews; their parents were part of a first wave of Jewish academics who got jobs in the late 1940s and early 1950s.[48] Still others grew up Christian and converted to Judaism later in life. Bettie Menchik's great-grandparents had been Jewish, but she was raised a committed Unitarian in the New York suburbs, and decided to convert only after she and Paul got married.[49] Liz Kaufman was raised by parents who were nominally Protestant and went to Presbyterian Sunday school in Salt Lake City; she became committed to Jewish practice and community when she and Don Kaufman began dating, but she didn't convert until much later in life.[50]

Migrating Jews thus came to East Lansing from a wide variety of locations, with a wide variety of experiences, but the majority had formative experiences in large Jewish urban and suburban neighborhoods of the 1930s, 1940s and 1950s that were notably similar. These experiences reflected an era when dense urban Jewish neighborhoods in the United States promoted a Jewish cultural identity mostly detached from significant religious practice and grounded in geography, institutional proximity, food, family and friendship networks. The vast majority of the men and women who would ultimately migrate to East Lansing were affected by this secular urban Jewish identity, either as part of their own experiences, or as a product of their spouses' experiences.

MOVING TO EAST LANSING

After a decade or so of college and graduate school life, where they typically engaged little in organized Jewish life and focused on education, career, and getting married, rather than any kind of Jewish religious or communal experiences, these men and women found themselves moving to East Lansing, Michigan—overwhelmingly because they or their partners had jobs at Michigan State University.

Most of them had experience in the Midwest before moving to East Lansing. Many, of course, were from Midwestern cities like Cleveland or Chicago. Others brought up on the coasts had gone to college or graduate school in the Midwest, especially to the University of Michigan and University of Wisconsin. The Midwest, and even Michigan, was not new for most of them.

But even many with significant experience in the Midwest paused when moving to East Lansing. East Lansing is part of the larger metropolitan area of Lansing, the capital of Michigan, and in the years after World War II, its population was booming, in part because of the national expansion of higher education, and specifically the growth of MSU, during this era. Nonetheless, in comparison to the major cities from which almost all of these men and women hailed, like Los Angeles, Cleveland, Chicago, and New York, the Capital area was tiny: in 1970, the combined population of East Lansing and Lansing was 178,943.[51]

And beyond its small size, Lansing was not an especially diverse city. Even the auto manufacturer centered in Lansing, the R. E. Olds Company, had historically hired its workers from surrounding white rural areas, rather than seeking out immigrant or Black workers, as had the Big Three centered in Detroit. Olds' goal was to preserve the homogeneity of its workforce and to discourage unionization, but the practice laid a foundation for a Capital area population that lacked ethnic and racial diversity.[52] Jews were a tiny minority in the overwhelmingly Christian city: in 1918, the Jewish population of Lansing was 450 out of about 57,000, only the sixth largest Jewish population in the state.[53] Forty years later, there were many more Jews in the mid-Michigan area, but they still remained a small proportion of the growing Capital-area region. In 1957, 350 Jewish families (perhaps between 1,000 and 2,000 people) were members of the only synagogue in town, Shaarey Zedek, while the Lansing population in 1960 was over 100,000.[54]

And perhaps surprisingly, the presence of Michigan State University did little to broaden this ethnic diversity in the 1960s and 1970s. Although similar state colleges that migrants were familiar with—particularly the Universities of Michigan and Wisconsin—had historically attracted a significant Jewish population and encouraged cosmopolitan college town environments, Michigan State's origins as an insular agricultural college shaped the culture of East Lansing, making it less of a typical college town with restaurants, theater, and other urban amenities. Stan Kaplowitz, for example, remembered that when he was an undergraduate, "people at U of M felt superior to MSU, which was called 'Moo-U,' because of its agricultural college origins," while he was told that people at MSU "referred to U of M as 'Jew U' because of its large number of Jews."[55]

A good number of migrants admitted to feeling alienated by the lack of cosmopolitanism and diversity, and particularly the lack of a Jewish community, when they got their jobs and first arrived in Lansing. "We came to East Lansing and it was so different from Ann Arbor. In Ann Arbor, there were Jews all over the place. There was a Jewish presence. . . . We came here, nothing," Toba Kaplowitz remembered.[56] Arthur Elstein's first impressions of East Lansing were entirely about the city's Christian identity: "The thing that I remember most [about arriving in East Lansing] was how difficult it was to be Jewish and how little the outside world got it. In the 1960s, East Lansing was a quintessentially goyish town."[57] And Don and Liz Kaufman both remembered that they planned to stay for only five years: "We thought we were moving to the ends of the earth," Liz said.[58] "The homogeneity here, the lack of diversity, the fact that even though this was a college town, there weren't any places to eat. I mean, it was white bread city and no Jews, except for those who happened to be at MSU, who didn't live out in Okemos [a suburb of East Lansing], where we did. . . . It was kind of a shock," Don remembered, adding that they both had wondered: "Oh my God, did we do the right thing?"[59]

It's important to note, though, that a number of Jewish academics reported little concern with East Lansing's lack of diversity at first, and few questions about their decisions to migrate. Many academics, especially as the job market dried up in the 1970s, were thrilled simply to be employed, and their top priority was to get their research done and to get tenure. Rich Block's early memories of East Lansing, for example, were that "it seemed like a nice place to live. . . . My focus was on the professional piece and the department was a good place to work . . . people let me do what I wanted to do."[60] "I was happy to have a tenure track job at a major research institution," Josef Konvitz explained.[61] And Emily Tabuteau remembered, "I was delighted and relieved."[62] In these responses, and others, we can see Jews accommodating to a new postwar economy, where upward class mobility was premised on geographic mobility, and the emergence of a "New Class" of information and service professionals promised young Jews exciting careers and national networks that expanded well beyond the urban Jewish neighborhoods of their youths. The promise of satisfying work, congenial colleagues, and a stable, prestigious career was more than enough to justify moving to a city with far fewer theater, art, music or food options than any other city most of the migrants had lived in.[63]

Unsurprisingly, spouses tended to be more unhappy than academics themselves. Fran Yelon made Steve promise her they would leave in a year.[64] Other spouses—all women—did not make quite such drastic demands, but they remembered being lonely, depressed, or frustrated at home with children, without jobs, and without a clear social network, while their husbands worked constantly in order to publish and get tenure. If Rich Block thought East Lansing "seemed like a nice place to live," for his wife Marcia Horan, "the first five years [in East Lansing] were probably the loneliest of my life. I think I was probably depressed . . . I didn't like it there at all."[65] Bev Wiener remembered that David "was always at a desk either grading papers or reading something," and she was responsible for both of their young children. "It was hard because we didn't know anybody and David was busy with his new job," she remembered, noting difficulties finding friends and staying home with her children alone. "For me it was a hard first year, it was a lonely year. We didn't even have a telephone. The city of East Lansing had not expanded its phone service fast enough. . . . I couldn't wait to be with other adult humans more."[66] The geographic mobility of academia was premised on a breadwinner ethos that brought only one individual (almost always a man at that time) to a university and assumed his spouse would travel gladly and care for his family; compounding matters, in the 1960s and 1970s, MSU had a policy of refusing spouses jobs.[67] As a result, women who themselves had trained for positions in education, labor relations, law, or the arts frequently found themselves unemployed in East Lansing, without a family or social network and often with the sole responsibility of caring for children.

In these circumstances—lonely for women and pressure-filled for men— Jewish migrants sought friends of any background. Although many reported being surprised by or disappointed in the lack of cosmopolitanism, diversity, and Jewish culture in East Lansing, few said they sought out Jewish networks or friends at the beginning. To be sure, some had Jewish members of their departments who reached out to them immediately; they formed close friendships and social circles that were both Jewish and professional right away. Others, however, became friends with members of their departments, or with neighbors, who were not Jewish; as women found jobs in the community and put their children in daycares and schools, they made non-Jewish friends through those avenues as well. [68] With backgrounds that had made Jewishness a part of the scenery, rather than an active engagement that was a necessary part of their lives, most migrants did not seek out Jewish life or Jewish community at the beginning of their years in East Lansing.

And indeed, there was little Jewish communal life to seek out. As noted above, there was only one synagogue in town, Shaarey Zedek (SZ)—a far cry from the multiple synagogues, shops, and restaurants with which most men and women had grown up. And many professors and their families did not find SZ in the 1960s and 1970s a hospitable or welcoming environment. It had begun as a traditional, Orthodox synagogue in 1918, after a number of Eastern European Jewish immigrant families had arrived in town and established businesses. In 1938, the synagogue merged with Temple Beth El, a Reform synagogue that had been established years earlier. Shaarey Zedek held both Reform and traditional services for years; in 1950, it affiliated with the Reform Union of American Hebrew Congregations, and in 1972, it affiliated with the national Conservative body, United Synagogue of America.[69]

But it was not really denomination that turned off most migrants. Instead, it was issues of class, gender, and decorum that concerned them. A number of academics who migrated to East Lansing in the 1960s viewed Shaarey Zedek as the province of the wealthy businesspeople of the community, most of them having been born and raised there. "They were . . . the people who owned the major Jewish businesses in the metro Lansing area," remembered Harry Perlstadt.[70] In 1969, the synagogue moved to a new, expensive, modern building on Coolidge Road in East Lansing, and the fundraising entailed for that construction was substantial. The synagogue required dues to belong, and tickets to pray on the High Holy Days. For some academic families, those dues symbolized the gulf between the wealthy business class of Lansing on one hand and the professors new to the community on the other. Several remembered one of their friends, Walter Kron, insisting that "You shouldn't have to pay to be a Jew."[71] Others found the environment of Shaarey Zedek at the time "too fancy," or dominated by "moneyed people whose values were different than ours."[72] "Shaarey Zedek at that time was very snooty," Art Seagull remembered, "they looked down on the academics."[73]

Gender too played a role in some migrants' discomfort with Shaarey Zedek. As was typical in Reform and Conservative congregations in the 1960s and 1970s, women could not lead services, read from the Torah or make *aliyah*. For some migrants, this inequality was insupportable; for example, Annette Weinshank was religiously educated, and in the wake of the second wave feminist movement, she sought to lead services.[74] Traditional voices at Shaarey Zedek rejected that possibility. Moreover, the culture of Shaarey Zedek was structured by gender division; men served as president, while women led the Sisterhood. Women's roles at the synagogue were auxiliary, dedicated to the kitchen and the gift shop far more than actual leadership. In an era of second wave feminism, young migrants—both men and women—found that culture traditional and stultifying. "Shaarey Zedek was a space in which women served coffee and tea; they ran the kitchen. Shaarey Zedek was not a space where women stood up and said this is what I think."[75]

As the above testimonies make clear, however, both gender and class were tied closely to an issue that scholars have identified as central to synagogue participation in the United States: decorum. Elements like "room arrangements, prayer tunes, and their style of praying," mattered more for young migrants than issues of denomination or theology.[76] Young migrants, many of whom had been politically active in protests for civil rights and against Vietnam and most of whom came to East Lansing as transplants from larger city environments, where synagogue attendance had been mostly a backdrop for daily life, found the decorum of Shaarey Zedek inhospitable: formal, traditional, hierarchical and stuffy. "I wasn't going to join a regular synagogue, not me," Toba Kaplowitz laughed. "I also felt the very limitations of expectations and the traditional stuff, the role of women, there were all sorts of issues. . . . My mindset was: no traditional shul. I'm not even going to give it a chance."[77] Art Seagull called Shaarey Zedek "a very formal place . . . They had a rabbi, had a chazan . . . Shaarey Zedek was the kind of place that I knew . . . from back in Newark and it seemed to me very old style, very stultifying, suffocating, you sat here, the rabbi was up here, he told you [what to do]."[78] "We were in our

20s, and [Shaarey Zedek] seemed so formal," Fran Yelon remembered.[79] These comments all suggested that concerns about decorum—the environment of the sanctuary, the style of the service, the very fact of tradition—were key concerns for Jewish migrants in East Lansing, just as they were for young Jews throughout the United States.

These cultural discomforts with the only significant Jewish institution in East Lansing had lasting and perhaps surprising impact. These men and women—who were mostly uninterested in religion, not particularly interested in seeking out Jewish community, and who were content to let Jewishness be only a silent backdrop to their lives, as it had been for quite some time—wound up constructing several vibrant Jewish institutions of their own in mid-Michigan in the 1960s and 1970s. This development placed East Lansing Jews squarely within contemporary currents of the Jewish counterculture, which was emerging at precisely this moment throughout the country. Independent *minyanim* and *havurot*—small lay-led prayer groups—were transforming American Judaism during this era, as young Jews sought to construct Jewish institutions that reflected their own politics and aesthetics.[80] At the same time, however, the academics who migrated to East Lansing responded to the Jewish counterculture in a fashion slightly different from Jews in Los Angeles, Boston, or New York. The fact that they were all separated from their natal and extended families and transplanted to an almost entirely non-Jewish environment, with only one other Jewish institution and a tiny Jewish community, meant that their new institutions were not solely designed to identify themselves as countercultural Jews different from establishment Jews. Those institutions also wound up constructing a substitute Jewish family, a viable Jewish identity for their children, and a more intense Jewish institutional life than most migrants had anticipated for themselves.

The first of these institutions was a fleeting and ephemeral one, but it reflected a belief among many Jewish academics and organizational leaders during the 1960s that Judaism needed to be connected to intellectual inquiry to keep young Jews engaged in the community.[81] Several Jewish faculty members from the American Thought and Language department in the late 1960s instituted a Friday-night discussion group for Jewish couples in the area—mostly, though not exclusively, faculty couples. Using a model practiced by secular Israelis, members would meet in one another's homes on Friday nights once a month for coffee and cake, and one person would give a lecture about their work, or about a subject of Jewish interest. "It was also a bit of a social event. . . . It was more about getting together with other Jews on Jewish topics,"

Bev Wiener remembered, noting that it enabled them to make friends with other Jews during their first year in East Lansing.[82]

Since a number of these couples had children approaching school age, they began to talk about developing a Hebrew school for them. By 1968, about a half dozen migrant families had established Rishon, a Hebrew school "where kids could learn the letters and learn about the holidays."[83] The school was determinedly secular, and it was shaped by the needs and proclivities of the new Jewish migrants moving into East Lansing: the founders were "young Jewish families, who were not interested in becoming members of the synagogue . . . but had kind of a secular humanist approach to Judaism [and] wanted to have a Jewish community."[84]

Rishon held classes for young children at the Hillel house off campus on Sunday mornings. They hired mostly MSU college students to teach, though they also recruited Ken Glickman, who had moved to East Lansing to be an instrumental music teacher at McDonald Middle School, to teach teenagers at David Wiener's house. While the younger children learned inside the Hillel house, their parents socialized on the porch outside, turning the school into a community: "we would take our children there and we would all bring our *New York Times* and our coffee and bagels and we would sit around and talk. We wouldn't actually read, we would sit around and talk to each other. And we really became close to each other," David Wiener remembered fondly.[85] Soon, members of Rishon began to celebrate the holidays together at one another's homes, creating services and inventing new rituals. "We made our own Sukkah . . . we would have a Purim celebration together and drink a lot and have fun. The biggest event of the year was the Passover seder. And we would make a big deal about it. We would write our own Haggadah. Some of us would perform. . . . People were really very involved with doing creative things for the Passover seder. It was a lot of fun."[86] They developed their own ceremonies for *b'nai mitzvot*. At least seventeen families were members of Rishon in its earliest iteration; perhaps forty to fifty people were members before it ultimately closed in 1977. Rishon served as a significant source of Jewish community and education for migrant families in the East Lansing area. "We felt comfortable with the people; it was a comfortable level of Judaism," Stan Kaplowitz recalled.[87] And Don Kaufman remembered that in the midst of his and Liz's shock over the transition to East Lansing, "the department was really our family here, and then gradually, the Rishon group became our family . . . and that made things a lot more comfortable." Rishon helped migrants to create a Jewish community in East Lansing.[88]

For a few influential members of the Jewish migrant community—especially Arthur and Rochelle Elstein, Lee and Judy Shulman and Don and Annette Weinshank—Rishon's focus on community and secular humanistic Judaism was not enough, however. Some of these men and women had joined Rishon, but they were not satisfied by its once-a-week secular school or its communal holidays. They believed they needed a more sophisticated religious education and a deeper religious experience, one grounded more in sacred Jewish texts, traditional liturgies, and the religious practices with which they had grown up, even though they were no longer observant Orthodox Jews. At the same time, a group of Shaarey Zedek members (some of whom were MSU faculty who had migrated from elsewhere and others who were not), including Martin Fox, George and Esther Kessler, and Jerry Faverman, had decided that they were unhappy with the synagogue, mostly because of its education for both adults and children, and began making plans to create a new synagogue.[89] "Probably the local congregation is weakest in the area of religious education. It has no adult program of any kind and its religious school program is outmoded, with no coherent curriculum or adequate administration, and is sadly underfunded," wrote Lawrence Alexander, an academic migrant, to the Reconstructionist Rabbinical College in 1970, seeking a rabbi for the new congregation.[90]

These dissatisfied Shaarey Zedek congregants and Rishon members worked together in 1970 to establish a new congregation, Kehillat Israel. In June 1970, they held an open meeting for Jews in the community to try to recruit potential members—predominantly from the expanding pool of academic migrants, along with a number of other transplanted Jews, some of whom worked as lawyers or professionals for the state.[91] By the fall of 1970, KI had written bylaws, attracted at least twenty-seven families as members, and held its first High Holy Day services at a local East Lansing church, with David Fass, a student from the Reform movement's Hebrew Union College, acting as rabbi. By the middle of 1971, it counted forty-four families as members, and rented space in a former fraternity house from the local Unitarian Universalist church.[92] The synagogue relied initially on Rishon as its primary educator for younger children, but established a classroom for children in grades five through eight, with teachers drawn from the MSU graduate student community.[93] The congregation also insisted upon the need for adult education in its very first mission statements, and planned to continue the Friday-night discussion group as part of their Shabbat services: "The Friday night service will not ordinarily include a sermon. Instead, following the service . . . for those who wish to participate, the Rabbi will lead a study or discussion session. The discussion of political and social issues, as well as religious themes, will be encouraged."[94] The third major Jewish institution created by academic migrants in East Lansing, Congregation Kehillat Israel, thus embraced and then superseded the first two. While Rishon and the Friday night group ultimately dissolved as separate entities, KI still stands after fifty years.

Kehillat Israel was purposefully egalitarian, reflecting migrants' earlier criticisms of the gender and class hierarchies operating at Shaarey Zedek. KI's very first documents made clear that gender equality was at the center of the congregation's rebellious self-definition: "Women will be called to the Torah and will be counted for a minyan," the "Prospectus for a New Jewish Congregation" read.[95] The synagogue's first bylaws spelled out membership and obligations in terms that were notably egalitarian for the era: "The unit of membership shall be either the individual or the family, both men and women, sharing alike the same rights, privileges, and obligations of membership."[96] These documents established female membership and participation at KI two years before the feminist group, Ezrat Nashim, called for the Conservative movement of Judaism to make such changes, five years before women were given *aliyot* in Shaarey Zedek's Reform minyan, and fifteen years before Shaarey Zedek tried to establish an egalitarian minyan for its Conservative services.[97] Kehillat Israel's finances were similarly designed as a radical break from the control of the local business elite at Shaarey Zedek. All KI members were required to contribute something to the synagogue, but they were not required to give any specific amount, and all financial commitments "shall be held in strict confidence . . . no financial commitment in any amount shall be deemed unacceptable for membership."[98]

Perhaps most significantly, Kehillat Israel was also self-consciously experimental and participatory, focused on education, community, and self-expression. Its first bylaws proclaimed that the synagogue "shall strive to meet the need of the local Jewish community for a new and different approach" to education and religion, and that it would "provide a wide variety" of activities "premised on a willingness of members to participate and to experiment in order to achieve these ends." "The overriding goal," the bylaws concluded, "is an atmosphere in which individuals may explore and develop more meaningful means of Jewish expression together."[99] In these bylaws, KI congregants reflected the countercultural Jewish moment, even though congregants report that they were unaware of the other *havurot* and independent synagogues emerging in other cities at the same time.[100]

Although the synagogue hired visiting rabbis at the beginning of its existence, its lack of finances, as well as its emphasis on radical self-expression, its lack of denominational affiliation, and its determined and educated congregation soon defaulted to making it a lay-led service for years. Some academic migrants who had gone to Camp Ramah or Orthodox shuls as children were capable of leading services "at the drop of a hat," and they worked to train others to do the same.[101] Despite this impressive training (or perhaps because of it), congregants sometimes engaged in "vicious arguments" over seemingly small matters of decorum—how to hold their bodies, for example, for the Cohanim blessing of the congregation during the Yom Kippur service.[102] As Riv-Ellen Prell has suggested, it was these arguments over decorum and aesthetics that were crucial to the countercultural Jewish movement's understanding of themselves. Just as significantly for the academic migrants of KI, it was in part the lay-led nature of the congregation, the emphasis on personal participation and experimentation, the rancorous argumentation over matters of decorum, and the absence of a rabbi that made their religious experiences far more intense, meaningful and even enjoyable than they ever might have expected their Jewish life would become. "It was such a thrill to have KI, where we asked questions," Art Seagull remembered, "We were without a rabbi for 18 years, that was terrific . . . that was more fun."[103] Arthur Elstein noted that he had not grown up going to synagogue regularly and that even at Camp Ramah, prayers had not been the most meaningful part of his experience. It was organizing the minyan at Kehillat Israel after the death of his mother that led him to make that experience part of his life.[104] And even a migrant like Fran Yelon, who attended a Reform synagogue growing up and could not initially read the Hebrew or sing the prayers, explained that the lack of a rabbi at KI was liberating and empowering: "At KI, we were all on our own, with many very knowledgeable people. And that [gave us] a sense of pride."[105]

To be sure, not all academic migrants joined Kehillat Israel by any means. Determinedly secular members of Rishon refused to join KI, for example, uninterested in the religious experiences it promised. Then, too, there were many secular Jews in East Lansing who resisted organizational affiliation of any kind. Lisa Fine and Emily Tabuteau, like many secular Jews throughout the university, simply had no interest in joining any Jewish organization—Rishon, KI, or SZ. There were also academic migrants who chose to join KI, but then left it to join Shaarey Zedek. Josef and Isa Konvitz joined KI when they arrived in East Lansing in 1973, but they did not make friends with many members and did not feel comfortable at the synagogue. With a family line that featured two famous rabbis, Josef found the lay-led experience to be chaotic, rather than meaningful, and Isa remembered that the synagogue's politics concerned them when the family returned from a sabbatical in France in the 1980s; like some other academic migrant families, the Konvitzes moved to Shaarey Zedek and helped to change that synagogue's culture and politics. Isa was the first woman to be called for an *aliyah* at the Conservative services in Shaarey Zedek in the 1980s. [106]

Yet for many Jewish academic migrants, the experience of building Kehillat Israel offered them not simply a chance to express themselves as members of an emerging Jewish counterculture, different from the established Jewish business class in East Lansing. It also allowed them to build a Jewish identity, community and family in a non-Jewish environment hundreds of miles from their nearest family members. "My family [in Brooklyn] didn't do the things that we do in East Lansing, [become] members of a synagogue," Paul Menchik noted. "Because everybody was Jewish, it was such a homogeneous community. Why join a synagogue? was the attitude. It's only when you're in the Midwest, I suppose, and you're Jewish [that] you want to identify by joining a synagogue. And if I'd stayed in New York . . . I might have stayed a non-member of a synagogue."[107] Rich Block too compared the Kehillat Israel community in East Lansing with the Chicago Jewish community of his youth, "It's our community and it's the community that we've made. . . . You go to New York and you walk into a ready-made community. Here you have to make it because it's not there. . . . I appreciate it a lot more because it's something I feel like I've had a piece in creating and everybody else has a piece in creating. And when I think about growing up, [Jewish community] was always there, but it's not something I did. This I feel that I had a little piece of creating. Here, everybody has a little piece of creating it. Whatever it is, it's because we've made it."[108]

For many secular urban Jews, it wasn't even their own Jewish identities that were most important; it was those of their children. Both Rishon and KI illustrated a signal dilemma for many secular urban Jews who had moved to East Lansing for MSU. As both Block and Menchik's quotations suggest, they themselves had Jewish identities formed by the particular circumstances of their urban Jewish neighborhoods: the dense structure of institutions, the presence of extended families nearby, and a wide range and dense concentration of Jewish neighbors and friends. When they were young, they could attend synagogue, or join a youth group, or not, and their understandings of themselves as Jewish were nonetheless embedded in their childhood experiences. But their own children raised in East Lansing would not experience any element of their parents' Jewish childhoods—indeed, they would probably know very few or no Jews or Jewish life at all in their own community without some form of organized institutional learning, which migrants felt they had to construct on their own. Many academic migrants discussed their decisions to join Rishon or Kehillat Israel as a product of this realization. "I think the lack of Jewishness we felt once we had a kid," Toba Kaplowitz remembered. "That was like, 'Oh my gosh.' We can manage fine, we thought. But . . . the kids wouldn't grow up Jewish because they would not only know nothing, they would know no one. . . . "[109] Another woman from Los Angeles noted that it was the fact that there was only one other Jewish child in her son's entire grade at elementary school in East Lansing that led them to join KI and put their children in Hebrew school: "We have often wondered if we'd stayed in [Los Angeles], would we even have joined a synagogue? Would [our kids] even have gone to Hebrew school? Because it's so much in the air in LA. . . . If we were just going to Canters and Juniors every weekend to eat, would we have just thought: 'Oh, they don't need to know anything.' . . . It's partially the fact that we came to this small town that they ended up getting all this Jewish training."[110] Harry Perlstadt was perhaps most evocative in describing the differences between his own childhood and that of his children: "I guess I have a Jewish identity. I've always known who I was and part of who I was was always Jewish. It's not that I was terribly religious but I knew I was Jewish. . . . My personality and my identity were established fairly early in life. . . . It was something that was a part of me and I wanted it to be part of [my children]."

And migrant after migrant testified that Rishon and KI provided them with Jewish community and family while they were far from their own natal families and communities. "I knew people outside of KI but they weren't my closest friends," Arthur Elstein remembered. "When my wife got sick, . . . we had a conference around our kitchen table in East Lansing and the people around that kitchen table were [people from KI]. When I was in trouble and I needed to figure out what to do or what was my next move, those were the people I talked to. . . . This was a relationship that went far beyond going to shul. It was a community. . . . It did the job."[111]

These poignant testimonies suggest that there are different experiences of migration in the twentieth century that American Jewish historians need to attend to. Jewish upward mobility in the years after World War II was frequently premised on geographic mobility—not only to the suburbs or the Sunbelt, but also to college towns like East Lansing, Michigan. Once in those college towns, at least some young Jewish academics and their families participated in the Jewish countercultural movement that was reshaping Judaism in the 1960s and

1970s throughout the United States, but that movement took on very different meaning for men and women hundreds of miles from their homes, families, and Jewish communities in New York and Los Angeles. They not only distinguished themselves from more established Jews in aesthetics and politics, but they created a Jewish community, family and identity in unfamiliar spaces far from home. The Jewish lives they made for themselves and the institutions they built suggest that there is greater richness, diversity, and texture in American Jewish history than has previously been considered.

Notes

1. David Wiener, interview by Kirsten Fermaglich and Chantal Tetreault, February 26, 2020, East Lansing, MI.
2. Ibid.
3. See Kehillat Israel, 1971–1972 Directory, November 1971, in "Membership Lists, Phone Lists, 1970–1972," in Congregation Kehillat Israel archives (hereafter KI Archives). Introductory material in this folder indicates that early phone lists included Rishon members. Sixty-seven percent of the families listed in the 1971–1972 directory were MSU faculty families; it's not clear whether this directory includes Rishon families or not.
4. David Wiener, interview.
5. For the influx of Jews into academia in the years after World War II, see, for example, Barry Chiswick, "The Rise and Fall of the American Jewish PhD," *IZA Working Paper No. 3384*, https://ssrn.com/abstract=1136189; and David Hollinger, *Science, Jews and Secular Culture* (Princeton: Princeton University Press, 1996).
6. See, for example, Adam Goodman, "Nation of Migrants, Historians of Migration," *Journal of American Ethnic History* 34, no. 4 (Summer 2015): 7–16; Matthew Frye Jacobson, "More 'Trans-,' Less 'National,'" *Journal of American Ethnic History* 25, no. 4 (July 2006): 74–84; and Marc S. Rodriguez, ed., *Repositioning North American Migration History: New Directions in Modern Continental Migration, Citizenship, and Community* (Rochester, NY: University of Rochester Press, 2004).
7. For the specific example of Solomon, see Hasia Diner, *The Road Taken: The Great Jewish Migrations to the New World and the Peddlers Who Forged the Way* (New Haven: Yale University Press, 2015), 72. Shari Rabin makes this argument powerfully in *Jews on the Frontier: Religion and Mobility in Nineteenth Century America* (New York: New York University Press, 2017). For texts that describe nineteenth-century Jewish internal migration, though they say less about these Jewish migrants' social and religious lives, see Adam Mendelsohn, *The Rag Race: How Jews Sewed Their Way to Success in America and the British Empire* (New York: New York University Press, 2014) and Rebecca Kobrin, ed., *Chosen Capital: The Jewish Encounter with American Capitalism* (New Brunswick, NJ: Rutgers University Press, 2012).
8. Lila Corwin Berman, *Metropolitan Jews: Politics, Race, and Religion in Postwar Detroit* (Chicago: University of Chicago Press, 2015); Deborah Dash Moore, *To the Golden Cities: Pursuing the American Jewish Dream in Miami and L.A.* (Cambridge: Harvard University Press, 1996); Etan Diamond, *And I Will Dwell in Their Midst: Orthodox Jews in Suburbia* (Chapel Hill: University of North Carolina Press, 2000).
9. Suzanne Klingenstein, *Enlarging America: The Cultural Work of Jewish Literary Scholars, 1930–1990* (Syracuse: Syracuse University Press, 1998); Hollinger, *Science, Jews and Secular Culture*. For sociological works that have traced the Jewish entry into academia, see Chiswick, "The Rise and Fall of the American Jewish PhD";

and Seymour Martin Lipset and Charles Ladd, "Jewish Academics in the United States: Their Achievements, Culture and Politics," *American Jewish Yearbook*, vol. 72 (1971): 89–128.

10. For the 1960s fears about academic Jews, see, for example, Norman L. Friedman, "The Problem of the Runaway Jewish Intellectuals: Social Definition and Sociological Perspective," *Jewish Social Studies* 31, no. 1 (January 1969): 3–19. Sidney and Alice Goldstein do offer an important sociological consideration of Jewish geographical mobility in the late twentieth century, but it is not focused on academic Jews in particular—and the Goldsteins do at times replicate anxieties about Jewish migration as a move out of the Jewish community. See *Jews on the Move: Implications for Jewish Identity* (Albany: State University of New York Press, 1990).

11. With a colleague, Chantal Tetreault, I interviewed twenty-eight members of the mid-Michigan Jewish community. Twenty-two of them fit the parameters of the study exactly: they were academics who migrated to the Lansing area in the 1960s, 1970s, or 1980s, or they were members of these migrant academics' families. The remaining six did not quite fit these parameters, but their stories are still highly relevant: three were born in the 1950s and raised in urban Jewish neighborhoods, but moved to East Lansing in the 1990s, having first found jobs elsewhere; three others moved to East Lansing for non-academic jobs: music education and rabbinical work (the last was the rabbi of Kehillat Israel from 2001–20).

12. Ken Glickman, interview by Kirsten Fermaglich, March 5, 2020, East Lansing, MI.

13. Marcia Horan, remote interview by Kirsten Fermaglich and Chantal Tetreault, June 2, 2020.

14. Paul Menchik, remote interview by Kirsten Fermaglich and Chantal Tetreault, June 1, 2020.

15. Emily Tabuteau, remote interview by Kirsten Fermaglich, July 6, 2020.

16. Don Kaufman, remote interview by Kirsten Fermaglich and Chantal Tetreault, June 26, 2020.

17. Lisa Fine, remote interview by Kirsten Fermaglich, June 23, 2020. See also Steve Yelon, remote interview by Kirsten Fermaglich, May 20, 2020; Don Kaufman, interview; Rich Block, Zoom interview by Kirsten Fermaglich and Chantal Tetreault, June 10, 2020.

18. David Wiener, interview; Marcia Horan, interview; Harry Perlstadt, remote interview by Kirsten Fermaglich and Chantal Tetreault, July 7, 2020; Art Seagull, remote interview by Kirsten Fermaglich and Chantal Tetreault, July 20, 2020.

19. See, for example, Don Kaufman, interview; Lisa Fine, interview; Rich Block, interview; Paul Menchik, interview. For close relationships with grandparents, see also Bev Wiener, remote interview by Kirsten Fermaglich and Chantal Tetreault, March 20, 2020; David Wiener, interview.

20. Rich Block, interview; Marcia Horan, interview; Karen Glickman, interview with Kirsten Fermaglich, March 5, 2020, East Lansing, MI; Steve Yelon, interview.

21. Beverly Wiener, interview.

22. Art Seagull, interview

23. Marcia Horan, interview.

24. David Wiener, interview.

25. Paul Menchik, interview.

26. Marcia Horan, interview.

27. Lisa Fine, interview.

28. Emily Tabuteau, interview.

29. See, for example, Jonathan Sarna, "The Rise, Fall and Rebirth of Secular Judaism," *Contemplate: The International Journal of Cultural Thought* 4 (2008): 3–13; Joshua M. Zeitz, *White Ethnic New York: Jews, Catholics, and the Shaping of Postwar Politics* (Chapel Hill: University of North Carolina Press, 2007); Annie Polland, "'May a Freethinker Help a Pious Man?': The Shared World of the 'Religious' and the 'Secular' among Eastern European Jewish Immigrants to America," *American Jewish History* 93, no. 4 (December 2007): 375–407.

30. Stan Kaplowitz, remote interview with Kirsten Fermaglich and Chantal Tetreault, May 4, 2020; Paul Menchik, interview; Don Kaufman, interview.

31. Steve Yelon, interview.

32. Lisa Fine, interview.

33. Paul Menchik, interview.

34. Stan Kaplowitz, interview; Emily Tabuteau, interview.

35. David Wiener, interview.

36. Marcia Horan, interview.

37. Karen Glickman, interview; Ken Glickman, interview.

38. For some interviews that helped to build this portrait of a traditional background, see Art Seagull, interview; Steve Yelon, interview; Bev Wiener, interview; Rich Block, interview; Arthur Elstein, Zoom interview by Kirsten Fermaglich, March 31, 2020. For an academic description of this fluidity between Orthodox and Conservative Judaism during these years, see Jeffrey S. Gurock, "From Fluidity to Rigidity: The Religious Worlds of Conservative and Orthodox Jews in Twentieth Century America," *David W. Belin Lecture in American Jewish Affairs* 7 (Ann Arbor: Jean and Samuel Frankel Center for Judaic Studies, University of Michigan, 1998).

39. Marcia Horan, interview; Steve Yelon, interview.

40. Arthur Elstein, interview; Josef Konvitz, interview by Kirsten Fermaglich and Chantal Tetreault, June 30, 2020; David Wiener, interview.

41. Bev Wiener, interview; Art Seagull, interview.

42. Steve Yelon, interview. For the goals of socialization and immersion in the Jewish camping movement, see, for example, Riv-Ellen Prell, "Jewish Summer Camping and Civil Rights: How Summer Camps Launched a Transformation in American Jewish Culture," *David W. Belin Lecture in American Jewish Affairs* 13 (Ann Arbor: Jean and Samuel Frankel Center for Judaic Studies, University of Michigan, 2006);

Michael M. Lorge and Gary Zola, eds., *A Place of Our Own: The Rise of Reform Jewish Camping* (Tuscaloosa: University of Alabama Press, 2006); Jenna Weissman Joselit and Karen S. Mittleman, eds., *A Worthy Use of Summer: Jewish Summer Camping in America* (Philadelphia: National Museum of American Jewish History, 1993.

43. Marcia Horan, interview; Toba Kaplowitz, remote interview by Kirsten Fermaglich and Chantal Tetreault, May 14, 2020; Lisa Fine, interview; Barry Goetz, Zoom interview by Kirsten Fermaglich, June 3, 2020.

44. Lisa Fine, interview.

45. See, for example, Rachel Kranson, *Ambivalent Embrace: Jewish Upward Mobility in Postwar America* (Chapel Hill: University of North Carolina Press, 2017), 164; Riv-Ellen Prell, *Prayer and Community: The Havurah in American Judaism* (Detroit: Wayne State University Press, 1989); David Glanz, "An Interpretation of the Jewish Counterculture," *Jewish Social Studies* 39, no. 1/2 (Winter/Spring 1977): 117–28.

46. Don Kaufman, interview; Lisa Fine, interview; Stan Kaplowitz, interview.

47. Fran Yelon, interview by Kirsten Fermaglich and Chantal Tetreault, May 22, 2020.

48. Josef Konvitz, interview; Judy Bisno Shulman, interview by Kirsten Fermaglich and Chantal Tetreault, March 6, 2020, Lansing, MI.

49. Bettie Menchik, Zoom interview by Kirsten Fermaglich and Chantal Tetreault, June 8, 2020.

50. Liz Kaufman, Zoom interview by Kirsten Fermaglich and Chantal Tetreault, June 29, 2020. See also Betty Seagull, Zoom interview by Kirsten Fermaglich and Chantal Tetreault, July 30, 2020.

51. For historical census data for Lansing and East Lansing, see World Population Review, Lansing, Michigan, found at https://worldpopulationreview.com/us-cities/lansing-mi-population and https://worldpopulationreview.com/us-cities/east-lansing-mi-population, August 6, 2020.

52. See Lisa Fine, *The Story of R.E.O Joe: Work, Kin, and Community in Autotown, U.S.A.* (Temple University Press, 2004), esp. 15–37.

53. Daniel Jacobson, "Lansing's Jewish Community: The Beginnings," *Michigan Jewish History* 16, no. 1 (January 1976): 12.

54. Of course, the membership of the synagogue does not reflect the entire Jewish population of the area. I have not yet uncovered good data for the entire Jewish population of the Capital area in the post-World War II era. "Historical Synopsis," *Congregation Shaarey Zedek 90th Anniversary Celebration* (East Lansing, MI, 2009), np; World Population Review, Lansing, Michigan, found at https://worldpopulationreview.com/us-cities/lansing-mi-population, July 22, 2020.

55. Stan Kaplowitz, email to Kirsten Fermaglich, July 30, 2020.

56. Toba Kaplowitz, interview.

57. Arthur Elstein, interview.

58. Liz Kaufman, interview.

59. Don Kaufman, interview.

60. Rich Block, interview.

61. Josef Konvitz, interview.

62. Emily Tabuteau, interview.

63. For contemporary literature about the rise of a "New Class," see, for example, B. Bruce-Briggs, ed., *The New Class?* (New Brunswick, NJ: Transaction, 1979); John Kenneth Galbraith, *The New Industrial State* (Boston: Houghtonn Mifflin, 1967); and idem, *The Affluent Society* (Boston: Houghton Mifflin, 1958).

64. Steve Yelon, interview; Fran Yelon, interview. They still live in East Lansing today.

65. Rich Block, interview; Marcia Horan, interview.

66. Bev Wiener, interview. See also Josef Konvitz, interview; and Anonymous Subject A, Zoom interview with Kirsten Fermaglich, May 21, 2020.

67. John Beck, conversation with Kirsten Fermaglich, July 18, 2019; Josef Konvitz, interview.

68. For people who made Jewish friends in their departments or through MSU connections, see Arthur Elstein, interview; Donald Kaufman, interview; Harry Perlstadt, interview. For people who made friends elsewhere, see David Wiener, interview; Stan Kaplowitz, interview; Toba Kaplowitz, interview; Bev Wiener, interview; Marcia Horan, interview.

69. Congregation Shaarey Zedek, *90th Anniversary Celebration*, May 9, 2009, np.

70. Harry Perlstadt, interview. See also Karen Glickman, interview.

71. Bev Wiener, interview.

72. Liz Kaufman, interview. Liz Kaufman, like others interviewed, made clear that Shaarey Zedek's environment has changed, and that they no longer hold these feelings about that synagogue.

73. Art Seagull, interview.

74. David Wiener, interview; Arthur Elstein, interview.

75. Arthur Elstein, interview.

76. Riv-Ellen Prell, "A New Key: Decorum and the Study of Jews and Judaism," *American Jewish History* 90, no. 1 (2002): 20. See also Prell, *Prayer and Community*; Leon Jick, *The Americanization of the Synagogue, 1820–1870* (Boston: Brandeis University Press, 1976).

77. Toba Kaplowitz, interview.

78. Art Seagull, interview.

79. Fran Yelon, interview.

80. See, for example, Prell, *Prayer and Community*; Glanz, "An Interpretation of the Jewish Counter-Culture."

81. See, for example, "Second Dialogue in Israel," *Congress Bi-Weekly* (September 16, 1963): 17–18; Jehudah Cohen, "Again: Jewish Intellectuals," *The Jewish Spectator* 30 (December 1965): 7–8; and Leonard J. Fein, "Let Us Stop Patronizing Jewish Youth," *Jewish Digest* 12 (April 1967): 1–6.

82. Bev Wiener, interview; Arthur Elstein, interview.

83. Bev Wiener, interview.

84. David Wiener, interview.

85. Ibid.

86. Ibid.

87. Stan Kaplowitz, interview.

88. Don Kaufman, interview.

89. For the names of Shaarey Zedek members unhappy with the congregation, see David Wiener, interview.

90. Lawrence Alexander, letter to Rabbi Arthur Gilbert, May 3, 1970, Folder "KI 1970 Prospectus for New Congregation," KI Archives.

91. "New Jewish Congregation to be Discussed Wednesday," *Lansing State Journal*, June 6, 1970, Folder "KI 1970 Prospectus for New Congregation," KI Archives; Harry Perlstadt interview.

92. See Financial Planning Committee, "Budget Recommendations, 1971–1972," and "Kehillat Israel—What It's All About" (1971?), Folder "KI 1970 Prospectus for New Congregation," KI Archives.

93. "Kehillat Israel—What It's All About" (1970?), Folder "KI 1970 Prospectus for New Congregation," KI Archives.

94. "Prospectus for a New Jewish Congregation," Folder "KI 1970 Prospectus for New Congregation," KI Archives.

95. "Prospectus for a New Jewish Congregation."

96. Congregation Kehillat Israel, "By-Laws (Draft of Dec. 14, 1970)," Folder "KI 1970 Prospectus for New Congregation," KI Archives.

97. For Ezrat Nashim, see Joyce Antler, *Radical Jewish Feminism: Voices from the Women's Liberation Movement* (New York: New York University Press, 2018), 205–18; for changes at Shaarey Zedek, see Congregation Shaarey Zedek, *90th Anniversary Celebration*, np.

98. Congregation Kehillat Israel, "By-Laws (Draft of Dec. 14, 1970)."

99. Congregation Kehillat Israel, "By-Laws (Draft of Dec. 14, 1970)."

100. David Wiener, interview; Arthur Elstein, interview.

101. Harry Perlsadt, interview. See also Don Kaufman, interview; Ken Glickman, interview; Betty Seagull, interview.

102. Harry Perlstadt, interview. See also Ken Glickman, interview.

103. Art Seagull, interview.

104. Arthur Elstein, interview; Arthur Elstein, email communication with Kirsten Fermaglich, August 2, 2020.

105. Fran Yelon, interview.

106. Josef Konvitz interview; Konvitz, email communication with Kirsten Fermaglich and Chantal Tetreault, June 30, 2020; Konvitz, email communication with Kirsten Fermaglich, July 31, 2020.

107. Paul Menchik, interview.

108. Rich Block, interview.

109. Toba Kaplowitz, interview.

110. Anonymous Subject A, interview.

111. See also, for example, David Wiener, interview; Karen Glickman, interview; Bettie Menchik, interview; Marcia Horan, interview.

Bibliography

Primary Sources

Bruce-Briggs, B., ed. *The New Class?* New Brunswick, NJ: Transaction, 1979.

Cohen, Jehudah. "Again: Jewish Intellectuals." *The Jewish Spectator* 30 (December 1965): 7–8.

Congregation Kehillat Israel archives, Congregation Kehillat Israel, Lansing, MI.

Fein, Leonard J. "Let Us Stop Patronizing Jewish Youth." *Jewish Digest* 12 (April 1967): 1–6.

Friedman, Norman L. "The Problem of the Runaway Jewish Intellectuals: Social Definition and Sociological Perspective." *Jewish Social Studies* 31, no. 1 (Jan. 1969): 3–19.

Galbraith, John Kenneth. *The Affluent Society.* Boston: Houghton Mifflin, 1958.

————. *The New Industrial State.* Boston: Houghton Mifflin, 1967.

Glanz, David. "An Interpretation of the Jewish Counter-Culture." *Jewish Social Studies* 39, nos. 1–2 (Winter/Spring 1977): 117–28.

"Historical Synopsis." *Congregation Shaarey Zedek 90ᵗʰ Anniversary Celebration.* East Lansing, MI, 2009.

"Second Dialogue in Israel." *Congress Bi-Weekly* (September 16, 1963): 3–85.

Secondary Sources

Antler, Joyce. *Radical Jewish Feminism: Voices from the Women's Liberation Movement.* New York: New York University Press, 2018.

Berman, Lila Corwin. *Metropolitan Jews: Politics, Race, and Religion in Postwar Detroit.* Chicago: University of Chicago Press, 2015.

Chiswick, Barry. "The Rise and Fall of the American Jewish PhD." *IZA Working Paper No. 3384.* SSRN: https://ssrn.com/abstract=1136189.

Diamond, Etan. *And I Will Dwell in Their Midst: Orthodox Jews in Suburbia.* Chapel Hill: University of North Carolina Press, 2000.

Diner, Hasia. *Roads Taken: The Great Jewish Migrations to the New World and the Peddlers Who Forged the Way.* New Haven: Yale University Press, 2015.

Fine, Lisa. *The Story of R.E.O Joe: Work, Kin, and Community in Autotown, U.S.A.* Philadelphia: Temple University Press, 2004.

Goldstein, Sidney and Alice. *Jews on the Move: Implications for Jewish Identity.* Albany: State University of New York Press, 1990.

Goodman, Adam. "Nation of Migrants, Historians of Migration." *Journal of American Ethnic History* 34, no. 4 (Summer 2015): 7–16.

Gurock, Jeffrey S. "From Fluidity to Rigidity: The Religious Worlds of Conservative and Orthodox Jews in Twentieth Century America." *David W. Belin Lecture in American Jewish Affairs* 7. Jean and Samuel Frankel Center for Judaic Studies, University of Michigan, 1998.

Hollinger, David. *Science, Jews and Secular Culture.* Princeton: Princeton University Press, 1996.

Jacobson, Daniel. "Lansing's Jewish Community: The Beginnings." *Michigan Jewish History* 16, no. 1 (January 1976): 5–17.

Jacobson, Matthew Frye. "More 'Trans-,' Less 'National.'" *Journal of American Ethnic History* 25, no. 4 (July 2006): 74–84

Jick, Leon. *The Americanization of the Synagogue, 1820–1870.* Hanover, NH: University Press of New England for Brandeis University Press, 1976.

Joselit, Jenna Weissman, and Karen S. Mittleman, eds. *A Worthy Use of Summer: Jewish Summer Camping in America.* Philadelphia: National Museum of American Jewish History, 1993.

Klingenstein, Suzanne. *Enlarging America: The Cultural Work of Jewish Literary Scholars.* Syracuse: Syracuse University Press, 1998.

Kobrin, Rebecca, ed. *Chosen Capital: The Jewish Encounter with American Capitalism.* New Brunswick: Rutgers University Press, 2012.

Kranson, Rachel. *Ambivalent Embrace: Jewish Upward Mobility in Postwar America.* Chapel Hill: University of North Carolina Press, 2017.

Lipset, Seymour Martin, and Charles Ladd. "Jewish Academics in the United States: Their Achievements, Culture and Politics." *American Jewish Yearbook*, vol. 72 (1971): 89–128.

Lorge, Michael M., and Gary Zola, eds. *A Place of Our Own: The Rise of Reform Jewish Camping.* Tuscaloosa: University of Alabama Press, 2006.

Mendelsohn, Adam. *The Rag Race: How Jews Sewed Their Way to Success in America and the British Empire.* New York: New York University Press, 2014.

Moore, Deborah Dash. *To the Golden Cities: Pursuing the American Jewish Dream in Miami and L.A.* Cambridge: Harvard University Press, 1996.

Noverr, Douglas A. *Michigan State University: The Rise of a Research University and the New Millennium, 1970–2005.* East Lansing: Michigan State University Press, 2015.

Polland, Annie. "'May a Freethinker Help a Pious Man?': The Shared World of the 'Religious' and the 'Secular' among Eastern European Jewish Immigrants to America." *American Jewish History* 93, no. 4 (December 2007): 375–407.

Prell, Riv-Ellen. "A New Key: Decorum and the Study of Jews and Judaism." *American Jewish History* 90, no. 1 (2002): 13–25.

———. "Jewish Summer Camping and Civil Rights: How Summer Camps Launched a Transformation in American Jewish Culture." *David W. Belin Lecture in American Jewish Affairs* 13. Ann Arbor: Jean and Samuel Frankel Center for Judaic Studies, University of Michigan, 2006.

———. *Prayer and Community: The Havurah in American Judaism.* Detroit: Wayne State University Press, 1989.

Rabin, Shari. *Jews on the Frontier: Religion and Mobility in Nineteenth Century America.* New York: New York University Press, 2017.

Rodriguez, Marc S., ed. *Repositioning North American Migration History: New Directions in Modern Continental Migration, Citizenship, and Community.* Rochester, NY: University of Rochester Press, 2004.

Sarna, Jonathan. "The Rise, Fall and Rebirth of Secular Judaism." *Contemplate: The International Journal of Cultural Thought* 4 (2008): 3–13.

World Population Review. Lansing, Michigan, July 22, 2020. https://worldpopulationreview.com/us-cities/lansing-mi-population.

———. Lansing, Michigan, August 6, 2020. https://worldpopulationreview.com/us-cities/lansing-mi-population; https://worldpopulationreview.com/us-cities/east-lansing-mi-population.

Zeitz, Joshua M. *White Ethnic New York: Jews, Catholics, and the Shaping of Postwar Politics.* Chapel Hill: University of North Carolina Press, 2007.

About the Contributors

LISA ANSELL is Associate Director of the Casden Institute for the Study of the Jewish Role in American Life at the University of Southern California. She received her BA in French and Near East Studies from UCLA and her MA in Middle East Studies from Harvard University. She was the Chair of the World Language Department of New Community Jewish High School for five years before coming to USC in August, 2007. She currently teaches Hebrew language courses at the Hebrew Union College-Jewish Institute of Religion. She also serves as the USC ambassador for academic partnerships in Israel.

NIR COHEN is Senior Lecturer in the Department of Geography and Environment at Bar Ilan University. Trained in International Affairs (Columbia University) and Human Geography (University of Arizona in Tucson), his research interests include relations between states and their Diasporas, the politics of migration and citizenship, and geographies of work in Israel. His work on policies towards skilled migrants, stratified citizenship and labor struggles against plant closures in deindustrializing cities have appeared in such journals as *IJURR, Cities, JEMS, Population, Space and Place, Environment and Planning D, Social and Cultural Geography* and *Geoforum*. In spring 2018 he was Visiting Fellow of Jewish Migration at The Parkes Institute for Jewish/Non-Jewish Relations at the University of Southampton, UK. In 2019 he was Visiting Professor for Urban Studies at TU Wien (Vienna University of Technology), Austria.

KIRSTEN FERMAGLICH is Professor of History and Jewish Studies at Michigan State University. Her most recent book, *A Rosenberg by Any Other Name: A History of Jewish Name Changing in America* (New York University, 2018) was awarded the Saul Viener Book Prize by the American Jewish Historical Society in June 2019. Fermaglich is also the author of *American Dreams and Nazi Nightmares: Early Holocaust Consciousness and Liberal America, 1957–1965* (Brandeis University Press, 2006) and the co-editor of the Norton Critical Edition of Betty Friedan, *The Feminine Mystique* (2013), with Lisa Fine. She is currently co-editor of the journal, *American Jewish History*, along with Daniel Soyer and Adam Mendelsohn. She has published articles in the *Journal of American History*, the *Journal of American Ethnic History*, and *American Studies*, and she has received fellowships from the YIVO Institute, the Posen Foundation, the Association for Jewish Studies, and the Frankel Institute for Advanced Judaic Studies at the University of Michigan.

LIBBY GARLAND teaches immigration history and urban history at Kingsborough Community College, The City University of New York, and courses on border studies and urban studies at the Master of Arts in Liberal Studies program at the CUNY Graduate Center. She is the author of *After They Closed the Gates: Jewish Illegal Immigration to the United States, 1921–1965* (University of Chicago Press, 2014).

STEVEN J. GOLD is professor and graduate program director in the Department of Sociology at Michigan State University. His scholarly interests include international migration, ethnic economies, ethnic community development, qualitative field methods and visual sociology. Gold is the author, co-author or co-editor of eight books including *The Israeli Diaspora* (Routledge/University of Washington Press 2002) which won the Thomas and Znaniecki Award from the ASA's International Migration Section for the best book on international migration in 2003. The chair of twenty-two PhD dissertations and author of over one hundred journal articles and book chapters, Gold received the Charles Horton Cooley Award for Distinguished Scholarship in Sociology from the Michigan Sociology Association in 2007 and the Distinguished Career Award from the American Sociological Association, International Migration Section in 2019.

LILACH LEV ARI is an Associate Professor at Oranim, Academic College of Education. Lilach heads the Faculty of Graduate Studies. She is a lecturer in Oranim and the department of Jewish History, Jewish Peoplehood at Haifa University. Her research interests include human migration, ethnic identity and intercultural encounters as part of the migration experience and multiculturalism. Her main research topic centers on emigration from Israel to North America and Europe. Lev Ari has published the following books: *The American Dream—For Men Only? Gender, Immigration and the Assimilation of Israelis in the United States* (2008); and *American Israelis, Migration, Transnationalism, and Diasporic Identity* (2010 with Uzi Rebhun), as well as various publications in scientific journals such as: *Contemporary Jewry, The Journal of Heritage Tourism, Higher Education, Tourism Recreation Research, Journal of Multilingual and Multicultural Development* and others.

LAURA LIMONIC is an Associate Professor of Sociology at the College of Old Westbury of the State University of New York. Her research is in the area of contemporary immigration to the United States and the integration trajectories of ethnic and ethno-religious groups. Her recent book, *Kugel and Frijoles: Latino Jews in the United States* explores issues of ethnicity, race, class and religious community-building among Latino Jewish immigrants in Boston, New York, Miami and Southern California. Laura's current work examines the rise of Chabad in Latin America as an avenue for Jewish identity construction and communal life among Jews in Latin America and abroad. Her work has been supported by the Berman Foundation, the Association for Jewish Studies and the Templeton Trust. Laura received her PhD in Sociology from the CUNY

Graduate Center in 2014. She has a Bachelor of Arts degree in Latin American Studies from Brandeis University and a Master of International Affairs degree from Columbia University. In addition to academic research, Laura has an extensive background in public policy research and advocacy.

NAHID PIRNAZAR received her PhD from the University of California, Los Angeles, in Iranian Studies and holds the Habib Levy Visiting Professorship of Judeo-Persian Literature and The History of Iranian Jews at UCLA. Dr. Pirnazar is the founder and president of the academic research organization of the "House of Judeo-Persian Manuscripts." She has edited the English translation of *The Women of Shahnameh* by Prof. Khaleghi Motlagh (2012) and an edition of *Habib Levy: A Personal Chronicle of Jewish Life in Iran from the Late 19th Century to the Islamic Revolution* (2016). Dr. Pirnazar's works have been featured in English and Persian in academic publications including, *Irano-Judaica, Irānshenāsi, Iran Nameh* and *Iran Namag*. She is also a contributor to the *Encyclopedia of Jews in the Islamic World* as well as *Encyclopedia Iranica*. She is the guest editor of the quarterly *Iran Namag* (Summer, 2016) and editor of *Farshihood*, Tehran, 2018/1397. Her forthcoming works are *Judeo-Persian Writings: A Manifestation of Intellectual and Literary Life* (Routledge, 2021) and *Ketab-Anusi*, "Book of Forced Converts" (Iran Namag Book Series, 2021).

GIL RIBAK is an Associate Professor of Judaic Studies at the University of Arizona. Born and raised in Israel, he came to the US on a Fulbright Dissertation Fellowship and completed a doctoral degree in History at the University of Wisconsin-Madison. After graduation, Ribak taught at Washington University in St. Louis as the Lewin Postdoctoral Fellow, and as the Schusterman Postdoctoral Fellow at the University of Arizona. Before returning to the University of Arizona for a tenure-track position, he served as director of the Institute on Israeli-American Jewish Relations at the American Jewish University in Los Angeles and taught at Oberlin College. His book, *Gentile New York: The Images of Non-Jews among Jewish Immigrants*, was published by Rutgers University Press in 2012. His articles appeared in journals such as *AJS Review, American Jewish History, East European Jewish Affairs, Israel Studies Forum, Journal of American Ethnic History, Polin: A Journal of Polish-Jewish Studies*, and *Modern Judaism*, among others. Ribak has published book chapters in books such as *Germany and the Americas: Culture, Politics and History; War and Peace in Jewish Tradition: From the Ancient World to the Present; Wealth and Poverty in Jewish Tradition: Studies in Jewish Civilization; American Jewry: Transcending the European Experience?; Reconstructing the Old Country: American Jewry in the Post-Holocaust Decades;* and *Anti-Zionism, Antisemitism, and the Dynamics of Delegitimization.*

STEVEN J. ROSS is Professor of History at the University of Southern California, and the Myron and Marian Director of the Casden Institute for the Study of the Jewish Role in American Life. His most recent book, *Hitler in Los Angeles: How Jews Foiled Nazi Plots Against Hollywood and America* (Bloomsbury Press, 2017) was named a Finalist for the Pulitzer Prize in History for 2018 has been on the Los Angeles Times Bestseller List for twenty-three weeks. His previous book, *Hollywood Left and Right: How Movie Stars Shaped American Politics* (Oxford University, 2013), received the Academy of Motion Picture Arts and Sciences' Film Scholars Award. *Working-Class Hollywood: Silent Film and the Shaping of Class in America* (Princeton University, 1998), received the Theater Library Association Book Award for 1999. Ross' Op-Ed pieces have appeared in the *Los Angeles Times, Wall Street Journal, Washington Post, Time, International Herald-Tribune, Hollywood Reporter, HuffingtonPost, Daily Beast,* and *Politico.*

The USC Casden Institute for the Study of the Jewish Role in American Life

The American Jewish community has played a vital role in shaping the politics, culture, commerce and multiethnic character of Southern California and the American West. Beginning in the mid-nineteenth century, when entrepreneurs like Isaias Hellman, Levi Strauss and Adolph Sutro first ventured out West, American Jews became a major force in the establishment and development of the budding Western territories. Since 1970, the number of Jews in the West has more than tripled. This dramatic demographic shift has made California—specifically, Los Angeles—home to the second largest Jewish population in the United States. Paralleling this shifting pattern of migration, Jewish voices in the West are today among the most prominent anywhere in the United States. Largely migrating from Eastern Europe, the Middle East and the East Coast of the United States, Jews have invigorated the West, where they exert a considerable presence in every sector of the economy—most notably in the media and the arts. With the emergence of Los Angeles as a world capital in entertainment and communications, the Jewish perspective and experience in the region are being amplified further. From artists and activists to scholars and professionals, Jews are significantly influencing the shape of things to come in the West and across the United States. In recognition of these important demographic and societal changes, in 1998 the University of Southern California established a scholarly institute dedicated to studying contemporary Jewish life in America with special emphasis on the western United States. The Casden Institute explores issues related to the interface between the Jewish community and the broader, multifaceted cultures that form the nation—issues of relationship as much as of Jewishness itself. It is also enhancing the educational experience for students at USC and elsewhere by exposing them to the problems—and promise—of life in Los Angeles' ethnically, socially, culturally and economically diverse community. Scholars, students and community leaders examine the ongoing contributions of American Jews in the arts, business, media, literature, education, politics, law and social relations, as well as the relationships between Jewish Americans and other groups, including African Americans,

Latinos, Asian Americans and Arab Americans. The Casden Institute's scholarly orientation and contemporary focus, combined with its location on the West Coast, set it apart from—and makes it an important complement to—the many excellent Jewish Studies programs across the nation that center on Judaism from an historical or religious perspective.

For more information about the USC Casden Institute, visit www.usc.edu/casdeninstitute, e-mail casden@usc.edu, or call (213) 740-3405.

9 781557 539984